That
Wondrous
Pattern

That
Wondrous
Pattern

Essays on Poetry and Poets

Kathleen Raine

Edited and with an Introduction by Brian Keeble
Preface by Wendell Berry

COUNTERPOINT
BERKELEY

Library of Congress Cataloging-in-Publication Data Is Available.

Jacket design by Kelly Winton
Book design by Megan Jones Design

ISBN 978-1-61902-923-1

COUNTERPOINT
2560 Ninth Street, Suite 318
Berkeley, CA 94710
www.counterpointpress.com

Printed in the United States of America
Distributed by Publishers Group West

10 9 8 7 6 5 4 3 2 1

CONTENTS

PREFACE

FOR A LONG time our world has been dominated by a "scientific"—hence economic and political—materialism, which "knows" that all of reality can be, and finally will be, explained by physics. A "theory of everything," a truth of the universe," will finally be derived from the observation of parts and particles. And this has involved a paradox increasingly obvious and fearful: The material world, which ought logically to be cherished by materialists, has instead by their influence and their processes been wasted, deformed, poisoned, and made ugly.

This has been accepted, even abetted, by a conventional religious dualism that involves another cruel paradox: Many Christians and Christian sects, which ought logically to cherish this world as the approved work of God and thus as a good gift and a privilege, regard it instead as a trap or prison from which the soul must escape by repudiating its earthly life and accepting a formula for "salvation." This sort of spirituality is little more than materialism's second face, for it abandons the world and our economic life in it to the materialists.

This curious alliance is opposed, and perhaps is opposable only, by the vision of the completeness of reality that is said to underlie the traditional cultures and religions of the world. This vision—attested by scholars and authorities far more learned than I am, though certainly confirmed by my own experience and reading—sees the "outer" world as completed and dependent upon "inner" realities such as love, reverence, goodness, and beauty. These realities, though they have belonged always to the actual lives of most people, the materialists dismiss as intangible and therefore unreal. The religious dualists see them perhaps as real enough while, like the materialists, seeing them also as irrelevant to the natural life and human economy of this world.

The consequent estrangement of body and soul, heaven and earth, time and eternity, leading to the further estrangements of utility and beauty, work and pleasure and all the rest of the divisions and divorces of our mechanical civilization, is owing to the loss of the ancient unifying vision, by which we have been enabled to see in the world the eternal light that everywhere informs it. This vision, this immemorial knowledge and way of knowing, sometimes called the Perennial Philosophy, sometimes simply Tradition, survives only marginally in the modern world. Inherently opposed as it is to the radical simplifications of the materialist explainers and devisers, it is assuredly the losing side. And yet its diminishment is just as assuredly consequential in the lives of people and the world.

Kathleen Raine wrote in one of her essays, "Waste land, Holy Land," that T. S. Eliot

> discerned in our world an absence—of all things the hardest to discern, still harder to identify. The death of God, the death of the soul—name as we will the withdrawal of the inner vision from the outer world—lays waste the earth.

Eliot situated the profane world in that place in the soul's order of values to which it belongs—in the hells, the kingdom cut off from life.

True of Eliot as that passage is, it can stand also as a fair summary of her own vocation and her work as both poet and scholar. All her long life she was experiencing and attending to our suffering of the absence, in the wastelands of the modern world, of the inner vision. In *Blake and Tradition*, she traced the ancestry of that vision as William Blake inherited and realized it in his work. And in many essays she showed us how the same sustaining vision, the same responsibility, has survived in the lineage of English poets from Spenser to Blake and Yeats, and on to her contemporaries, David Jones, Edwin Muir, and Vernon Watkins.

This survival has been little noticed in our time because most of the keepers and teachers of our economic life, of the Christian gospel, and of the arts have not known where to look for it and would not have known what to make of it had they found it. And so by publishing this selection of Kathleen Raine's essays, her friend and editor, Brian Keeble, and Counterpoint have filled a need much felt though little recognized, and so have rendered a distinguished service to writers and readers of our time.

These essays speak more than capably for themselves and need little comment from me. But because I fear it may be necessary, I want to draw attention to their practical import. When she spoke of "the inner vision" whose absence "lays waste the earth," Kathleen Raine meant what she said. When she wrote an essay on "the use of the beautiful," she was thinking, and asking us to think, as seriously as possible about questions that are

in part practical. The issue is that of context, as with anything
that is of use. A thing that is useful cannot exist "for its own
sake." Beauty moreover is not an attribute of parts and fragments, but of the whole, or the wholeness toward which the arts
and our human lives aspire. It is ultimately the wholeness of that
immeasurable, hardly nameable reality that we call "creation"
or "life" or "world." And so the context of the beautiful is the
whole world and our need for the world's wholeness. This is the
context, I think, of Aldo Leopold's question, when defending
the entire plant community of the American north woods, which
is to say "the health of the forest as an organism":

> Is there not an esthetic as well as an economic issue? Is
> there, at bottom, any real distinction between esthetics and
> economics?

Within the context of our departmented schools, within
the context of our departmented economy, there is an exhila-
rating boldness in Kathleen Raine's demonstration of the use
of the beautiful. She wrote that "the beautiful is an order of
wholes, and of wholeness . . ." Insofar as they remind us of
this paramount order and our need for it, and insofar as they
embody such order in themselves, "works of poetry and the
other arts are necessary for our survival; survival, that is, as
human beings . . ."

The arts, in their fullness, teach us to live and so to survive in
the fullness of our humanity, as living souls, not as the brainiest
of the apes. The alternative is our present materialist struggle to
survive by means of technological and political "solutions" our
technological destructiveness of the world's order of wholes. We

are betting our lives on the triumph—in the future, of course—of our small cleverness.

But our problem, as Kathleen Raine understood and made clear, is not technical and political but cultural. It is poverty of soul. We destroy the world's wholeness and our own because we have forsaken the ability to see the order of beauty, which is wholeness and good health and holiness. William Blake wrote that "Everything that lives is holy," and nothing more practical in its force and implication was ever written. If we believed, if we saw, the holiness of everything that lives, a principle sufficiently corroborated by the Bible, our economic lives and all of our work would become immediately better, because they would become consciously subordinate to the order of beauty, which is the order of wholeness and holiness which is the order of the world.

But one cannot learn the holiness of everything that lives by dissecting a frog. The holiness of frogs, and of the rest of us creatures, can be revealed only to imagination and by the works of imagination. Of the many gifts we receive from Kathleen Raine, surely one of the best is her understanding of the use, the life, and the learning of the imagination in its highest, truest sense. The power of imagination exactly, in the poetry she loved and served and in her own poetry, is to see that everything that lives is holy.

—WENDELL BERRY

INTRODUCTION

WE ARE IN need of a counterbalance. In a world that is in relentless pursuit of a quantitative evaluation of everything, an age that has forgotten that a phenomenal world necessarily entails a noumenal that is transcendent to it—a recognition that every existent being is the effect of a preceding cause—there must arise from time to time a voice to reaffirm the timeless, universal order that relates the one world to the other: joins the realm of ultimate principles to the manifest world where we find the embodied wisdom of our imaginative life in which things are known *sub specie aeternitatis*. Such a voice was that of Kathleen Raine.

To read the essays presented here is to find oneself negotiating a spiritual and intellectual landscape far removed from the preoccupations of what we currently think of as 'culture': those diminishing returns of 'self-expression' we call 'art' sustained by a new elite of purveyors and explainers of banality, anxious to convince us of its superiority to our common-sense reaction, in the face of it, of uncomprehending bewilderment. For this 'culture' the imaginative arts are limited to the expression of the mundane through personal emotion as having a legitimate claim to be the substance of art. What has become entrenched is the exclusive idea that the arts can no longer meaningfully relate to anything beyond such evidence as the senses might suggest. This follows from what has been the cumulative acceptance, based on the material sciences, that reality is in essence quantitative and that any appeal to a higher order of thought is at best mistaken, at worst amounts to a subversive heresy. It is a type of prejudice that chooses to ignore the obvious fact that it is in the intuition of conscious awareness, not itself available to scrutiny, that we know all that we can know, and in which all things possess any reality they can be said to possess. All such diminishments these essays challenge head on.

How has this narrowing of the possible accomplishment of the arts as a depository of beauty and wisdom come about? In keeping with the order invoked in these essays it is necessary to recognise the metaphysical depreciation of history; the entropy inherent in the passage time as it is taught (though not exclusively) in the Hindu theories of the unfolding of the cosmic cycles. Each complete cycle's unfolding is divided into four Yugas and with the passing of each Yuga a quarter of reality is removed from common apprehension until the complete cycle is exhausted—from the highest qualitative possibilities to the lowest: from the 'golden age' to the age of metaphysical poverty in which material qualities are the determining measure of all values, in which state, as Kathleen Raine often points out 'ignorance passes judgement on knowledge'. At this point the higher, qualitative wisdom is excluded from contributing to the contextual understanding of the arts of life. As becomes evident from, for instance, her essay 'On the Symbol', in addition to its inherent presence in the 'learning of the Imagination' of the poets studied herein, the guiding source of the teaching of the perennial wisdom the author draws upon she found in René Guénon's seminal text *The Reign of Quantity*.

The Hindu teaching of the Yugas, as Kathleen Raine pointed out in her monumental study of the sources of William Blake's iconography (*Blake and Tradition*, 1969), allows us to infer 'that the natural world may . . . degenerate and withdraw its qualities and powers from degenerate civilisations like our own, following the loss of certain faculties of (qualitative) perception'. This seemingly bleak assessment is none the less, on the evidence, a realistic one, and the poet did not shy away from its wider implications in her attempt to demonstrate the deforming of the arts of our time when isolated from the perennial wisdom. In her essay 'Poetic Symbols as a Vehicle of Tradition' (not included here) the poet asks whether or not 'we are the last of the old', and wonders if it is at all possible that there could yet be a late flowering from the seed of the ancient knowledge in the degenerate civilisation we have created by default, according to the prevailing deprecatory conditions. T. S. Eliot went so far as to suggest our civilisation might perhaps be the first to leave behind no culture.

In the same essay Kathleen Raine posits, of the cosmic decline of the gradual movement from qualitative to quantitative possibilities, that it is not from a 'failure to be or become what they should be, but rather through their own fulfilment, when all the seeds sown at the beginning have come to fruition', and the 'governing spirit' (as Plato called it) of the universe recedes. The Platonic teaching is fully in accord with the Hindu in its metaphysical essence.

Transposed to the study of European culture, the poet repeatedly traced (as she does in her essay 'On the Symbol') the line of descent of the life-giving learning of the traditional wisdom in the West, from Plato and the Neoplatonists to the Florentine renaissance to Edmund Spenser and beyond to the poets studied in the following pages, each in their way making a stand against the unfolding diminishment of the temporal exhaustion. Far removed as they might seem, such desiderata lend a powerful advocacy to Kathleen Raine finding in Eliot the most eloquent spokesperson among her contemporaries of the loss of vision of the sacred that is the hallmark of what Henry Corbin called modern man's 'agnostic reflex'. A revealing indication of the gradual erosion of the transcendent as a vital attribute is in the absence in contemporary arts of a sense of hierarchy as the embodiment of beauty informing the creative process.

The further we go back in history the more readily we must acknowledge that the arts immemorially served as the means by which man integrates himself within the total cosmic fabric in accordance with their reciprocal spiritual nature. In her essay 'The Use of the Beautiful' Kathleen Raine points to this rejection of beauty in the contemporary arts as indicative of the unconscious reaction to the absence of any relation to the total cosmic reality. Beauty, the poet suggests, possesses an inherent reproach, which reproach—given the active presence of an adequate perception—harbours a proof that the essence of our human state lies beyond the limitations of mundane reality. In the sensory consolation that beauty offers we might find some intimation of our perfection in the eternal. Perhaps it should be said, in parenthesis, that it is not so much a rejection of beauty in the modern arts, so much as that beauty simply becomes beyond the reach of the artist for want of its adequate perception. The consequence is clear. The all too evident 'realism' of the demotic unfailingly equates the human condition with the lowest possibilities rather than the highest. Its stock-in-trade is to reflect the least significant dimension of our common experience, founded as that is on no more than the 'fortuitous concourse of memories accumulated and lost', as Blake pertinently observed.

Time and again in these essays, in arguing for the value of poetry as a living presence in 'the house of the soul' (the phrase is I. A. Richards's) the poet questions whether the arts of 'self-expression' can serve any purpose, beyond being a minor diversion from the business of maintaining our economic survival.

The comprehensiveness of the author's standpoint enables her to point up the terms by which the arts might enhance and enrich the human condition, but also the terms on which they debase and pervert that condition.

Despite their commitment to the perennial wisdom, which nonetheless includes a recognition of its by now almost complete obsolescence—at least so far as the arts are involved—these essays are offered in the hope of retrieving some reverberation of the archetypal order in which knowledge is a vital, intuitive state of being rather than an accumulation of observed and rationalised information largely handed down, often on questionable authority and rarely verified in the direct understanding of the knower. The essays underwrite a recognition that 'culture' is much more than the outcome of 'what people do'.

They are a reminder that the word culture has its semantic roots in the notion of cultivation (the horticultural world is an honourable exception in this respect); and what is to be cultivated is, precisely, the potential spirituality of the integral human state.

The traditional hierarchy of values that comprises the perennial wisdom cannot, by its very nature, be destroyed. 'Reality', as the poet reminds us, 'is always and everywhere itself.' According to the primordial wisdom the soul and the world are mirrored in each other. Man looks into nature to find the soul of the Creation so that the world is apprehended as a living presence, an incarnational immediacy of Being that is experienced as the world's noumenal significance. The living source of love that makes this mutual embrace possible is timelessly captured in Kathleen Raine's poem 'Amo Ergo Sum', among others.

In the poetry of each of her chosen subjects there is the implicit acknowledgement that the function of *poesis* is to guard the inviolate world of Imagination as the bond that joins the transcendent to the concrete. In her commentary on these poets the author relentlessly points to the catastrophe that is the abolition of poetry's guardianship in the modern world. The crisis is stark and unequivocal: the Creator can be found only in and through the reciprocal love of the Creator and the Creation. Even more: in the final, metaphysical analysis there is only God: there is only God to witness God. The materialism against which the poet was embattled does not present us with a 'face' of the real with which we might conduct a dialogue concerning the divinity of our personhood. All cultural meanings and values rest, finally, on such an exchange. In the world view, based on sensate awareness of modern science, as the poet writes in the essay on Yeats, 'the age old search for truth and beauty and the good has been replaced by the observable, the immediate, and the process of change as values in themselves'.

✸

ARGUABLY THE MOST important overarching theme of Kathleen Raine's thought is that of the nature and function of Imagination. Whether explicitly or implicitly these essays raise the broader question: What is the ontological status of an image held in the mind?

It will not escape the attentive reader's notice that throughout the essays the word imagination is given a capital initial. For the poet, as for her master, Blake, Imagination is the supreme faculty by which true poetic vision achieves the fulfilment of its intrinsic quality as the agent of spiritual perception. Here we are far from the commonplace idea of imagination as simply the passive mirror of images drawn from the sensorium, a view that leaves unanswered the question, in what sense can it be said that such images are 'real' or 'unreal'?

For Kathleen Raine Imagination is theophanic vision and is thereby a transcendent faculty. The capital indicates the distinction. In Imagination we are the very act of apprehending the Sacred in participative mode in and through images that render cognitive experience as inherently meaningful. True Imagination does not invent or impose meaning. In the truly Imaginative image the soul arrives at the necessity to inhabit experience as an act of participative Being, facing the Presence of its meaning in relation to the Supreme Reality—an act of ultimate sympathetic correspondence. This is not to suggest that the poet's conception of Imagination is illustrated in her poems. I would draw attention to, for instance, her 'Northumbrian Sequence' as a poem that inhabits the conception outlined above.

These essays are nothing if not an impassioned argument for the recovery of the poetic image as an authentic approach to sacred reality. The author's argument starts from Blake's

assertion that active Imagination presents images of 'what eternally exists, really and unchangeably'. But from that position to
confronting the materialist bias of the modern mind for which
imagination is a passive faculty, and for which anything that
is not quantitative substance is in some way unreal—in other
words, a fiction—involves a considerable leap.

Although the concept of a spiritually active Imagination,
largely learned from Blake, is present in the poet's earlier scholarly work, in the essays of her later years the poet took strength
from the work of Henry Corbin. Expounding the Sufi doctrine
of the *mundus imaginalis*, based mainly on the Illuminationist
School of Persian mysticism (Suhrawardi, Ibn cArabi and Mulla
Sadra), in order to recover for the West the true cognitive status of the Imagination, Corbin showed how *mundus imaginalis*
is an intermediary domain in the mystic's journey to the One
'where the spiritual takes body and the body becomes spiritual'.
It provides therein the essential link that joins in total continuity the forms of the corporeal world as subsisting in the forms
of the spiritual substance or the intelligible world. The *mundus
imaginalis*, so understood, Corbin called the 'exultation' of the
Imagination.

There is no doubt room for a close scrutiny of Kathleen
Raine's appropriation of the concept of the *imaginal* world
(Corbin himself invented the term *mundus imaginalis* to denote
the realm in which imaginative consciousness is spiritually
active) in order to counter the modern acceptance of imagination at having a merely passive function. This appropriation does
give rise to certain problems, the most serious of which is the
danger of divinising Imagination itself. I must leave others better qualified to examine the problems that arise in any attempt

to transpose from the cadre of Islamic spirituality a framework for understanding the spirituality of the poetic Imagination. However that may be, it should be clear why the poet made use of Corbin's studies.

In light of this it is not difficult to see what the ultimate aim of Kathleen Raine's challenge to the materialist premises as to the nature of mind was. The imaginative discourse of the poet, if it is to have an authentic spiritual status, must have a place from which to speak of the 'unseen' realities that inform the significance of the world of sensible appearances. And that discourse must possess a language whose voice is capable of embracing and therefore speaking of *things* beyond the transient world. In short the language of the poet must identify with the ultimate source of which it speaks. This is the alchemy of metaphysical analogy. It has always been acknowledged that the voice of the poet occupies the highest eminence when it comes to articulating the intrinsic spiritual aspirations of man to inhabit his ultimate home. It is where he locates the *meaning* of his mundane life. As the poet states in 'The Inner Journey of the Poet', 'to the Imagination everything in nature speaks of the mind which it reflects'.

As Kathleen Raine has argued in her essays and has presented in her poetry, and from a position within a literary convention so long confined to the ephemeralities of 'self-expression', it seems likely that the only dependable way to the restoration of the poet's true vocation is through heightened perception in a manner akin to the experience of the contemplative mystic providing a sort of template as to how forms of the natural world are to be truly perceived. Certainly, mystical experience has in all cultures been taken to be evidence of how 'nature' is illuminated in being a shadow of the supernatural. We are back to those bright shadows on the wall of the Platonic cave. Perhaps the question of whether the poetic symbol can ever have quite the ontological status of the *imaginal* image must remain unanswerable. Be that as it may, these essays, devoted as they are to the 'learning of the Imagination', cogently suggest that such study can support the transmutation if guided by the predilections of the illuminated soul. In a world of impermanence it is the nature of mind to arrest the fleeting: to find confirmation beyond sensory perception, not a substitute for the real, but the Real itself; a world made evident through the poetic language of symbolic discourse. As Frithjof Schuon has pointed out, 'the symbol is a suggestion aiming at an intuition, not an explanation addressing a thought'.

Each of the poets featured here took their stand against the secularism of their time which, as Kathleen Raine puts it in her comments on 'Ash Wednesday', seeks 'to obliterate from modern experience the old vision of human love as something holy, sacramental'. These pages are not so much a contribution to 'literature', but to an enlargement of our being as a corrective to those diminishments that have ended up converting imaginative consciousness into cyber-space where there is no principle or measure of significance and where profundity and platitude are indistinguishable.

We can hardly doubt that this is largely the reason why the arts now fight to secure a modest territory from which to make a meaningful contribution to the quality of life. With each generation the gulf between the cultures that gave us, in Yeats's phrase, 'monuments of unageing intellect' and contemporary culture grows wider. At the same time ever more sophisticated means of retrieval and storage of those past cultures is pressed into service. This making available in curatorial form the material remains of so many past cultures is paradoxically accompanied, not by a sense of illumination as to their spiritual wealth, but a pervasive sense of surfeit and exhaustion. In the light of this it hardly seems audacious of Kathleen Raine to suggest that we live in the first society to build no environment for the arts—that is to say worthy 'monuments' of our own. Do these essays hint at the coming barbarism? Without what is *signified* we are mere creatures of biological process. If so by what principle of permanence do we measure the flow? Without a value of permanence what must be the obvious function of intelligence, to evaluate, is neutralised in the face of an incomprehensible mystery. At the end of an earlier essay on Vernon Watkins (not included here) the poet noted:

> What we did not know thirty years ago was how extreme would be the isolation of those who hold to tradition. It then seemed that there were at least some values which were agreed upon between the profane positivist world and the world of the 'ancient springs'. . . . We can no longer deceive ourselves. It seems that there no longer exist any common terms or values; beyond a certain point of divergence communication becomes impossible. . . . Tradition, which recognises a difference between knowledge and ignorance, cannot come to terms with a world in which there are no longer any standards by which truth or falsehood may be measured.

We are living the ever-widening divergence.

That there could never be a return to the old order of cultural values should be perfectly obvious. It would, were it even remotely possible, amount to such a reversal of premises as would rend what, over countless generations, we have recognised to be the properly human fabric of life. The 'signs of the times' are that the unfolding cycle must exhaust *all* its possibilities, the lowest not excluded, before a new cycle can begin. Are we then to conclude that our lot is one of unabated confusion and further degeneration? Is there nothing we can do to alleviate the now almost total erosion of even the humanist culture, itself an attrition of the traditional cultures founded, ultimately, on sacred principles? Are we to be forever imprisoned by the futility of living in a world where our subjectivity is bound within a closed circuit of accounting and measuring its existential substance without recourse to its ineffaceable source? The poet offered her response to such questions in the final paragraph of 'What is Man?' For all our failings we remain human and on that evidence it is worthy to believe that to recognise an 'end' is already to acknowledge a criterion that transcends whatever powers carry us to the end and is not itself a component of the final collapse.

✹

KATHLEEN RAINE (1908–2003) was a prolific essayist. Collected, these would fill several volumes. In making the present selection I have followed two guidelines: that the essays should be relatively unavailable, and that the book should have a structure that reflects the values that the author, throughout her long life, upheld in her elucidation of the individual poets whose voices she was heir to. There is no exaggeration in pointing out that these essays are addressed to the soul of the reader.

They are not academic exercises in erudition as a contribution to 'Eng. Lit.'

In her essay 'On the Symbol' the poet writes:

> These images seem put into our hands like clues which we are invited to follow back and back. . . . By their numinous nature we recognise them; and not with academic curiosity do we pursue them to their mysterious source, but as we follow the beloved person, unable to keep away. . . . We live under the power of their compulsion: for they do not present themselves, like academic problems, from outside, as tasks to be taken up by will-power. . . . They arise, rather, as living impulses, urges of our own being and therefore compelling. We cannot rest until we have followed them to their source, as far as our understanding allows.

Much in the spirit of this passage I have removed what few references there were in these texts: in the case of the essay on Yeats, all the footnotes, which were, in any case, source references. I must hope that the reader does not find this any sort of barrier to the living spirit of comprehension.

Considering the extent of the author's scholarly writings on Blake and Yeats I at first favoured leaving them unrepresented here. They deserve to be collected in their own right. Then it seemed that a collection of essays that excluded the two poets the author was most indebted to was untenable—something of a distortion of her poetic loyalties. In the end I chose an essay on each that is more or less free-standing. Needless to say the reader is advised to avail himself or herself of all else the author has written on these two—her seminal—poets which forms the context of these two papers.

I

THE PRESENCE
OF POETRY

What Is the Use of Poetry?

THE WORD *POETRY* can mean many things to different people, in different times and places, but however understood it has from time immemorial been something humankind has created and felt to be essential to life itself. It remains true that 'man does not live by bread alone'. We need poetry in our lives, as we do music and dance and the other arts, because our souls need their proper food, as do our bodies—'The Bread of sweet Thought & the Wine of Delight', as Blake wrote. 'Poetry, Painting & Music' he calls 'the three Powers in Man of conversing with Paradise'.

But towards poetry attitudes have greatly changed in the course of my own lifetime, and I have had to question and examine many of my old assumptions and attitudes. What, for example, does 'conversing with Paradise' mean in a secular materialist society for which the word paradise is meaningless, belonging as it does to a context which presumes a heirarchy of 'worlds' in an ascending scale of value and reality? In a society which supposes all knowledge to belong to one level only, that of the shared material order, it can come about that the popular voice can claim for the opinions of some journalist an authority in no way different from the inspired writings of a prophet, 'revealed' (that is to say 'inspired') from another level altogether. The freedom to voice opinion is a democratic right, but that does not make the hierarchic order of truth and values any the less real. However, in the domain of poetry there has been what one may call a democratic revolution.

Looking back to my own, excellent pre-war education at a County High School attended by by no means rich or privileged children, and like many others at that time, accessible to any intelligent student, I inherited (in my measure) the unbroken tradition of civilized Europe as this has descended from Homer and the classical world, through Rome and Christendom, and English literature from Chaucer to the twentieth century, each age inheriting, building on and adding to the heritage of the past. That past was, for the educated (I say 'was' — I hesitate to say 'is'), an extended present in whose whole each generation lived. As Eliot wrote, 'We know more than the past: yes, and the past is what we know.'

My father was the English master at the school I attended, in a London suburb; and the poetry he taught—and loved—was that of the great English poets from Chaucer to Shakespeare to Herbert and Marvell, to Pope and Gray and the Romantics, and ending, for him, with Tennyson and Browning. He also knew and loved the most illustrious Latin poets, and, coming as he did from County Durham, he had a special love for the Anglo-Saxon language and poetry, which he felt to be the language of his ancestors. There was also the King James Bible, familiar at home, and heard every Sunday in the Methodist church we attended (the Bible was in most homes in those far-off days). Its words, we were given to understand, were divinely inspired; and the words of the poets were, though not in the same degree, also 'inspired' from some source not accessible to the common-place, everyday mind. Probably I would have scorned such ideas in my Cambridge student days, but, essentially, such would be my present view, having come full circle through the 'modern movement' and the reductionist ideologies fashionable in my youth, and still widely current; though no longer unchallenged by an ever growing number dissatisfied with ideologies which so restrict the range of human experience.

For my mother poetry was an inheritance of a different kind (though she shared, of course, my father's love of the poets of England). She, being Scots, knew by heart—as did my aunts and grandmother—a seemingly inexhaustible fund of the songs and ballads of Scotland and the Borders. These songs afforded words and music for every mood, tender or warlike, gay courtship or scathing contempt. These came to my mother and her sisters not by way of 'education' but as an inheritance, a birthright, along with the language of Scotland itself, which bestowed the sense of her Scottish identity and participation in an age-old culture. I loved and received those songs and ballads in a different man-ner from anything learned at school. It is something that must be known to all nations before reading and writing puts an end to the rare, rich inheritance of oral tradition, and in England something lost, perhaps, with the rural world Thomas Hardy knew, though by no means so in Scotland, Ireland and Wales. Poetry taught in school, however beautiful, was not a birthright, but an acquisition: the songs and ballads of Scotland did not so much belong to us, as we to them. They were anonymous— and Robert Burns who collected so many songs himself merged into anonymity. Authorship was really of no great importance. It was as if they had forever existed and belonged to no one

and therefore at the same time to everyone. A Spanish friend of
Lorca's described to me how once in Andalusia he had been with
the poet in a village when someone began singing one of Lorca's
songs—no one knew who had written it. This, Lorca had felt,
was the supreme attainment of the poet—to become anonymous.
Even if the authorship might be known this scarcely mattered,
for the stamp of ballad or song was that of a nation's imagination, not such individual 'style' as readers admire in Donne or
Browning or Hopkins.

As for the English poets—to return to England—they seemed
to us people apart, born into the world with shining names—
Keats, Shelley, Coleridge, Wordsworth, Tennyson. In my home
these were venerated names, as it seemed of another race than
ours. What a poet had written had authority, if not quite as
the Bible had; at all events we received their words as *truth*.
It was not in my childhood yet fashionable—as it was in my
student days at Cambridge—to scrutinize, to criticize, to pull
a poem to shreds and stamp on the fragments. (I was not, let
me add, reading English—I had that much good sense—but
Natural Sciences.) F. R. Leavis edited a literary journal which he
entitled *Scrutiny*, and 'scrutiny' was a new, reductionist attitude
brought to the reading of poetry utterly alien to the imaginative
receptiveness without which the enchantment of beauty cannot
be experienced. The purpose of reading seemed to be the detec-
tion and exposure of bad verses rather than the delight of lifting
the soul above the mundane. My generation had expected to
participate, to be enchanted, not to analyse. What these critics
did was to bring to bear on an imaginative art the apparatus of
conceptual rational thought. My generation had been prepared
to be receptive, in a spirit of reverent expectation of receiving

wisdom or delight, not of a (envious surely) desire to find fault. 'The best in this sort are but shadows, and the worst no worse, if but imagination do amend them', Shakespeare wrote; he was writing about drama—a bad play, one might say, concocted by the craftsmen of Athens. Or, I think of the Holy Pictures (of Ireland, or of India, it's all the same) or plaster statuettes of the Madonna; yet these may possess miraculous power, be invested with the presence of the Mother of God for those who bring to them love and imagination. However, scrutiny too is an attitude to poetry that seems now to belong to the past.

Now I edit a literary review whose title—*Temenos*—likewise indicates its attitude to the arts. The name means a sacred enclosure around a shrine or temple; and we hold that the arts are normally to be found—should properly be found—within the precincts of the sacred; they grow on hallowed ground. The sacred is not indeed to be confused or identified with the religious—religions also, according to Blake, being 'derived from each Nation's different reception of the Poetic Genius, which is every where call'd the Spirit of Prophecy'. A steady stream of bulky envelopes comes through my letter-box. Usually it is poetry, and it is as far from Keats and Shelley and Milton and Marvell as it is from the songs of Scotland or the Border Ballads. It is written, as often as not, by people who have perhaps read none of these. For nowadays, so it seems, poetry has come to mean something people write, not something they receive.

Multitudes of people seem to be moved by a compelling urge to express themselves in poetry; not any longer to memorize passages from the Bible, or poems from Wordsworth and Shelley and the rest, or to know, almost without the effort of learning, from hearing their mother sing old songs.

To this day poems and passages from the Bible come to my remembrance, often, at need, bringing their beauty and wisdom to some situation of later life unforeseen in school days. Who, in later life, can or would wish to remember the poems they themselves have written?

Much poetry is now a 'pop' activity, like the music the younger generation listen to, or themselves take part in. Instead of deploring the lowering of standards—which is obvious enough—we must ask why such a radical change has taken place, for it cannot be dismissed in purely negative terms. While at the Universities the study of literature has tended to become something analytical and reductionist and joyless, there is a flood of verse being written by people of all ages, women and men, and the barely literate, who have one thing in common—the writing of poetry is of great importance to the writer. Often it is the most important thing in their lives—one is tempted to say 'too important' if one judges by the results. But perhaps we should not be judging by the results at all, but by the inner activity which impels so many to write. We should ask ourselves what poetry, good or bad, is for, how it operates, what we may hope to find in it.

Certainly there is little enough poetry in the lives of most modern urban-dwellers—I mean in the kind of activities at which men and women spend their hours, and for which they are paid salaries or wages. The profit-motive scarcely provides food for the soul that perhaps the daily life and daily work of craftsmen and women's arts of making beautiful garments and embroidering the adornments of their homes once did provide, the rich craftsmanship of other times and places, now practised rather as 'occupational therapy' than as a part of life. We find our deepest expression and fulfilment rather in spite of than through our daily lives and occupations—something to be fought for, sometimes heroically. I think of a young man who wrote to me that he lived on national assistance because if he took a job he would not be able to give his time to the writing of poetry. Perhaps very wrong of him, but also we may ask what is wrong with a society which sets intelligent and feeling people so at odds with its values. Even that extreme case (and I am sure there are many such) is surely a criticism of a world that does so little to satisfy our spiritual hunger and thirst, but merely feeds the body and educates the young for the performance of practical skills in the service of the profit-motive.

What, then, do all these hope for in the writing of poetry? At its simplest it is like the song of the birds, even the chirping of crickets, just affirming our presence, to say 'we are here, this is our voice in the chorus'. That is how it is with children, it comes naturally. A revolution took place in our schools some fifty years ago (was it?) partly through the writings of Herbert Read, who introduced the idea of 'education through art'; not, that is, by looking at paintings or absorbing, almost unawares, the beauty of architecture and carved stone, in village church or cathedral, reading or memorizing poetry, or listening to, or learning, music, but through making paintings and writing poems. Read was among the first to say that it is the act of creation, not the result that is vital. Now we have gone to the other extreme and our schools no longer educate young people in the mainstream of the poetry and the language, the inheritance without which they cannot express anything at all.

By no means all writers of spontaneous verse are children. Writing verse is now commonly used as a form of 'therapy'— that, in plain English, means healing—by many psychiatrists and others concerned with enabling people to cope with their lives. Again, the results scarcely matter. The method can go to absurd extremes, as with the young American (I suppose and hope he was young) who sent me his poems with a letter saying that his psychiatrist had told him that getting into print would be good for him! I was unable to oblige his psychiatrist by printing them—they were quite worthless, objectively considered—and I wonder what good could have come from feeding an illusion? His analyst would surely have been wiser to concentrate on the activity of writing—the desire to reach some deeper self-knowledge—rather than to attempt to float his patient on a bladder of inflated egoism. Better still, he might have set him to memorize, as we did in my school days, a real poem every week!

Then there are all those poetry workshops, poetry competitions, poetry festivals and all manner of organizations that cater for this wave of anonymous creativity. All this gives a great deal of pleasure; and while some may write in the hope or expectation of recognition of a talent they do not possess, I do not believe that is the deeper or true motive that drives so many to write. When we have written a poem we desperately want someone to read or listen to it. I believe this is not so much because we want to be told that it is a good poem, but arises from a desire to communicate, to be known not as in merely social encounters, for our outer mask, but at a deeper level, as we really are. To be known—understood—to be loved, if you like. This is a lonely world and I see all these scribblers of verse rather as one may watch sea-anemones, dull blobs of jelly when the tide is out, opening their beautiful flower-like forms in the incoming tide. Or simply like birds who sing because they have to—we do not criticize or scrutinize the birds, be they sparrows or thrushes. Though I could wish that the anonymous chorus had better models. No doubt they feel that they themselves could do as well as the kind of poetry currently published— commonplace language reflecting commonplace attitudes and very little 'poetry' in it, if by poetry we mean some glimpse of higher or deeper experiences of the imagination.

There are those who would say that the function of the arts is to 'hold a mirror up to nature'; a phrase that can be read in more senses than one. A mirror may, like a television screen, simply multiply appearances ad infinitum, or it may show our true nature reflected in the magic mirror of art. Such art mirrors imaginative truth, the invisible nature of things, 'the true man' as Blake would say; 'the human existence itself' is not the warty face but the unseen face of the soul made visible. Social realism may reflect in the smallest detail the outer aspect of things; or a reductionist art the state of mind that produced it, and which it in turn serves to spread, like an infectious disease. But unless a work of art comes from a higher, a deeper, source than the trivial daily mind how can it enlarge, expand, or heal that mind? England and the westernized world has developed a prodigious structure of material science, and this concentration on natural appearances has doubtless been reflected in the outward realism of writers like Dickens, who reflect and caricature mannerisms and externals, without a trace of that imaginative transformation that far greater chronicler of society, Proust, accomplishes, and which entitles him to the claim he himself made, to be a 'poet'. As indeed did Balzac, whose Paris is built of the inner no less than the outer lives of its inhabitants. Such is the present state of our culture; yet it would be untrue were we to deny that much verse is indeed written in the attempt to open the springs of imaginative life, perhaps just because there is so little food for the soul in the writings offered as models by contemporary writers who, however clever and observant in things of this world, are too often imaginatively illiterate, and themselves spiritually starved.

It is our misfortune to live at a time when, the material order being deemed to be the whole of the totality of the cosmos, there is no recognition of a hierarchy of values, all is on the same level, a horizontal externality with no vertical dimension. English poetry has become description of natural appearances ad nauseam and a record of human adventures in this externality, yet poetry from the beginnings of civilization has been the language of human feeling and thought at the highest level. There are, of course, exceptions, even since the Second World War (when England parted company with European civilization and became mainly open to American influences)—I think of David Gascoyne, or the Bardic poetry of Sorley MacLean, or the deeply rooted traditional simplicities of George Mackay Brown. Yet virtually all civilizations prior to our own have seen living spirit, not dead matter, as the ground of reality, and within that order, the material phenomenal world being but the outermost, and lowest plane of inner and higher causes, a 'ladder' on which the angels (spiritual intelligences) are forever 'ascending and descending'. More and more people are increasingly dissatisfied with the materialist view of things, and among the ways in which many are seeking to break through to deeper levels of reality is the writing of poetry. We are not content to live in a world of mere facts and objects, but seek to reach the 'souls', the real, essential being alike of rock and stone and tree, and of the subtler and higher regions of human thought. I am not speaking of 'another world' but of this world, seen differently, within another context: of experience. For a materialism which sees all objects of nature as lifeless and meaningless products of blind chance sets in motion a reductionism which ends in the disintegration of the human image also. We too are meaningless products of dead matter in collision, which we can observe, but not love. In this situation, the writing of poetry can be a form of meditation, a spontaneous incantation to bring us into rhythmic harmony with the powers of life; it may be an extempore prayer or psalm—indeed, what are the Psalms but the spontaneous words of the heart addressing Being itself—call it God if you like—the ultimate and living reality towards which the words of prayer rise like fire? A spell to evoke, an incantation, a prayer, an utterance of ecstasy, poems can be all these, and our own spontaneously uttered, and secret, words may seem the most appropriate.

Thus by seeing the writing of verse as an act, rather than the poem as a finished product, we place its value in the act of writing and the value that act may have to the writer; the fashionable word 'creativity' takes its meaning from this view of poetry. Not indeed that act and result are wholly separable, for the ill-written is also likely to be the uninspired—there is a formative (Coleridge's 'esemplastic') power, a rhythm of life, that at a certain intensity of imaginative thought and feeling, takes over. The ill-written is most often also the superficial, the self-centred and the facile. Something comes through, however limited the vocabulary (think of negro Spirituals) or artless the writer (children's poems can be most beautiful) if the source is true.

BUT NOW TO speak of the real poets, whose task begins where self-expression, therapy and the rest, end—those who do not choose to write, who do not send their work accompanied by a stamped addressed envelope, hoping for a word of praise to increase their confidence, but who are, as it seems, chosen by some other mind as the vessels and vehicles of communications whose source lies beyond the individual in deeper and universal regions of the spirit—who are, to use a word quite out of fashion, inspired; by the Muses, as it used to be said; by the Queen of Elfland of the Scottish ballad of Thomas the Rhymer; in more abstract terms, from the transpersonal ground of our common humanity. Jung has written of the 'collective unconscious' common to all, that same knowledge, perhaps, of which Plato said we had only to be reminded, we who are (as Blake continually says) 'sunk in deadly sleep'—the Platonic forgetfulness of higher and inner worlds. Of these worlds the poet is (in Blake's words again) 'the Awakener'. The poet indeed tells us nothing new—he awakens us to our true selves. And I suggest that the inspired words of true poetry can tell us more of ourselves than can all the 'education through art' of the Modern Movement, and the 'art therapy' psychiatrists. That, one may say, is the very purpose and nature of true art; which is indeed educational and healing also. What is civilisation if not a shared participation in the perpetual discovery and expansion of the regions of universal Imagination, the shared archetypal ground by which every individual is supported and sustained? Traditionally, there are four worlds, or levels, and poetic inspiration may take its origin in any one of these four—that of the natural world, the world of the individual soul, that of universal archetypal reality, or, it is claimed for certain sacred scriptures, from a source beyond the human order altogether. Mystery is in its nature immeasurable. Names are not important: we cannot know who the Inspirers are (Yeats called them 'instructors') but it has at all times been known *that* they are.

The most important question to be asked of poems is, from what level, what region of the mind, does their inspiration originate? Much comes from the description of the commonplace daily world; many beautiful poems and songs and sonnets of love speak from the feeling soul of the human individual; what in the past has been acknowledged and recognized as great poetry speaks for the universal mind all share—Dante and Shakespeare, Shelley, Rilke, Yeats at times (for no poet remains always at this level), and these it is whom Shelley called 'the unacknowledged legislators of the world'—legislators because they communicate thought and beauty from the deeps of the mind alike in all, though unawakened. This inner source which inspires and illuminates these realities of the invisible order, are made current within civilisations, not through sermons and political oratory, but by mythological stories, heroic epics, odes that proclaim the divine attributes and celebrate the nobility of human virtues as expressed in the living and the remembered dead; or that in love-poems bestow on men and women the aspect of their mutual beauty. It is Homer who gave to Greece—and to all succeeding ages—the heroic virtues of Hector and Achilles, and the beauty of Helen of Troy. And who but Shakespeare has created for us—held a mirror up to nature if you will—all the diversity of the English national character in his kings and queens, in Lear and Hamlet, Iago and Macbeth, down to Falstaff and Nick Bottom the weaver with his immortal ass's head?

Poets who have played their traditional part—and there have been such poets in our own century also, Eliot and Yeats, Rilke and Lorca; St. John Perse, Tagore, Robert Frost, David Jones, besides many less famous, like Edwin Muir, Vernon Watkins, David Gascoyne (to name but three I especially love)—have with the authority of their vision taken upon themselves the task—the 'labour' as Blake called it—of total imaginative absorption and transmutation of their own time and place in terms of timeless imagination. For it is not enough for the poet to be 'modern'— of his time and open to its currents of fashion—there are many such—he must at the same time be aware of the invisible order— the eye of the poet 'doth glance from heaven to earth, from earth to heaven' as Shakespeare describes him whose 'imagination bodies forth the forms of things unknown'. In every period it has been, and must be, poets, painters, musicians and architects who have embodied human meanings, visions, intellectual understanding, adding new regions to the kingdom of the Imagination which future generations may inhabit. Within the terms of the secular, materialist ideologies still current in the West and westernized world, the role of the poet as legislator of values cannot rise above the level of political spokesman or protestor for some sort of civil rights. This might lead to some reform or change of government, but not to the raising and widening of consciousness itself. The current role of the poet (so conceived) is not in this sense an essential one, but at best an adjunct to the 'politics of time', not a vision of 'the politics of eternity'. Severed from their spiritual roots the arts themselves can only present a reductionist view of humanity that can but lead to a *nihil* no less threatening to our inner universe than are our weapons of destruction, our pollution of seas and rivers, forests and cities, to the earth and its inhabitants. The arts themselves then become agents of corruption and of destruction, for the soul of humanity, without the imaginative vision, is starved or poisoned.

Worst of all perhaps is the trivialization, everywhere to be seen, which inevitably follows from a denial of the vision of other worlds—I use the word, of course, in the sense of regions of consciousness, not in the sense of 'science fiction' or of the scarcely less damaging fictions of 'science' that quantify and devaluate immeasurable life.

Blake called the poet 'the Awakener'; for is there not in us all something we feel we have forgotten, which we seek to retrieve from our unawareness, to 'remember', as Plato says? Plato's word is *anamnesis*, which means, literally, 'unforgetting'; for Plato taught that the soul knows everything, but has in this life forgotten what it knows 'in eternity'. Inspired poetry awakens us to the recollection of what is already within us, bringing with it a kind of recognition, as if we had always known these things. Inspired poetry is not 'difficult', in the sense of requiring many notes before we can understand it—on the contrary, what is inspired from this deep source comes with a sort of simplicity, like the music of Bach or a melody of Schubert, a sense of familiarity, like the landscapes and the Fools and Angels of Cecil Collins; almost one might say of a homecoming to our native country.

Blake wrote that 'One Power alone makes a Poet: Imagination, The Divine Vision'. His greatest disciple, Yeats, wrote that 'genius is a crisis that joins that buried self for certain moments to our trivial daily mind.' Both poets make the Platonic assumption of a greater knowledge accessible to us through an enlargement, an expansion of consciousness. The poetic 'Muse' is no mere literary fiction, but a reality experienced by the poets themselves, who are aware of another mind, presence, or person who inspires, instructs, 'dictates' knowledge from some source beyond the empirical ego. Plato wrote of 'the Garden of the Muses', which is the world of Imagination accessible at such times. Yeats wrote of his 'instructors' who brought their 'mysterious wisdom'. Blake wrote of two distinct kinds of poetry, that inspired by the 'Daughters of Memory'—by which he meant conscious, personal and historical memory—and that inspired by the 'Daughters of Inspiration'. Absolute distinctions cannot be made, of course, and Blake himself admits that the lesser kind is 'seldom without some Vision'; but the distinction in kind must be respected (in Blake's words) 'for the Sake of Eternal Life'.

In the absence of a recognition of any sacred tradition—or tradition of the sacred—Yeats recognized everywhere 'a certain evil, a certain ugliness that comes from the slow perishing through the centuries of a quality of mind'. It is a sense of the qualities of things that has been lost. My father used to speak of 'the *poetry* of life'; and without that poetry—that magic—the body may be fed by planners and economists, but the soul dies.

It is for this that the arts exist, not as entertainment, or as a pastime, a hobby, therapy and the like, but as the living mainstream of any civilization. A culture is precisely this inheritance, within a society, of a language and a literature, a *corpus* of music, painting, and all the arts. It was, surprisingly enough, I. A. Richards, inventor of so-called 'scientific' criticism, who called poetry 'the house of the soul'. Indeed each of us 'inhabits' an inner world, and the arts are, in every age, the collective embodiment of that inner order. Within a traditional society the shared mythology and rites of a religion and, related to these, architecture and music, painting and sculpture, dance, and all the arts provide a spacious habitation for the human spirit, at once expressing and evoking rich and deep experiences shared by all. But that house has fallen into disrepair. There has surely never been a time when the images that meet us wherever we may look have been so meaningless, so false, so valueless, not to say distorted, corrupt and soul-destroying. An appalling world is presented to us as 'the real world'. There has been a betrayal by those who transmit the heritage of culture—the schools and the Universities—and indeed among those who claim the name of poet, painter and musician themselves, whose work, instead of illuminating and redeeming the time, too often merely reflects the decay. Instead of building cathedrals, poets lament that the vision that built them was mere self-delusion. In the Universities, the meanings and intentions of the poets there studied are swept aside to give place to the 'deconstruction' of their works by so-called 'critics', in a world where knowledge is a transmission of information, not of understanding. We live in a world of imaginative illiteracy. Not through a clearer knowledge of reality but through our inability to create realities which mirror the order of the Imagination, we have built for ourselves a habitation of cement and plastic—not confined to architecture, these substances have invaded our dreams, our 'house of the Soul'. The houseless soul is driven, screaming, like Munch's famous painting, into the inner and outer dereliction which continues to proliferate around us. The frontiers of our consciousness have been narrowed and narrowed until, like Edgar Allen Poe's hero, we are driven into the pit to escape the pendulum. And this modern nightmare is not, for most of western mankind, war, starvation and torture, but, in our own society, reductionism, trivialization and profanation of the human image and the images of nature brought about by materialist ideologies which have desacralized the world by a diminishment and denial of our inner life. Yet, even now (to quote Blake again), 'If the doors of perception were cleansed, everything would appear to man as it is, infinite'.

Causes and effects are inextricably bound together so that it is hard to say whether the present impoverishment of the English language is the cause or the effect of the decline of an imaginative and spiritual culture. Just as a musician must learn to play an instrument or a sculptor to work in wood or stone, so must a poet learn the instrument of language. Indeed, every poem is a duet—a love-affair might be a better simile—between the poet and the language he inherits—there is no such thing as pure 'originality', and the American who refused to read Shakespeare because it would interfere with his own creativity was doomed to a liaison with the language of the television commercial and the chat-show. No one's language is his own, it is a collective inheritance. The poet can say only what the language permits; and language is the speech of the ancestors, not the great poets only, but all the men and women, wise and foolish, whose thoughts and feelings, intuitions, knowledge, joys and sorrows have created and sustained the words we use, filled them with meaning, the thought-structures of grammar and all the sensitive shades of thought and feeling words have gathered through the whole history of a nation. Not only the words themselves, but all their uses in all the contexts in which they have been used in the past by poets and philosophers, orators and satirists, as our language has linked generation to generation. In Yeats's 'singing-school' we must learn to bear all those echoes and resonances by which poets can—or could while the texture of the language held—remind us of those words in other contexts, evoke overtones, weaving an unbroken web of memories, allusions, echoes.

The English language was long held together by the King James Bible, the one book, very often, in a poor man's house, in which all perforce learned a rich and beautiful speech. The words of the sacred book communicated a whole range of meanings, on many levels—the literal fact, the stories of human joys and sorrows and questings, and beyond that again prophetic intuitions of a sublime order. Have we allowed words to perish because we no longer have the capacity for deep feelings and subtle thoughts? Or can we no longer enter that world of a culture slowly created over centuries to be the house of the soul, because the words have been lost? The uneducated are semantically deprived, certainly—I believe that the vocabulary in use in some notorious 'inner city areas' numbers only a few hundred words; but it is not simply a matter of the number of words we can muster, it is their content. What kind of language does our contemporary world offer, in a commercial and technological society concentrated on material skills directed to material ends?

We have many words for our fine new technology, but what words for things of the heart, the inner universe from which we are continually distracted by the stream of empty salestalk from television and newspapers? Even for our inner worlds technical terms are taking over—we do not speak of joy and sorrow, love and virtues, but of manic-depression, schizophrenia, and all the vocabulary of sex, boy-friend, girl-friend, the 'gay' (neither boys, girls nor friends, so manhood, womanhood, friendship and erotic love are all evaded and trivialized) devalue and sever bonds between parents and children, undermining the natural loves by a vocabulary invented by the psychologists to replace that of the mutual respect and duties of relationships within a civilized society. Within such societies as were held together by oral tradition, its language, songs and stories, and codes of behaviour, few words could contain much meaning; I think of the oral traditions of Scotland and even now of Ireland and Wales; or the negro people of America and their rich culture of music and 'spirituals'. But the dispossessed of our inner cities inherit no ancestral language, only the trivia of the television-screen—information, not wisdom. Nor has the new technical vocabulary of the University thesis much to recommend it. All has to be rebuilt from the ruined foundations of language itself, the present and future somehow re-grafted on to the severed roots of the past; and how will that come about? This was a theme that much exercised David Jones, who wrote of what he called 'The Break' in our culture (a break affecting both the arts and the religious roots from which these grow) and he reminded us that the arts 'abhor any loppings-off of meanings, or emptyings out, any lessening of totality of connotation, and loss of recession or thickness through'.

Doubtless great genius can accomplish the unforeseen, but can there be such genius outside a living network of a shared culture? Is not such genius itself a collective expression through the agency of one man—a Homer, a Dante, a Shakespeare? What is written is what time and place and language permit, we are instrumental, obedient to the collective, the transpersonal mind which 'inspires'. The poet knows 'the intolerable wrestle with words and meanings'. Words 'slip, slide, perish,/Decay with imprecision', Eliot wrote; there are no individual words or individual meanings. Yeats knew that there can be no 'unity of being' without 'unity of culture'. In the multitude of versifiers and scarcity of poets at this time it is hard not to see the final breakdown and fragmentation of our civilisation.

With deep reluctance I have relinquished many of the assumptions of my youth—the unquestioned assumption that civilisation, the heritage of poetry and the other arts, of language itself, were as enduring as the seasons, that the shining names would remain in their places like the stars, that other shining names would join them, that nothing could ever be lost from that heritage, that more and more people would come to participate in a shared universe of the visions of the Imagination. It seems that the civilisation I inherited is nearing its end. Eliot foresaw a new Dark Age; Yeats saw the advent of his Rough Beast the reign of Ubu Roi. David Jones asked, in his Preface to *The Anathemata*, what remains of our inheritance when 'the bulldozers have all but obliterated the mounds . . . when where was this site and were these foci there is *terra informis*'?

Of the poets writing now, I see none of major stature to be compared with the generation before the Second World War. To be truthful, I believe the age of great poets in the old sense is over, in this late phase of our civilisation. The mass media are against it, these being mainly visual, not verbal. Genius can speak through any medium, at need, and Tarkovsky has spoken through the film—his message, too, apocalyptic. Yet is not the only certainty the unforeseen, unpredictable miracle? Between the writing of this paper and its publication there have been unpredictable changes enough—even the election of a man of the theatre as President of Czechoslovakia. However, every civilisation reaches an end. Or transformation. Our own has, after all, made its great contribution.

Still, I would like (be it end or transformation of my own heritage) to consider the great value of the unity of culture which civilisation bestows. It is from the entire context of such a culture that individuals draw; without such a culture how can there be transmission of the treasuries of a shared knowledge? Civilisation is a wholeness, it is the context of human life, it is all or nothing, indivisible, a state of mind. In the modern academic world I see a tendency to break down that wholeness once the birthright of all educated people, and in older cultures to all without exception, for literacy is by no means a pre-requisite for a shared culture, and can be a destroyer when literacy is only a means of manipulation of a public in the interest of commerce or some other interest. The academic specialization in some jealously guarded 'subject' has nothing in common with the participation in a certain way of being and a shared heritage that makes us what we are—French, or Italian, or Irish by right of that participation and love. I suppose that finally it is love that gives us our place within that culture. Rilke said that to read a poem demands of the reader almost the same effort of imagination as that of the poet—giving, thereby, a wisdom and delight also equal to that of the poet.

Edwin Muir confessed himself a Platonist; and Plato sees our task as remembering the eternal world—the 'fable', as Muir calls it, the archetypal pattern. I believe that the true purpose of poetry and the other arts is to remind us, to help us to remember the eternal world within ourselves. When the old supportive structures of civilisation fall away, is our time perhaps compelled to look within? Jung speaks of this time as demanding of us individuation, the inner journey there to discover the fountain all share. Muir was also much indebted to Jung and placed his faith in that inner world. In his poem 'Day and Night' he writes:

The night, the night alone is old
And showed me only what I knew,
Knew, yet never had been told;
A speech that from the darkness grew
Too deep for daily tongue to say,
Archaic dialogue of a few
Upon the sixth or the seventh day.

And Yeats himself, lamenting the blotting out of old civilisations in a time when 'Conduct and work grow coarse, and coarse the soul', speaks of the 'dark' out of which all things will come again: 'Those that Rocky Face holds dear' shall,

From marble of a broken sepulchre,
Or dark betwixt the polecat and the owl,
Or any rich, dark nothing disinter
The workman, noble and saint, and all things run
On that unfashionable gyre again.

We know what is ending; for what is to come, is not the responsibility ours? Or are we but instruments of an eruption from the Cosmic Ground whose knowledge is beyond our imagining?

(*c.* 1990)

The Writing of Poems

I AM VENTURING TO state my own experience of the process of writing poems, as I have found it—purely as a personal testament, not as a doctrine.

Poems are not made up. A fabric of words can be made up, but if it does not tell the truth, the result is not a poem. What the truth is, depends, of course, on one's view of the nature of man and his universe, but whatever the stuff we and the world are made of may be, I do not believe that the truth, for poets, is anything less or anything different from truth in general. It is much more than a mere personal expression of opinion or point of view. The words of a poem lay bare the truth—that is, the poem. They do not construct or compose or adorn it. We learned as children how to compose sonnets, ballads, *vers libre*; to match words in rhymes and meters. We learned our language. The discovery of the poems themselves is another process.

Rimbaud—that idol of bad poets—himself a stern enough technical disciplinarian—described very well one wrong starting-point from which much bad poetry has sprung. The heresy of the 'deliberate derangement of the senses' has a large following, because it seems to offer a short cut to poetic inspiration. One can induce in oneself a sort of poetic frenzy, in which one has the sensation of knowing the world in quite a new and special way; as one has under gas or chloroform, or under the influence of alcohol or drugs. They are altogether too easy, the states of mind outside the control of the reason. But the true mystical vision cannot be reached without intense spiritual effort. And this fake mysticism bears no relation to truth, but is rather a source of attractive falsehood. It is the most amusing pastime in the world, this spinning of fantasies. It is when they do this that poets are close to lunatics—both are then subject to the control of their lower faculties of mind. The poets, of course, are only playing. The really insane cannot help it. The danger is, that poets have the power to deceive others with this web of idle make-believe—like Peer Gynt, who with his story-telling cheated his dying mother even of her death's reality.

There are those who may think that it is better to be so deluded. Such profound denial of the value of existence can only produce a decadent art. It is not for poets, who should be the guides to truth, to add to the illusion in the world.

The muscles of the body are normally controlled by two sets of nerves, one of which releases, while the other inhibits, an action. The abnormal but short-lived strength of the lunatic or the drunkard can be induced by relaxing the inhibiting nerves. In the same way, the relaxing of the reason, the judgement, and the will, liberates a stream of images, and the relaxed mind finds the writing of such poetry easy and pleasant. Only the result is not that kind of poetry that, as Shelley saw it, is the legislation of the world. Only a mad world would put the Surrealists in office.

There is another wrong way of writing that all poets know. It is the error of putting ideas into words. Only the poem can state itself, it is the thing in itself. To use the form of poetry as a way of paraphrasing some other truth, is to falsify. Why indeed should something that has already been adequately stated, gain from being stated in verse? Seen from the point of view of the poet, the error is in the way of living that such an approach to writing implies. That one should expect both to have an experience, and then to make a poem of it. I truly believe that no poem ever written transcribes an actual experience that the poet ever, apart from the poem itself, had. To write a poem about an experience, in the Byronic sense, is to admit the incompleteness both of the poem and of the experience. There is more than a superficial truth in Coleridge's assertion that the poet is a man of action *manqué*. And yet the idea is largely current among intellectuals at present, that a man of action is the lowest kind of man—a mere lout who uses his body but not his mind. This is profoundly to underestimate and to misjudge the nature of action. What it can mean for a soldier to give his life—even though it does not always mean all that it can mean; or for a woman to bear a child—while, again, it does not necessarily mean all that it can mean; or for a saint or a working man, for that matter, to work in the medium of the actual texture of the world, of life itself, of history; should never be forgotten by any poet. To work in the medium of reality is the highest of the arts, and overlooked by those who fail to see the potential greatness of the actual deed, that needs no poem to glorify or justify it. Nothing so magnificent as a birth, or a death, or a life, needs the poet to make it immortal.

Nor, on the other hand, is the poet a mere reporter and scribe of action, history or of nature itself. For poetry is itself one of the manifestations of life. A poem is the thing it states. It is the love, it is the history, it is the rose; it is the battlefield. The experience, the action, the landscape, the love, lives and is lived in the poem, not otherwise. For every epic a bard was blind, for every immortal poem, a man gave his life to the poetry. The man who writes a poem lives his life in the poetry—and does not live that piece of his life, otherwise. He is a man of action, but not *manqué*. All art is an act of sacrifice, and only those who sacrifice much can ever be great artists.

Such sacrifice is no mere abstinence or negation. That is a process that can deaden but never quicken the spirit. By sacrifice, for the poet, I mean the living in the process of writing, of a piece of life. Keats spoke of the negative character of poets. The rule seems to hold generally true.

Poets are seldom outstanding or attractive figures in their private lives, which, as a rule, they conduct singularly badly. And yet, poets must not live apart in a private world. The poet must know humanity, history, love, hate, vulgarity and beauty, intimately and personally. He must experience, endure, and enjoy the whole gamut of experience. But know it, endure it and enjoy it, not in a personal way, but through and beyond himself, vicariously, like a priest. The spirit of a poet must be entirely chaste. And chastity is not a virtue of abstaining from loving, but of experiencing love not personally, but universally, selflessly; as it is said of St Thérèse of Lisieux, that she burned with the flame of love 'as a victim of charity for mankind'.

There are those who think it must be pleasant to be a poet, and to be able to write down experiences, thereby having the cake and eating it. But the price of that immortal gift is the experience, nothing less.

Many of us, too, when we were young, wanted to be poets, because it seemed easier to live in a world of words, than in the world itself, where there are no signs to guide us. So it was—when the words were Chaucer's or Shakespeare's. But we ourselves, did we know what was demanded of us? Poverty, chastity, and obedience are easy words when we do not know what the alternatives offer us—but they are the way that saints must always travel. And for the poet, it is something very like it, in a limited medium, and a restricted sense.

By a strange paradox, the rebels against convention, the long-haired young poets who are the bohemians of any period, end by learning the necessity of obeying the stringent rules of their art. Like Cézanne, who late in life wrote that to be a painter was to submit to an order comparable with a religious order. Yeats, too, spoke of the poet's experience leading him into a world where there are many monasteries. We stray into this world, sometimes unawares. And then we find that 'to go back were as perilous as go o'er'.

The poet is the ascetic of his own solitude. There are not, after all, so very many things that we must do entirely alone. Birth, prayer, death; and creative art. Very few people like to be alone, and many cannot endure it. Poets must have a strong power of enduring active and arduous solitude. Solitude, even in the midst of the world.

What is it, then, to write a poem? If it cannot be made up in a trance, or constructed by the skilful use of words, or transcribed from life, what is this legendary inspiration that comes to poets, from a source outside the mind or within the mind, from a level of experience, in which the self scarcely partakes? Practice and experience are the best guides to this mental state that artists all know very well. But so far as I have experienced this inspiration it appears to me like this.

One sees the poem in a flash of light on the mind, as one sees a fish dart in the stream. Perhaps held in the vision for a moment or two, or even longer. Sometimes gone almost immediately. Sometimes it is a phrase or a line, sometimes a visual image, but more often, it is a mere glimpse of the Grail, of the Questing Beast, that makes the heart leap with the conviction that it has seen a vision. That there is a poem there. It seldom happens when one has leisure, pencil, or notebook, but rather when one is receiving impressions, from walking along in the country or the city or reading a book. The flame kindles out of the mechanical and habitual *terre-à-terre* of existence. Whence that light? From outside or within the mind? At the level of poetry such barriers no longer exist.

Once it has flashed into the mind, it can be recaptured by concentration, by remembering. One marks, so to speak, the pool where it lies in the mind, to return later to fish at leisure. The line, or the image, one can usually recapture exactly as it was. Then one works on it as on a dissection, lays it bare, brings it to light, fixes it as a botanist fixes a section on a slide. A wrong word, a wrong meter, can spoil it, and then, like a spoiled dissection, there is nothing to do but to discard it. Once a poem is written wrong it is hard to right it. Once a poem is commenced, fixed, one can leave it and take it up again; for, being a thing in itself, a platonic idea, one might suppose, it will not change. The process of digging it out, laying it bare, making the statue emerge from the stone, can be continued intermittently. If anything changes, it is the poet. One loses touch with the poem, forgets it, grows away from it. The work should be completed before this happens. For though some poems may be eternal, poets' minds are not. This must be particularly so with fragile lyric poetry. On the other hand, one remembers Gray's Elegy, that the poet worked over for years. Or Milton, who knew that he had an epic to write many years before he was able to turn his attention to writing it.

Writing a poem demands not only prolonged concentration but a rapidity of thought, at which the reason works at the speed of intuition, like the vibrating wings of an insect that are controlled by muscle-contractions repeated at a speed far greater than the speed required for other kinds of movement. The process of thought demands an output of energy no less great, because it is more rapid, than pages of prose. For the poem is conceived as a whole. It is like a living thing, a spirit. It has not parts, except within its whole. Each poem is like a living spirit-made incarnate.

Seen from the point of view of the poet, discussions of the rules of poetry and its forms are meaningless. What are the proportions, the dimensions, proper to a thought? Should it be a sonnet or a ballad or an ode? Every thought has its own living form, as has every insect, flower, bird, beast, or man or woman born. There are generic types, there is heredity and evolution, but all are born, not made.

What determines the form—sonnets for Petrarch, Chaucer's stanza, Milton's line—is nothing arbitrary. Poets can but reap what history sows, the words, the shapes of sentences, the cadences, that are in men's minds, ripen into poems, each in its generation. So it happens that often, by accident, poets write alike who have never seen each other's work. There is no magic about this. The work of different poets springs from a common source, literary and historic; so that others, who are not poets, can recognise as true for themselves the work of their contemporaries. Their roots are in the common soil, and their validity is for all minds that speak the same language.

The artist's place in society is always much discussed. To this question there are two opposite approaches. There are those who regard human rights as fundamental, and others who think rather in terms of human duties. The Marxist materialist puts the rights first. From this point of view the question is whether the poet should be supported by the State, or paid according to output like any other workman. Herbert Read in discussing this question, comparing the position of painters and architects with that of the poet, rightly sees no place for the 'divine *literatus*', in society on such terms. One cannot pay a poet by results, any more than a nun or a priest. There are many who see the religious life as superfluous in a world based on materialist values, and who would therefore abolish it. The artist and the poet, no less than the nun and the priest, is threatencd in the downfall of the spiritual order. The painter may take refuge for a time as a designer, and the architect as an engineer, the poet as a propagandist. But these alibis are a postponement only of the inevitable discovery that a materialist world has no place for the artist. Let the politicians make no mistake—the poet stands in the world for spiritual values, and for spiritual values only. And these, as such, have no place in Caesar's realm.

If, on the other hand one takes not the materialist approach— man's rights—but the spiritual approach—man's duties—the poet has his place. It is not the State who should support the poet, but the poet who should save the State—the poet together with the saint and all lovers of the three verities. For civilisation depends finally upon those who give more than they receive. If artists claim to be a nobility, their standards must be those that gave the word *noblesse* its connotation. As was said by one of the kings of France, nobility implies not privileges, but only duties. The poet's part in the world can only be with those who are prepared to give all and to take nothing.

As for earning a living, the inner dedication of the mind to poetry can be made at the same time as following some other profession, as Chaucer, Spenser, and Milton did; and giving hours and years to strenuous work of another kind. A lifetime's poetry—even epic poetry—can be written in a matter of weeks or months. The inner training that prepares for it covers years, and can be a life of almost any kind. A poet must undertake more, not less of life, than uncreative souls. I would not exempt a poet from anything in the world, on account of his being a poet.

Rather, impose more, since he must know more, suffer more, and understand more—a process that demands hard work and other kinds of hardship of many kinds. Poets are not like painters, who require daylight and space to work in; nor musicians, who must devote their whole time to their skill. The only living space that a poet requires is within himself. And that is both easier and harder to obtain than economic security under any political system.

(*c.* 1943)

II

THE WISDOM
OF POETRY

What Is Man?

I N CONSIDERING EDUCATION it is before all else necessary to ask that oldest of questions, 'What is man?' We find
the question in the Book of Job, who asks, 'What is man,
that thou shouldst magnify him? and that thou shouldest set thine
heart upon him?' Job is quoting from a Psalm which reminds us
of the paradox of human littleness and human greatness:

> When I consider thy heavens, the work of thy fingers, the
> moon and the stars, which thou hast ordained;
>
> What is man, that thou art mindful of him? and the son of
> man, that thou visitest him?
>
> For thou hast made him a little lower than the angels, and
> hast crowned him with glory and honour.
>
> Thou madest him to have dominion over the works of thy
> hands; thou hast put all *things* under his feet.

This Psalm is quoted in the Epistle to the Hebrews, in order
to present to the Jews, familiar with the scriptures, the new concept of Jesus as the divine humanity incarnate; and all these texts
look back, finally, to the first chapter of Genesis, where the creation of man is described:

So God created man in his *own* image, in the image of God created he him.

—and the passage goes on to describe the dominion given to man over all living things on the earth.

When Job reminds God of his exaltation of man he does so in bitterness, complaining that man is a creature of dust who goes down to the grave unregarded. Nevertheless the theme which runs through the Bible, from Genesis to the Epistle to the Hebrews, is man as the image of God, bearer of the divine imprint; Jesus, as the Son of Man, is the realisation of the first-created humanity, the *anthropos*, as imagined by the Creator before the Fall; which Fall is the result of Adam's 'sleep', a loss of consciousness, a 'descent', as the Greeks would say, from a spiritual to a natural mode of consciousness, with a consequent self-identification not with the spiritual but with the natural body; which is, as Job complains, a thing of dust.

The Greeks too asked the question 'what is man?'—the riddle of the Sphinx: 'What is it that in the morning goes on four legs, at midday on two legs, and in the evening on three legs?'—a bitter evocation of the mortal worm who creeps from helpless infancy, through a brief and precarious prime to the helplessness of infirm age. Oedipus guessed the riddle, and, by implication, acknowledged the truth of the Sphinx's description of man.

Which is of course the widely accepted view of mankind in modern secular societies. Week in week out the evolutionists describe natural man on the mass media; the schools assume the finality of the scientific description of reality, including natural man (who dares question the infallibility of science—natural knowledge—or its pronouncements?). Thus in our secular society man the mortal worm is, paradoxically, denied the only dignity which properly belongs to us—our spiritual nature—and at the same time proclaimed as the lord of creation. Education of the mortal worm for a brief life on earth is inevitably therefore designed to fit men and women to the performance of tasks concerned with bodily life, tasks more or less skilled, but all alike directed to the production of material goods and the construction and control of machines, also utilized for material ends. Ultimately man becomes, within such an order, a replaceable spare part in the great machine a materialist society has constructed, with a built-in obsolescence after fifty or so years of efficient functioning. The modern state is a self-perpetuating machine built to last longer than any individual lifetime and we like to pretend that the state, or the world super-state, will last forever—well, nearly forever, and what difference is there between eternity and a very long time indeed? The world will last our time, we shall not be here at the end; at most we wonder about our grandchildren, but who cares about their own progeny six generations hence? 'They are destroyed from morning to evening: they perish forever without any regarding it.'

This is the implicit, and sometimes explicit, view of the materialist Western society to which we belong, and it is difficult to remain totally untouched by the evolutionism of materialist science, which recognizes only a material order, with humankind as part of that order—the most complex and 'evolved' species which has produced man as the cleverest of the primates, by a process of natural selection. This process may produce cleverer primates yet and (as many hopefully believe) is bound to do so, because evolution, guided though it is by blind chance, can result only in Utopia; (Utopia, be it said, in the modern sense of the word, as a society in which all temporal mankind's aspirations and desires will be realised. The catholic Thomas More would not have expected a society without any spiritual order to have any such result). In the modern Utopian dream every disease will be 'conquered', and so perhaps will death, and no one will go cold or hungry or unintegrated within the social structure; as for living, our machines will do that for us, thereby freeing us to enjoy this hell of spiritual meaninglessness for as long as we can endure it.

Utopians never give up their myth: the plain evidence goes to show that the English nation (to look no farther afield) simply cannot stand it, that the schoolchildren do not want to be trained for the kind of 'jobs' that the machines provide, in the technological Utopia where thinking is something computers do, where the brain, is synonymous with mind and thought. We have even had it claimed that a computer can write poems, and truth to say the examples given were all too like many produced by human beings who conceive themselves in terms of a mechanistic science.

Students engage in revolution, destruction making small demands in comparison with the complex programming of the university syllabus; besides satisfying some unformulated and baffled sense of frustration engendered by the secular society. The mass of mankind—the worker-ants—misled by the ever-present advertisements which tell us that Utopia is in every packet of this or that, grasp what they can, forever deceived by the trash of the machines which cheats their dreams of realisation. Who can blame them that they are dissatisfied? Clever cynics who know about human dreams paint for them those desert-islands, those far shores and clear paradisal streams, unfelled trees, unbulldozed meadows, unravished Eves, that forever elude the purchasers of cigarettes and convenience foods, underwear and insurance policies, cosmetics made from slaughtered whales whose rotting carcases stink upon the real shores, and all the celestial omnibuses are driven on oil and coal and steel from Paradise Lost, and the tasteless bread and canned vegetables harvested from a waste land where the wild flowers and the bees are sprayed with poison, the rabbits, so popular on children's cot-covers, die of myxomatosis, and as the motorist fancies a tiger in his tank the real tigers of the earth are threatened with extermination. The world has never been more hideous, more uninhabitable, than the world created by an ideology which proclaims that this world is all, which gives matter a primacy, an all-importance unknown to other civilisations. Decidedly the way to Utopia is long and hard for the last of the primates.

If man is indeed what Blake calls the mortal 'worm of sixty winters' and 'seventy inches long', 'born in a night to perish in a night', what can education be? In a world of pure materialism education can only be utilitarian, a training to fit the human spare part for the function it is to perform during its few useful years; after which there is nothing to expect but death: and death is the end, as birth was the beginning of life. The satisfaction of natural appetites is presumed to give the mortal worm, or naked ape, those satisfactions of which we are capable; including music, whose rhythms serve to stimulate or soothe, food and shelter, sensual pleasure, freedom from pain, hunger, cold, or the disorientation of those habits to which we are conditioned; 'programmed', as it is nowadays called. And so, 'distracted from distraction by distraction', as T. S. Eliot wrote of the dwellers in the waste land, we 'get by'. Drugs can alleviate whatever states of anxiety our souls may cause us, and there is yet another industry to cater for our inevitable dreams or day-dreams; for these are an as yet unexplained flaw in the perfect adaptation and functioning of mortal life: mankind continues to imagine quite other things.

The Utopian view of humanity is of course untrue; untrue not because the deductions of science concerning natural law are incorrect within their own terms—the great merit of the scientific method is its respect for evidence and, in that sense, for truth—but untrue because the assumption—the premise of Western science, that nothing exists other than the quantifiable natural world—is false. Consciousness—to take the most obvious thing in the world—cannot, for example, be quantified, cannot be dealt with at all in terms of weight and measure, of those extensions in space or in time which are the only terms proper to material science. Mental and physical entities are incommensurable not because science has not 'as yet' found a way of describing mental events in physical terms but because these belong to distinct orders. In measuring the brain-waves of dreamers or of meditators, scientists have not come one whit nearer to measuring the dreams themselves; nor can they ever do so within the terms of their proper field of knowledge. This is no reproach to natural science, which has its own field, and whose account of natural phenomena is impressive indeed—a field which rightly includes man's physical frame, its anatomy, physiology, and place within the natural universe.

But so overwhelmed are we by wave after wave of information about man's natural evolution and affinity with nature on the one side, and on the other by medical explanations of whatever concerns the psyche, that we easily forget that man is *not* merely a clever primate; we forget that the brain is *not* the mind, that consciousness is *not* a property of the sense-organs of which it makes use. We forget, in fact, that man is *not* a species of animal but a new kingdom, as distinct from the animal kingdom as mammals are distinct from rocks. Each kingdom, from the mineral to the vital, from the vital to the animate, from animal consciousness to the human kingdom of the Imagination, is subject to new laws proper to itself. This Teilhard de Chardin has made very clear to our generation, but he still has not clearly enough reminded us that mankind, as human (for of course we share the laws of chemistry with the mineral world, the vital physiology with plants, and our bodily senses with the animals) is an invisible kingdom whose world is a mental world, subject to laws proper to itself which do not conform to the categories of time and space, or to any of the laws of nature. Because this is in reality so, and equally so for atheists as for Christians, for Marxists as for Buddhists, the extreme picture of man as a spare part of his own machines can never altogether come about. We cannot altogether dehumanize ourselves.

Whereas our opinions can make us very unhappy and raise in us all kinds of conflicts between what is so and what we opine to be so, they cannot alter the reality of what we are. We continue to be human, and insofar as we are human we are spiritual beings.

Western materialism is an unprecedented departure from human culture, as it has existed and developed from the stone age to the present time. From the oldest examples of human art we see humankind seeking to express ideas, to discover a mental order; to explore our inner worlds in terms of pantheons of 'gods' who personify the qualities of human consciousness, our moods and modes of experience. From the earliest known human records we see humankind creating abstract patterns and forms not found in nature; gods of strange unnatural aspect—the more unnatural the more profoundly 'human'. Modern Amazonian savages asked Lévi-Strauss, that civilized Frenchman, why he and his kind did not paint their faces with abstract patterns in order (like the Amazonians) to affirm their humanity, their difference from the animals around them.

They knew what Western anthropologists would seem to have forgotten, that to be human is, precisely, to live our myths, to live according to an inner order which is not natural, which is, in terms of natural law, unnatural. The distortions and deformations of the human face and body, the paintings and tatooings practised by primitive, from the land of El Dorado to Borneo or the Congo are supremely, specifically human, being expressions of a mental, an inner world, affirmed in opposition to, in challenge of, a natural order. The pantheons of more advanced societies are more psychologically complex and subtle explorations of those inner regions of human consciousness. The familiar gods of Greece—still, in many respects, our own self-knowledge personified—are not mere moods and passions but intellections of great subtlety, related each to certain fields of knowledge. The Orphic theology in all its complexity of hierarchic relationship and causality is unsurpassed as an account of mankind's invisible worlds, a system no less elaborate in its structuring than the scientist's description of the kingdoms of nature.

To name only one or two of the most obvious examples of the distinctness of these inner fields, Apollo is the principle of all mental clarity, knowledge of music and number, medicine, the ordering principle that belongs to the enlightened mind, to the rational; the changing moon goddess to dark knowledge of the blood, to parturition, witchcraft, all kinds of feminine regions of experience. Dionysus is the genius of ecstatic possession by irrational states of consciousness, an exaltation unknown to the clear reason of Apollo's kingdom; while Ares takes over the warrior when, like the Irish Cuchulain, the battle-warp seizes him, his hair stands on end, his face is distorted with rage and his body filled with the berserk courage the Vikings delighted in, a transport of rage in which the warriors scarcely felt the wounds of battle. To each god his kingdom. In our own century these principles or energies of the psyche which materialist science had thought to dismiss as unrealities, or as primitive attempts by mankind to describe the 'laws of nature', have been renamed by C. G. Jung the 'archetypes', which are, as he says, self-portraits of the instincts. Jung was the tireless reminder of our forgetful age that the psyche is real; that it is also most dangerous. It is not from nature that this world stands in danger of destruction, but from the human mind which has invented hydrogen bombs and the ideologies in whose service such weapons may be used. If the most appalling apocalyptic prophecies are realised it will have been ourselves who have brought them about. The author of the Book of Revelation read only the possibilities within the inner worlds of mankind. We are inclined to read that book as a threat from an arbitrary and cruel (but fortunately, so the scientists reassure us, non-existent) God; but read that terrifying book as the story of inner events within the human psyche reflected—as our thoughts inevitably must be—in the world of history, and we must tremble, not at what 'God' might do to us, but at what we ourselves have it in us to do to ourselves and to our world. Is not that prophecy of poisoned seas and rivers, of Armageddon, of shelterless refugees, of destruction falling from the skies, already realised, nor by some cosmic catastrophe or arbitrary act of 'victimization', as it is called, of innocent humankind by a demon-god, but by the demons who inhabit the human soul?

All the great religious traditions have been attempts to cultivate the human soul. But any attempt in our materialist civilisation to bring order to the inner worlds, to nourish the specifically human, has gone by default. Not altogether so, of course, for the past is still powerful and two thousand years of Christendom and all the wisdom of the Greek and the Hebrew traditions before that are still with us; or at least with the educated sections of society, who are less at the mercy of current ideologies. Pythagoras continues to impose upon the soul the order of the diatonic scale through such music as is still composed according to its laws. Christian art continues to remind us of the celestial hierarchies of angels, of the lives of saints lived in accordance with the laws not of nature but of the spirit; of the Christian myth of the birth of the Divine Principle into the world of generation, fully manifested in that sublime figure of Christ Pantocrator, the ruler of all, depicted in the dome of every Orthodox basilica; and whose suffering under the world-rulers for whom man is natural man, the armed ape and the toga'd ape, Western Catholicism, in the image of the Crucifix, has never allowed us to forget. For the struggle to rise from the natural to the human kingdom is hard and endless, and none of us has succeeded so well that we can afford to dismiss the symbol of the Crucifixion, which Utopians would like to banish from their brave new world; which is the hell of the human spirit whose kingdom, as it is said in the Christian Gospel, is 'not of this world'.

Let me remind you that we are still considering the question 'What is man?' I have suggested that man is, in truth, nor a mortal worm but a spiritual being, immaterial, immeasurable, who is never born and never dies, because spirit is not bounded or contained within the categories of the material world of time and space, of duration and extension. In this sense, we are immortal, eternal, boundless within our own universe. Yet of the kingdom that is truly ours, specifically human, we have realised very little.

Nowadays the term 'human' has been inverted to the point of signifying precisely what is least human in us, our bodily appetites and their gratification, and all that belongs to natural man; while the study of philosophy, for example, or the practice of some religious asceticism is considered 'inhuman'. Nothing in our 'permissive' society is held to be more 'human' than the act of sex; but Alexander the Great—Aristotle's pupil—said that man was never *less* human than in that act. He was not, of course, speaking of love, which is of the soul and has no necessary connection with the sexual instinct. Sex is an animal function, love a human experience. It is all too easy to revert to the animal which we, as humanity, must labour to transcend in order to come into even a small portion of our potential kingdom. The late Dr Schumacher, who in his book *Guide to the Perplexed* made many things so clear, liked to quote Aquinas's words, 'Even the least knowledge of things superior is of greater value than the most extensive knowledge of things inferior'.

Having, therefore, reminded ourselves that humanity, in so far as we are human, is a kingdom not in nature, 'not of this world', but an invisible inner universe, let us consider this universe a little more closely.

While every pantheon is a less or more perfect, a more or less crude and simple, or subtly complex representation of the structure of the human inner worlds, certain elements seem to recur and to represent the abiding structure of the psyche. The sphere quadrated by a six-armed cross, or the circle quadrated by a four-armed cross; four-ness under many symbols— the four-faced gods of India; the four 'sons' of the Egyptian Harpocrates; Jesus Christ with the four evangelists, the four 'living creatures' of Ezekiel's fourfold Chariot of God, or the lion, eagle, ox and angel of the Book of Revelation. C. G. Jung in his *Psychological Types* has made the Four familiar as the 'functions' of the human psyche: reason, feeling, sensation and intuition. Blake, basing his symbol upon Ezekiel and St John, describes the four 'Zoas' or 'living creatures' whose conflicts and rebellions form the drama of his Prophetic Books. These Four are in every man; and Blake speaks of the Four Zoas as the four 'faces' of the Universal Man; as the four rivers of Paradise; as four 'worlds' or 'universes'—distinct worlds, each with its own mode of knowledge, distinct and incommensurable, as feeling or intuition with reason, or sensation with the other three. Blake, at the end of the eighteenth century, had already diagnosed what he calls 'the sickness of Albion'—that is, of the English national being—as the usurpation by the rational function—Urizen—of the throne and sceptre of supremacy which properly belongs to the Imagination, the 'human existence itself ' and divine anthropos, made in the image of God, which is above the Four. Urizen is the rational mind, basing its deductions upon what Blake calls a 'ratio of the five senses', and his creation is scientific materialism. The rational mind is aware of no form of knowledge higher than itself, calling the

Imagination 'delusion and fancy'. This spiritual sickness of the English nation Blake saw typified in those culture-heroes of science, Bacon, Newton and Locke (to whose number others have since been added—Darwin, Huxley, Russell and so on), who share the false premise of all, that 'matter', a substance existing apart from the mind which perceives it, is the only ground of the 'real'. Under the rule of Urizen, feeling becomes no longer a mode of knowledge, but a selfish emotion; while intuition, refusing the rule of Urizen, rebels in vain. Although Blake was well able to argue the case against rationalism in its own terms—and did so most trenchantly—his most powerful weapon was the depiction of man the rationalist, anxious and purblind, unable ever to complete his conquest of the rebellious energies of life; a foolish travesty of God the Father.

Blake describes the 'sickness of Albion' under the usurping rule of Urizen as a 'deadly sleep', using the Platonic term, which sees unconsciousness, oblivion of the real, forgetfulness of the eternal worlds within, as the mark of the human condition described in the Jewish-Christian tradition as the Fall. Mankind is 'fallen', specifically, from a human (imaginative) into a natural mode of consciousness. Thus understood, the Fall has nothing to do with the commission of certain specific 'sinful' acts, but is a descent from a higher state of being into a lower, from the Imagination to the natural body; as symbolized, in the Biblical story, by the eating of the apple.

Every 'revealed' tradition is agreed upon the essential structure of the human psyche, of that invisible inner universe which is the properly human kingdom, from which we have 'fallen' into natural life; all holding our present state of consciousness as imperfect in relation to that which we essentially are, man as first created in the order of 'origins', by which a temporal beginning in the sense of the scientific evolutionists is not of course meant, but rather the type, pattern, archetype of the *anthropos*, 'made in the image of God', as described in the first chapter of Genesis. The 'human', according to tradition, is not, as for our own society, natural man but the archetypal perfect humanity, of whom every average man is a more or less obscured and distorted image. Our own secular society has sought to make everyone happy by taking as the norm 'fallen' man, Plato's dwellers in the Cave; but flattery of our fallen, or forgetful condition can only superficially and briefly deceive us into believing that all is well, that we are all we should be, since each of us carries within ourselves, however obscured, the image of the *anthropos*.

This is a goal few have attained. The Buddhist world holds that Prince Siddhartha attained perfect enlightenment; Christians believe that Jesus was the Christ, fully incarnating the archetypal first created Son of God. The Hindu tradition holds that there have been several revelations of the divinity in human form; that whenever the world has fallen into spiritual darkness a new revelation of the divine Person has again made known to us our own forgotten reality. All traditions are agreed that the divine humanity, although the type of all humanity, has scarcely ever been realised: for the Christian world, once only; for the Jews, not yet but some day; no religious tradition flatters us, as do the Utopians, by allowing us to believe that we can come within reach, or barely within apprehension, of that which we essentially are. Few attain enlightenment, few are saints. One of the most deplorable features of the secular West is the universal complacency of a mankind often barely human at all, in properly human terms. Many 'primitive' races—many American Indians, or the illiterate country people still to be found here and there in the West of Ireland or of Scotland, live upon a higher and more properly human level than the sophisticated products of our technological culture. I do not doubt that many powerful commissars could learn much of the real nature of humanity from village grandmothers with shawls over their heads and a corner of icons; icons which are, by definition, depictions of invisible spiritual essences. You find their depictions in the interior of any Orthodox church—in the Mother of God, the Pantocrator, angels, saints; or in Italy's pre-Renaissance basilicas—in the Church of Saint Francis at Assisi, where the episodes of the saint's life Giotto has depicted are all of them spiritual events—dreams, visions, the casting out of demons, the beholding of the eternal Christ. In the secular world the facts that make up our news—the events narrated as biography or as fiction—are all of the natural order; how few belong to this human order, which we of the West have so deeply betrayed.

If, then, in order to 'educate' a human being it is first necessary to answer that old question 'What is man?' are we to process, to condition, to 'form', to 'brainwash' natural mankind to fit human beings for a longer or shorter lifespan in the natural world and the performance of more or less skilled tasks in the great mechanism? Or ought we not rather to consider man's invisible kingdom, the boundless interior regions we inhabit, the almost unguessed, undiscerned spiritual regions within us, so close to childhood, but later only to be attained through aspirations and disciplines which have little to do with the amassing of facts or the learning of technical skills which passes for education in our secular society?

Blake called the Divine Humanity, the imprinted archetype, the Imagination. Imagination, he said, is 'the true man', the unifying life of which the Four are the faculties, the instruments.

Whereas the soul, with its fourfold universe, is individual, the Imagination is universal—the universal self alike in all. The word 'Imagination' suggests, in common parlance, the arts; and in so far as, in a normal society, music, painting, poetry and architecture are depictions of mankind's inner worlds, the proper language of the soul, this is true; for, whereas science measures the natural world, the arts alone can depict the inner worlds.

But while it is true that the arts are the proper expression of the inner worlds, of mankind's imaginative self-knowledge, from the caves of Ajanta or Lascaux to Santa Sophia and Chartres, we must remember that not all that goes by the name of art is an embodiment of inner reality. Plato condemned naturalism in art, the mere imitation of natural behaviour. If the soul and its world—and, above that, the universal Imagination and its order—is not known, how can it be expressed? And that we live in an age of spiritual ignorance is everywhere evident in our art-forms, which are for the most part self-portraits of states of ignorance, not of knowledge.

Imitative, naturalistic art of the kind fashionable in the nineteenth century was not always without some vision, some reflection of paradise seen in the forms of nature; we think of Samuel Palmer, of Calvert, Constable, Turner, for whom nature is itself the glass in which Imagination beholds itself; but, for many more, realistic depiction is mere trick photography of natural appearances; as is the 'social realism' of Marxist materialism.

The newer fashions, from abstract expressionism to the present, proclaim art as 'self-expression', sometimes glorified by the name 'creativity'; American universities have classes in so-called 'creative writing', and in our own schools there is endless talk of teaching children to express themselves 'creatively'. But self-expression is, unfortunately, very far from being an expression of imaginative vision and imaginative knowledge. The final result of this century's guiding principle in the arts of 'breaking with the restrictions of the past' in order to be totally 'original', has been a school of scribbles whose total originality expresses only the ignorance of its authors; expresses nothing at all. The only 'originality' that has any value is a return to the origin, the lost knowledge of the Imagination.

The art of a secular society has suffered fatally from the identification of 'knowledge' with natural science. It has been forgotten that there can be 'knowledge', in any precise or universal sense, of the invisible worlds; knowledge no less exact than science's knowledge of the natural universe. Therefore, whereas we know very well that in order to be a mathematician or a chemist we must study the laws of mathematics or of chemistry, we have forgotten that there is knowledge proper to the soul. It is true that the mathematical and chemical laws of nature are everywhere expressed in the world about us, but we do not for that reason expect our schoolchildren to go and find them out for themselves by observation or to practise 'free expression' in chemistry, or to 'liberate themselves' from traditional mathematics in order to become original astronomers or physicists. We have far too much respect for science to turn it, as we have turned the arts, into a children's playground. We cannot expect our children, our 'young' poets and painters to discover for themselves the abiding order of the invisible worlds. Just as those who study mathematics or chemistry or plant morphology respond with recognition to what they are taught, so, far from inhibiting talent and 'creativity', knowledge of higher things can only awaken a similar response and widen the field of the individual imagination. But we have denied or forgotten that the invisible worlds can be fields of knowledge which can be taught and learned and transmitted and communicated. Other civilisations have taken this to be so as a matter of course. From Indian metaphysics, Platonic theology, Christian doctrine, down to the religiously preserved sacred stories of the most primitive tribes, every race has preserved its own embodiments of a 'revealed' tradition concerning the inner nature of things, the order of the soul. These theologies, theogonies, sacred rites and tribal myths are not pastimes or self-expression, they are the self-knowledge of the human psyche upon which alone a culture can be based, be that culture simple as that of the Bushman or metaphysically rich as Vedanta. It is we who are the barbarians—spiritual barbarians, that is—who lack this collective language, this shared knowledge, upon which the goldsmiths of Byzantium, the builders of Chartres, the musicians of the diatonic scale, the painters of Florence, down to Yeats and the poets of the Irish renaissance, drew.

MY CONCLUSION, THEN, is that our materialist secular society, well though it may educate in the natural sciences, altogether fails to educate the human soul, the invisible humanity which is, in Plato's words as well as Blake's, 'the true man'. We are simply not educated in these things which above all make us human. Those who inherit—who have not yet lost, under the cancerous impact of Western ideologies—some metaphysical, religious and iconographic tradition, some language of symbolic images built up throughout a civilisation, are fortunate indeed. For the rest of us, all is to be remade; not altogether as if it had never been, for in the relics, the survivals of the past, we can rediscover lost knowledge, piece by piece reconstructing something, perhaps, which will serve a broken culture without a tradition of its own. Reality is always and everywhere itself; but who shall say whether we can use the language of Christendom, of the Far East, of Islam (the last prophetic revelation), of Cabbala, of the American Indians? In all the arts there is a confusion of tongues. Blake knew everything except how to find symbolic or linguistic terms to communicate what he knew; he was eclectic in his symbols but orthodox in his Christian theology. Yeats's lifelong labour was to test, to discard or to retain, a great range of symbols and terms drawn from many traditions, Rosicrucian, neo-Platonic, Far Eastern. To recreate a common language for the communication of knowledge of spiritual realities, and of the invisible order of the psyche, is the problem now for any serious artist or poet, as it should be for educators. Yet the problem of language would resolve itself once these worlds were re-opened to our experience, for the knowledge itself is primary, the terms—symbols—secondary. This rediscovery, re-learning, is a long hard task—a lifelong task for those who undertake it; yet the most rewarding of all tasks, since it is a work of self-discovery which is at the same time a universal knowledge, 'knowledge absolute' as the Vedas claim. So-called 'creativity' and 'self-expression' will not get us very far. The Grecian goldsmith, the Gothic sculptor, the painter of churches or elaborator of Islamic geometric patterns in a mosque were none of them 'expressing themselves' in the modern sense of the term; far less breaking with the past, or being 'revolutionary'. They were making use of the shared knowledge of a spiritual tradition that illuminates their work, as it illuminated the inner lives of those who participated in its unity of culture.

(1979)

Premises and Poetry

ALTHOUGH IN THIS paper scholarship would be inappropriate the conclusions I shall suggest have been reached through much reading, though of books not generally considered necessary to the understanding of 'English Literature' as taught in the universities. But I claim poetic licence—and poetic precedent—for the unorthodoxy of my studies. The poets do not read the same books as the academics, or even the same kind of books; or if the same books, read them in a different way. Thomas Taylor the Platonist, whom Emerson called the best 'feeder of poets since Shakespeare', for example, was veritably persecuted by the reviewers of the end of the eighteenth century and the early nineteenth century because he read Plato, Plotinus and Proclus for the truths they taught and not for the sake of mere erudition (which Taylor himself castigated in no uncertain terms). 'Feeder of poets' is true of 'the modern Plethon', as Taylor called himself; for it was through his translations and commentaries of the neo-Platonists and Plato himself that the Romantic poets learned their Plotinian aesthetics and their symbolic language of mythology, their doctrine of imagination and the soul. Blake and Flaxman were among his friends, Shelley's intimate friend Thomas Love Peacock (who

put Taylor in his novel *Melincourt*) his admiring follower.
Coleridge had read his works while still at school, and we may
trace Wordsworth's mind and Keats's also, I believe, travelling over the pages of his paraphrase translation of Plotinus's
Concerning the Beautiful (*Ennead* I, book VI), which went into
a second edition and was most obviously a source book among
the Romantics. Samuel Palmer in Italy planned to read Plato on
his return to London; presumably in Taylor's translation, since
there was no other at the time. Emerson and Bronson Alcott made
of Taylor's works (scorned by the dons of Oxford) the foundation of the American Transcendentalist movement. His translation of Porphyry's *De Antro Nympharum* was early known to
Yeats, doubtless through the Theosophical Society and John M.
Watkins, the theosophical publisher and bookseller who reissued
Porphyry's *Cave of the Nymphs*.[1] called him 'the uncrowned
king'. And for all this, his very name, until recently, was not to
be found in academic works on the Romantic poets. His books,
even the few reprinted by the Theosophical Society and by John
M. Watkins (and one or two in America), are extremely rare and
to be found on no university syllabus, so far as I know. But I
name Taylor as an example—though a central one—to illustrate
my argument that there is a great field of excluded knowledge
which the schools, dominated by the materialist climate of the
time, do not recognize.

I was fortunate in not reading English Literature at the university (I read Natural Sciences). I did not do so because I saw no
reason why educated people cannot read for themselves the literature of our own language. But from my own point of vantage

---

1 George Russell.

(or disadvantage) I saw something of the revolution in the reading of poetry, whose beginnings lie outside the universities, in larger social changes; and whose consequences likewise go far beyond the English schools. I was spectator, but never participator in this cultural revolution; which may conceivably mark the beginning of a new civilisation but assuredly marks the end of what C. S. Lewis has called 'old western' culture; of which (so he told Cambridge in his inaugural lecture as Regius Professor in the mid-1950s) he was among the last examples. But, as a student of natural sciences, I did come under the influence of the materialist ideology, and have, over the intervening years, piece by piece and with much toil and some pain restructured my thought. I do not know how many of my own generation have shared my experience; when I meet old Cambridge contemporaries I find most of them still of the party I deserted. It is in a younger generation that I see a questioning of the materialist premises of the kind which led me to discover the excluded knowledge; which indeed is not far to seek when once we know what we are looking for.

What I saw happening (and indeed I attended several of Dr I. A. Richards's open lectures on Practical Criticism, delivered in—I think—1925 or '26) was, as I now see it, a brilliant exercise in the reading of a whole body of English poetry—almost, though not quite, of *the* whole body of English poetry—in the context of a culture not only unlike, but in its fundamental premises, opposed to that which had produced the literature of 'old western' culture. The method is now well known to all who have taught English in the universities; a poem is taken, preferably one unknown to the students. The exercise of dating and ascription is a secondary one, and the real purpose of Richards's now famous method is to see the poem in itself and precisely 'out of context'. This way of reading a poem works best (works only, perhaps) when the culture of the student is, in general, the same as that of the poet. Only then does the answer to the question 'What does the poem mean to me?' approximate to what the poem meant to its author.

It was never Richards's intention that his 'scientific' criticism should replace the reading of poems in the context of the poet's whole work and thought, or poets in the context of their culture. But what he had designed as a teaching method, a way of focusing vague minds upon the text before them, happened to coincide with that social change which was sending for the first time to the universities students from classes hitherto uneducated. In this cultural revolution it was Leavis who made of Richards's teaching method a weapon. For it was an excellent way of encouraging such students, burdened with the sense of their own ignorance, to say 'Never mind the past, or the poet, read the poem word by word and register your own responses'. The poem was, as it presently became fashionable to say, 'the words on the page'. Add to this Leavis's performances in the art of demolishing some trifling poem by an obscure poet (with an occasional hit-and-run on the great Milton, or Shelley) and his popularity in the decades of the 'inferiority complex' is understandable. But again, Leavis, and his magazine *Scrutiny* (how well the word expresses the attitude, carried over from that phase of the natural sciences that murdered to dissect), rose on the tide of a world revolution with a new religion—scientific materialism. In this situation it could be said that the new 'scientific' criticism was an attempt to save for the new age the literature of the older culture by demonstrating how much remains to be admired and understood even when the system of thought of which it is an expression is discarded and replaced by another, whose answer to the question 'What is Man?' is so radically different. Recently, to the English television audience (popular culture in the early 1970s having overtaken Cambridge undergraduate culture of the mid-1920s), Dr Bronowski, another Cambridge contemporary, interpreted the cathedral of Rheims in terms of its construction. The vision of God and his Mother, the theology of Aquinas, the aspiration of worshipping multitudes, might never have existed. Of course Gothic architecture is, as Bronowski demonstrated, a marvel of engineering; but can it be explained in terms of the curiosity of the master masons about the stresses and strains in stone? Is Michelangelo's statue in the marble to be understood in so literal a way? Bronowski too was clearly concerned to save the bare ruined choirs for the post-revolutionary world in which it is supposed that materialism must prevail even in those countries where Marxism as yet does not. Why the same passion for engineering has in our own time produced not Rheims or Chartres but Megalopolis Dr Bronowski did not say; or did he see no significant difference in meaning between a Gothic cathedral and one of New York's temples of commerce?

Plotinus in *Concerning the Beautiful* takes architecture as his example in illustrating a very different thesis. For him the building is not a 'construction in space' (to use a phrase popular among modern sculptors) but an idea in the artist's mind. Architectural harmony is a matter not of engineering but of intellect. (I quote Taylor's paraphrase translation of 1787.)

But how can that which is inherent in body accord with that which is above body? Let us reply by asking how the architect pronounces the building beautiful, by accommodating the external structure to the fabric in his soul? Perhaps, because the outward building, when entirely deprived of the stones, is no other than the intrinsic form, divided by the external mass of matter, but indivisibly existing, though appearing in the many. When, therefore, sense beholds the form in bodies, at strife with matter, binding and vanquishing its contrary nature, and sees form gracefully shining forth in other forms, it collects together the scattered whole, and introduces it to itself, and to the indivisible form within; and renders it consonant, congruous and friendly to its own intimate form.

For Plotinus, a building is beautiful in so far as it expresses a triumph of mind over matter's innate formlessness. Matter 'is base, and separate from the divine reason, the great fountain of forms; and whatever is entirely remote from this immortal source, is perfectly base, and deformed. And such is matter, which by its nature is ever averse from the supervening irradiations of form.' The principle of form, which Bronowski (speaking for his time and place) found in matter, Plotinus finds in mind. The 'construction in space', is redeemed from being that conglomerate heap of stones that works so named very often appear to be, by the organizing form of the idea. A circle is a circle whether it be drawn in ink or chalk or inscribed on the stone of New Grange or the turf of Stonehenge; and is neither 'the ink on the page' nor the 'construction in space'.

The poem as the 'words on the page' is the literary equivalent of Bronowski's view of architecture. The student of literature begins with the words on the page; the poet with an idea which does not yet exist in words but which does exist as an idea, a mood, an intuition; even as a wordless form, somewhat like music. My own experience as a poet is that, like Plotinus's builder, one attempts to match words to an idea, the poem in the mind; or, rather, hovering just beyond the reach of the conscious mind. But our success in communication (in this the poet is less fortunate than architect or musician) is dependent upon the reader's knowledge of words, his range of literary associations. For words mean nothing in themselves; they are only a currency supported by meanings; the gold is in the bank, as it were, and the paper currency has more or less value against the reader's own equivalence in the realms of gold. The poet's too, of course; which in the present literary situation is very often more meagre than his reader's. When the reader's field of association, which alone gives meaning to words, is very different from that of the poet, he will not be reading, through 'the words on the page', the same poem as the poet wrote. He 'speaks a different language', though the words he uses may be the same on the page. But they do not carry the same meaning.

In my own lifetime I have seen—indeed experienced—the sleight of hand by which the central canon of English poetry has come to be read in a context of thought, and according to premises alien to the poets themselves. Poets of the imagination write of the soul, of intellectual beauty, of the living spirit of the world. What does such work communicate to readers who do not believe in the soul, in the spirit of life, or in anything that can be (unless the physically desirable) called 'the beautiful'? For in René Guénon's 'reign of quantity' such terms of quality become, as the linguistic philosophers would say, 'meaningless', because there is nothing for which they stand.

This is only in part a matter of period; far more it is a matter of culture; for not all who are contemporary share the same culture. Take Hopkins, who can be said to have been I. A. Richards's great discovery. Two of his pupils—William Empson and E. E. Phare—wrote on poems by Hopkins using the method of Richards's 'scientific' criticism. William Empson in his book *Seven Types of Ambiguity* wrote on 'The Windhover'; as brilliant a misreading of 'the words on the page' as could be found. I remember he made much play with the key word, 'buckle':

> Brute beauty and valour and act, oh, air, pride, plume, here Buckle! AND the fire that breaks from thee then.

'Buckle', William Empson argues, could mean that the priest will 'buckle' these virtues on (like St Paul's 'whole armour of God') in the life he has chosen; or that these virtues 'buckle like a bicycle wheel'; and he draws from that crumpling of the wheel those conclusions about the Jesuit's life which we should expect from the Cambridge of Russell and Wittgenstein in the heyday of Freud; who so conveniently permits the critic to argue that the poet knew not what he wrote; the dire ambiguity is there on the page. Father Arthur Thomas, S. J., has surely settled the matter once and for all by his discovery that 'buckle' is a term of falconry, and that Hopkins knew the term.

I remember secretly and rather sadly contrasting with the brilliant game my Cambridge friends were playing my own first acquaintance with Hopkins; in another world altogether, as it then seemed, in which I had, as a child, imagined I loved poetry for quite other reasons than for the barbed pleasure of picking the prickles from a hedgehog. I first heard poems by Hopkins recited by a young musician, then hovering on the brink of a monastic vocation, who had recited to me (as though in the words of the poem his own tormented aspiration found expression) those early poems Hopkins wrote in a mood of religion (or religiosity) which to many of his own generation, and a few even of mine (though not in Cambridge), was a living reality. Which had read the poems more truly? Hopkins indeed was interested, as Empson was, in what could be done with words. In some ways their minds are alike, highly literate products of the classical education of the English public schools. They might have greatly enjoyed an exchange of letters; just as the freemasons of Rheims would have found much in common with Mies van der Rohe. The 'how' of construction—the quantifiable part of knowledge—they would have shared; but as to the 'what'— the qualitative—they would have spoken different languages. The materialist scientific mentality supposes the 'how' to be the 'what', the meaning of a building to be no other than its engineering.

Yeats, whose thought and whose poetry are related to a world-order totally other than the atheist humanism of his time, has suffered from radical misreading by the critics. John Wain, in an essay, 'Among School Children,' dismissed Yeats's own allusion to Porphyry as of no account, and, for the 'drug' Lethe that brings forgetfulness to the generating soul, substituted the chloroform of a modern maternity ward. Clearly he had no thought of injuring Yeats's reputation—on the contrary, his misreading of the poem is an attempt to save Yeats from himself and reshape his image in a way more congenial to his own society. And Mr Wain is by no means alone in his attempt to cover up the great poet's supposedly ridiculous beliefs and discreditable studies. We are not so much concerned with 'period' (though of course the premises of societies do change) but with the changes, the losses of meaning that come about when the reader's premises are nor those of the poet, when they are in the most literal sense living in different worlds.

What can be saved from a culture whose premises are of a spiritual order in an iron age peopled by Plato's 'men of clay' (the human primate of the scientist) is the quantifiable; the mechanics of construction, in whatever art. And the engineering element in the making of a poem is negligible in comparison with that of that most impressive and typical work of the reign of quantity, the spaceship. What meaning is there, in materialist terms, to the word 'poet'; or the essence—the 'poetry'—and the quality—the 'poetic'—of works of art? The adjective 'poetic' carries a certain contempt as the critics use it, and the 'poetic' element (as we use the word of the music of Schubert or Chopin, the painting of Claude or Palmer) is avoided by those typical of the 'modern movement'. Proust and even Balzac called themselves 'poets', indicating by the word at least the intention of giving expression to precisely this intangible quality that used to be called the 'poetry' of life. The preferred word in the modern movement is 'the artist'—placing the emphasis on the execution rather than the informing idea. A sculpture is a 'construction in space', a musical work a 'construction in time'. The 'work of art' is no longer an embodiment, but a body.

Beyond the question of how much a materialist present can understand, in its own terms, the art and poetry of a spiritual past, there is the question of the kind of art—the kind of poetry—the reign of quantity can produce. The modern megalopolis, for all our understanding of the stresses and strains (in ferroconcrete if not in the soul of man), is not encouraging. It has yet to be demonstrated that, once a materialist society has exhausted the excitement of sacking the treasuries of the past in such 'revolutionary' anti-art movements as surrealism and 'pop' art, spent its nostalgia for tastes and manners inherited from a rejected culture (whose values these manners reflect), it can, or will even wish to, include poetry or 'the poetic' in its way of life.

A new culture, a new civilisation, is born of a change of premises. At the height of Roman power the seed of Christianity began to germinate among slaves and social outcasts. In the age of apparent triumph of materialism, is there a comparable process already at work among a younger generation who reject the materialist Utopia?

Knowledge, in any culture, is only an agreed area of the known and the knowable; 'Let X equal knowledge' is premised and the proofs follow. Every X can of course yield its results. But there is always an excluded knowledge; and as the crude beginnings of science were the excluded knowledge of pre-Renaissance Christendom, so theology and all the wisdom of the spirit is the excluded knowledge of a materialist society. As R. P. Blackmur (apropos Eliot and Yeats) wrote in 1911, 'the supernatural is simply not part of our mental furniture'. But reality does not change its nature because we are unaware of it; a fact which the scientists themselves would not deny.

Just as science has its *gnosis* within its own terms (the quantifiable) so there is a *gnosis* of mind, which has been known and formulated in every civilisation. Coomaraswamy wrote of a universal language of which the several theologies, mythologies and arts are dialectical variations. If mind is premised—is the 'X' of knowledge—the same truths will always be rediscovered. Plotinus. who wrote that 'there is nothing higher than the truth', was not a scientist; though only from scientists, in our society, is that appeal recognized. This *gnosis* (implicitly or explicitly) is the ground of all works of imagination. A work of art is precisely an expression in words of some intuition of imaginative reality. Poets may or may not have been religious men (who knows if Shakespeare was?) but all poetry of the imagination is the language of spiritual intuition and spiritual knowledge.

This is not the place to give chapter and verse in support of what is not after all a particularly original view, that our European variation of 'the universal and unanimous tradition' has been, with variations and accretions, neo-Platonism. Christian theology has itself its roots in Greek philosophy, and differs in no essential first principles from Platonic (or Aristotelean) metaphysics. From the point of view of religion neo-Platonism might seem a dead language; the Mysteries of Hellenic civilisation no longer exist as religious cults with places of worship, rituals, a priesthood and so on. From the standpoint of the poets this very freedom has perhaps made the Platonic theology more amenable to poetic purposes than the Christian religion with its involvement in history and its other worldly ramifications. Cult belongs to time and place; and this aspect of the Christian Church itself is now assailed by inevitable change. But the first principles themselves, from which have sprung many cults and their various rituals, are defined in the Platonic theology, which is itself an embodiment of tradition. Religion is, after all, a collective art embodying a vision shared by a nation or an age. The essence of reality cannot be captured or held in any of the forms, however wonderful, which may at some time embody it. Involvement with a cult may be as dangerous to the poet as involvement in politics; however sincere, such involvement is, for the imagination, at best a symbol and at worst an irrelevance. But, as a symbolic description of the nature of things, all myths whose origin is in the imagination are unageing and may live again in poetry (as Hyperion in Keats, Prometheus in Shelley or the Greek gods in Hölderlin) after centuries. 'Religious' poetry is only a small category (unless we beg the question by calling all profoundly imaginative poetry 'religious') and often a somewhat uneasy one, since the self-searchings or conflicts of the poet as a personality often obscure and impede the imaginative vision, which comes from a deeper and impersonal source, the Muse, the *anima mundi*, the Holy Spirit, the God. The name varies, the experience is constant. It is not the religion (if any) of the poet, in the personal and moral sense, that is in question. Even among poets professing the Christian religion (in forms so various as to include Dante and Spenser, Milton and Vaughan, Blake and Edwin Muir) their metaphysics—their spiritual geometry—commonly proves to be neo-Platonic in essence. Coleridge, a Christian in his prose, is a neo-Platonist in his poems.

Obviously every poet's field of culture is different; but in my own detailed study of Blake's sources I have been astonished to discover how many of these he shared with the poets named, and with Yeats, Shelley, Wordsworth and others not professing the Christian faith. The canon of the learning of the imagination is constant. Such knowledge does not, like the discarded hypotheses of science, become obsolete; for it is not cumulative but a priori; or as poets and metaphysicians alike would say, not amassed by experiment but 'revealed' by inspiration; or as Plato says, by 'recollection'—*anamnesis*. To our European canon the present century has added many texts from the spiritual literature of the world without changing the essence of the knowledge

or the intelligibility of its language. Such additions are no confusion, but an enrichment which in no way alters or weakens the
structure. Yeats, typical of the eclectic modern situation, through
theosophy, and later through his teacher Shri Purohit Swami,
learned from Hindu philosophy. Early in his intellectual life he
had read Swedenborg; studied Christian Cabala; the Buddhism
of the Japanese Noh plays, besides Spiritualism, the folklore of
Ireland and the primitive beliefs of the whole world, formed, for
him, together with Plato and Plotinus, the Gnostic texts and the
Hermetica, a body of imaginative learning as self-consistent as
(within its own terms, as an account of the phenomenal world)
modern science. This structure, within which human consciousness finds its ultimate orientation, stands the test not only of
intellectual analysis but of experience; opening ways that materialism can but close. I believe that this knowledge (whether intuitive or learned, or, as is usually the case, more or less of both),
is no less essential to the production of works of imagination
than is knowledge of, and respect for, the 'laws of nature' essential to those who launch space-missiles. Certain experiences are
not otherwise attainable than by exploring regions of experience
whose very existence is destroyed by the materialist philosophy
which denies access to them. For if the supernatural be 'no part
of our mental furniture' how can we discover those modes of
being, experience our own nature, or know

> What worlds, or what vast Regions hold
> The immortal mind that hath forsook
> Her mansion in this fleshly nook:
> And of those Daemons that are found
> In fire, air, flood, or under ground?

The imagination opens, now as always, into heavens and hells of the mind, beyond which lies boundless mystery.

The scientists seek in vain to quantify such knowledge; whereas, conversely, nature itself, for the Imagination, becomes a living image, reflection, expression, incarnation, and language of spiritual realities, 'higher' in that they are causes of the phenomena of nature; which is 'lower' only insofar as it is the world of the effects of these causes. To the scientists themselves the Berkeleyan argument—that mind, or spirit is the only substantial reality—must, in terms of modern physics, seem unanswerable as an account of all that we actually see, hear and touch, and call a world; *māyā*, as the Eastern philosophies have always understood. To the imagination everything in nature speaks of the mind which it reflects; of qualities; of 'the beautiful', that highest concept of Greek philosophy. *Nihil vacuum neque sine signo apud deum.* Without this implicit doctrine of the *signatura rerum*, the 'signatures' and 'correspondences' of things earthly to things heavenly, poetry cannot operate, being precisely the language of such correspondences. Such discourse, whether the poem be the *Divina Commedia* or Yeats's 'little song about a rose' is, I would say, what poetry simply is, if it is anything at all. It is a sacred language because it speaks of qualities; and behind qualities, and sustaining them, mysteries, meanings; the holy ground of the soul's country.

Poetry, God knows, does not deal in certainties so much as in the glimpses of that country seen at certain moments by that eternal exile Psyche. The Russian Metropolitan Archbishop Anthony Bloom reproved me when I said to him that atheism could probably have no poetry. No, he said, 'poetry is the language of longing'; only when the soul is dead can there no longer be poetry. But what can the atheist (the materialist, that is, not the a-theist of Buddhism, who in no way denies the spirit) long for, unless that things should be otherwise than he believes?

What if all traditional sources were to be lost and the learning of the spirit forgotten? This of course cannot happen; since virtually the whole human inheritance of the arts, all the literature of wisdom, proclaims the 'universal and unanimous tradition' which forms the structure of all possible experience. But if—unimaginably—this were to be so; or—and this is the actual situation of innumerable people in the modern world—a generation were to grow up in ignorance of traditional spiritual teaching, yet the nature of the soul must reaffirm itself. Jung has described the 'individuation process' by which, through our own dreams and intuitions, the ego discovers its hidden and holy 'ground'. Or truth may come, as Yeats heard it spoken, 'out of a medium's mouth'. Reality being always such as it is, it must be discovered and reexperienced countless times and in various ways. And those who discover the matter will soon discover the books of knowledge and works of art which bear witness to such experience; for our own enlightenment makes accessible all that tells of what we have ourselves perceived. As Plato says, we can learn only what we already know, but do not yet know we know. The learning of the Imagination can remain an excluded knowledge only so long as the premises of material science remain unquestioned and their exclusions undetected.

(1977)

The Inner Journey of the Poet

O F ALL THOSE great contemporaries in whose times I have lived, C. G. Jung is one of the two or perhaps three minds to whom I am most indebted. Nevertheless I am not a Jungian. In two senses this is so. First, of course, I am not a trained psychologist, and although I have read most of Jung's published writings with pleasure and profit I have never attempted to master his terms in the exact sense required by professional rigour. In the second place I suspect—though with Jung one can never be sure, for he is himself often deliberately ambiguous, or evasive—that in some important matters I would not share his point of view. What, for example, in *Answer to Job*, does he mean by the 'God-image'? Does he mean that 'God' is a psychic image, amongst others? Or does he mean that man bears in his psyche the image of God? Since I unambiguously adhere to the traditional teaching that man is made in the image of God, it may be that here I part company with many Jungians, if not with Jung himself; and probably in other contexts where metaphysical questions are involved—though Jung disclaims metaphysics and a poet would also be wise to do so; poetry, like psychology, being in essence the language not of intellect but of the soul.

I have been persuaded by a fellow lecturer at a weekend conference on The Inner Journey to talk upon that subject: not because of my knowledge of Jungian psychology but as an example of what that lecturer called 'a natural Jungian'; though we poets might equally say that Jung is a 'natural' poet, thinking in terms of myths and symbols long current in the language of the poets. The inner journey is certainly a theme poets and psychologists have in common; one might almost say that journey has, one way or another, been the theme of most of the imaginative poetry of mankind. And since there is not one of us who must not sooner or later set out upon that journey we may expect to learn from the poets some of the stages on the way all must travel. For, as Blake wrote, 'these States Exist now. Man Passes on, but States remain for Ever; he passes thro' them like a traveller who may as well suppose that the places he has passed thro' exist no more, as a Man may suppose that the States he has pass'd thro' Exist no more.'

In the middle of the road of life Dante, supreme poet of Christendom, came to himself (*mi ritrovai*) literally 'found myself again'—to discover that he had lost his way and was in the middle of a dark forest. How he came to be there he did not know because, as he tells us, he was 'full of sleep' when he missed his way. The great *Divina Commedia* is an allegory; and yet the opening scene has upon us the impact of a dream we might ourselves have dreamed. Dante's fear, when he finds himself entangled in natural life, in 'the forests of affliction', the 'forests of the night' as Blake was later to call that place, communicates itself to us because the symbol evokes in us a resonance at a far deeper level than mere allegory. There Blake met his Tyger; and Dante too met a beast, 'burning bright';

not a Tyger but a fierce creature at once leopard, lion and wolf. He allegorizes the beast; and yet the encounter has the quality of some dream or vision in which forest and beast alike arose from the unconscious mind which creates such encounters for us.

The encounter was, in any case, the determining moment of his inner life, the starting-point of his own interior journey.

As the poet fled bewildered by the forest and terrified by the beast, there came towards him one of those figures we meet on the road of life at the moment of need; sometimes in dream, sometimes in the person of a human being: the poet Virgil, an Italian like himself who, more than twelve hundred years before, had made (in the person of the hero of his epic poem, Aeneas) his own descent into Hades. Virgil is said to signify, in Dante's poem, human wisdom and tradition, and on one level this may well be so; yet in terms of the psyche and its symbolic figures, Virgil is recognizable as the archetype Jung has described as 'the wise old man' who counsels many a dreamer, or whose knowledge we project onto some teacher or master. Virgil becomes Dante's protector, companion and guide; and the two poets, Virgil, the shade, and Dante, the living man, set out upon an inward journey into 'an eternal place'; the same that Aeneas had entered, guided by the sibyl of Nemi. For those who have so 'found themselves' there can be no going back; the beast, when once we have discovered it in ourselves, forbids return; we must flee, literally for our lives, in the hope of escaping the monster we have discovered within.

But the first stage of the journey takes us, not to Paradise as we might hope, or at all events to some better and safer place or state, but into the hells.

To the ancient world those shadowy regions of alienation were thought of as external to ourselves; regions not of memory or of fantasy but the real habitations of discarnate spirits both human and non-human. So the descent into Hades is presented by Virgil, whose Aeneas there met the discarnate spirits of many he had known in life: his father, happy in the Elysian fields; Dido, whom he had deserted, who turned away in silence, still unforgiving. Virgil's Hades is in its turn based upon the still more primitive account given in the *Odyssey* of Ulysses' visit to a temple (which some have thought to be Stonehenge) in a dim northern land there to consult the spirit of the wise Nestor, who in life had advised the Greek heroes, on how he should get home to Ithaca. There he met his former companions—Ajax, and Achilles, still striding in his wrath—who bitterly said that it were better to be the meanest labourer on earth than a hero among the dead. We are in a world of primitive necromancy, the kind of consultation with the ancestors to be met with in all primitive tribes. If the journey is inwards those who make it are not aware that this is so.

I must here say that I hold it, on the evidence, as probable that in our inner journey we do encounter such discarnate beings as Homer, Virgil and Dante describe; our own dead, and whatever spirits besides may inhabit the unexplored regions of mind on which our own consciousness impinges. Here again I may well hold a view Jung himself may not have shared; yet he was at one time a physical researcher and in his *Septem Sermones ad Mortuos* he is nearer to Virgil (whom he so often quotes) than to Freud.

Dante's inward journey stands midway between the ancient and the modern world. In his hells, his heavens and his purgatories he did indeed meet, like Aeneas and like Odysseus, many he had known in life, besides persons who had lived in former times. But the *Commedia* is also something else: it is an exploration of the psyche, of the inner worlds and states of the poet himself. And 'the lost traveller's dream under the hill'—as Blake was later to describe that journey through the hells—begins with a descent into the depths under the mountain of Purgatory on whose summit is Paradise. Every pilgrimage must begin in the same way: if Freud did nothing else at least he made us aware that these regions are in each of us, and that the only way out is through; the way that Dante took into the dark regions of human souls.

His journey follows a descending course through ever-narrowing circles, each representing some of the sins that deform the soul; and there, in each of the states, the poet is moved, now with pity, now with horror, to find persons he had known on earth. But each successive hell is at the same time a recognition of what lies within himself. In his encounter with the adulterous lovers, Paolo and Francesca, he is so moved with pity that he faints; for had he not loved Beatrice to that extreme by which he knew he might have become like them, aware only of one another? T. S. Eliot has in *Little Gidding* recaptured Dante's dismay at another meeting, with his old teacher Brunetto Latini, in the 'What, are you here?' of his own encounter with the 'familiar compound ghost' of his literary masters. The empathy that so shook Dante to the heart is surely an identification of ourselves with the state of another soul; we discover ourselves in them, and them in ourselves. For the hells through which Dante moved are not places but states, all of them recognizable to every one of us.

At the bottom of the abyss, that narrows and narrows to those self-enclosed, ice-bound prisons in which the souls have

lost all freedom, the poet comes to the throne of Satan. I have
never undergone analysis (otherwise than through poetry and
the other arts, which is after all the more ancient and normal
way of self-exploration) but I understand that at an early stage
of self-discovery the patient may expect an encounter with the
figure Jung calls the Shadow. This figure may appear in our
dreams as a sinister, repulsive alter ego whom we are as loath to
recognise in ourselves as was Shakespeare's Prospero to accept
Caliban; and yet to the monster of his isle Prospero said at last,
'This thing of darkness I acknowledge mine'. Perhaps Dante's
meeting with the beast in the forest was his first glimpse of the
Shadow, as a protean, theriomorphic form, like some dream
monster who may inspire terror without obliging us to recognise in so alien a shape an aspect of ourselves. But, just as in a
series of human dreams the same archetype may present itself in
a series of guises, Dante was to meet the Shadow again, in more
terrible and inescapable form. He confronts Satan, the ruler of
evil who has his throne within each of us, in the most hidden and
remote depth of those regions of evil we in vain deny.

The limit of the descent into Hell is the point of total inertia, the centre to which everything falls. The narrowing circles
whose terraces the poet, led by Virgil, has all the while been tra-
versing, lead to this place where no further freedom is possible.
As in Poe's story of the pit and the pendulum, Hell narrows
and narrows until the point is reached at which the final terror
is inescapable. Here Satan is enthroned, the hidden ruler of all
the hells; Jung's Shadow encountered unavoidably at the heart
of the soul's labyrinth. Dante can see no way of escape; but the
confrontation with the principle of evil face-to-face proves, on
the contrary, to be the point of reversal. The journey had been,

hitherto, always a descent into darker and worse places, the claustrophobia closing in until Hell's ruler is encountered and identified as the Shadow; or, as Blake called Satan, the Selfhood or ego which in each of us perverts our acts to selfish ends. Now that the ruler of the hells has been seen and identified, Virgil half leads, half carries the horrified Dante through a narrow passage under Satan's throne, below the hairy thighs of the half-animal, half-human figure of the Devil. What takes place is a kind of rebirth through 'a round opening'; and like the new-born Dante can now for the first time see the sky and the stars. Now there is literally—and how dramatically—a change of point of view: Satan on his towering throne is seen reversed beneath the travellers' feet; his power gone. He is no longer the ruler and the centre of the psyche. What has taken place Jung has described as re-integration of the personality when we find the Self—the 'other' mind within us—and not, as we had hitherto supposed, the ego, to be the ruler and centre of the soul.

Dante's journey surely meets the experience of many whose first step in self-knowledge has been the discovery of the hells within: under the volcano; the waste land; Blake was surely thinking of Dante when he wrote of

The son of morn in weary night's decline,
The lost traveller's dream under the hill.

Dante at the beginning of his spiritual adventure had no idea of even the existence of these hells; and so it is in perhaps every interior journey. Those who have read Bunyan's *Pilgrim's Progress* will remember that his journey to the Celestial City also began in the City of Destruction. But the Pilgrim had lived for many presumably contented years in that city before he recognized that familiar neighbourhood for what it was, and set out to flee from it, leaving his own family and the friends and neighbours of a lifetime. Bunyan's City of Destruction; Dante's City of Dis whose domes glow in a red sky, so like a modern city; Milton's Pandemonium, adorned with all the skills and arts of architecture and technology; or those terrible false paradises of Aldous Huxley's Brave New World where nobody is allowed to suffer or to desire anything better than perfect adaptation to existing conditions—all these are adorned with every amenity of civilized living. None of the poets has ever suggested that Hell is a place of pitchforks and boiling tar.

Dante, emerging through the opening at the bottom of Hell (the extreme limit of his own inner darkness), finds a new orientation. Whereas in the hells he has been enclosed within the caverned world of his own subjectivity, he now emerges into the greater universe and beholds the heavens and the stars above him. In Hell, native inertia had facilitated the poet's descent; but from this point he will have to climb. Did Dante here think of the line of Virgil Jung so often quotes, 'easy is the descent into Avernus, but the renascent—*hoc opus, hic labor est*'? And yet the poet undertakes the climb gladly, for he knows, now, where his journey is leading him. Once there is a goal, and that goal is seen, there can be no going back. The wise teaching of the Church is that none who has entered Purgatory can thereafter return again to Hell, the closed world with no outlet, no greater context to give meaning and orientation to life. In the hells the poet had witnessed and experienced each of the human energies misdirected in the service of the satanic ego; in the purgatories, whose states he must now traverse on his ascending spiral path, each of these energies will be set right, and the poet freed, one by one, from each of those faults we all share. In the heavens beyond, opening in widening circles, each of the seven energies or functions of the soul which in the hells had found and distorted expression as the 'seven deadly sins' will be seen in their aspect of seven cardinal virtues; for they are the same energies now operating in obedience to the divine order.

Dante's reorientation involves a new way of seeing even the hells; for now he understands that what had seemed an endless descent had all the time in reality been the first stage of the upward climb towards Paradise: while he had thought he was descending he was in truth already spiralling upwards towards the point of transformation of consciousness. Had he not emerged through that dimensionless point of reversal, to see the stars overhead and the light of dawn rising over the sea, he would never have made this discovery; for the hells are states of, precisely, absence of this light of hope, and ignorance of the whole of which even they form a part. While we are in Hell it seems that there is no way out; we are there, as it seems, eternally. Only as we emerge do we see evil in its true proportion. Once we have set foot on the Mountain of Purgatory we are free from those inner prisons—the self-enclosed worlds of the ego cut off from God—and are already aware of belonging to a greater whole.

At the summit of the mountain is the Earthly Paradise: the state of unfallen man. Thus far Virgil has led him—wisdom, or reason, or whatever may be symbolised by that figure of the 'wise old man'. But in order to enter the heavens, the worlds of the blessed spirits who behold God, wisdom does not suffice; and it is here that Beatrice comes to meet him; and it is she, the embodiment of love—of heavenly love, the love of the soul—who must lead him into those higher worlds or states that knowledge alone cannot enter. Jung's figure of the anima, the soul-figure, is said to be ambiguous, at once desirable and cruel, angel and temptress, beyond good and evil. We may find the shadow of Beatrice in Francesca blown by the winds of passion; but Beatrice is the soul-image purified and transfigured by the transforming experience through which the poet has passed. But when the poet invites us to gaze with him into the great cosmic mandala of the mystic rose of the heavens of which Eliot wrote—

> When the tongues of flame are in-folded
> Into the crowned knot of fire
> And the fire and the rose are one

—he leads us beyond the range of experience to which most of us have attained; yet he enables us to glimpse the goal we are even now travelling towards. In this poet's supreme vision of the numberless multitudes of the heavenly spirits, even Beatrice herself becomes but one among the numberless blessed souls who draw their life from God.

Dante's *Commedia* may serve to remind us that, whereas our present knowledge of the inner worlds is uncertain and fitful, there are old maps of that country. But at the end of a civilisation whose concern has been almost exclusively the exploration of nature and physical space, we have all but forgotten what country it is the old maps are describing. Materialists imagine that because the hells are not to be found among the rocks or the angels where the astronauts fly that these are unreal. But there is at this time a complete withdrawal of the old projection of the hells and the heavens into an external elsewhere; a recognition that all the old supernatural population is to be found in ourselves. Not outer, but inner space promises to be the theme of a new age; and the old maps are being brought out again.

A recent volume of poems by Thomas Blackburn reflects, in many fine and deeply self-searching poems, this change of standpoint; like this on the Scandinavian demon Grendel, another shadow-figure:

> After the marsh was drained and its vast monsters
> Had gasped their lives our in the well-rinsed air,
> Our city corporation cleaned the fosse up
> And charged us sixpence to see Grendel's lair.
> We thought that with the great Panjandrum banished
> An era of sweet dreams was sure to start;
> But gracious no, only his cave has vanished;
> Don't look now, but he's walking in your heart.

Perhaps we meet Dante again not full-circle, but on a higher turn of the spiral of development. Dante suffered from the dualism of medieval Christianity which makes redemption from the hells eternally impossible. Blake was perhaps the first Christian poet (or prophet, as he called himself, for he held poets who speak for the Imagination to be the prophets of the modern world) to challenge his dualism, and to say that though all the hells remain as eternal possibilities, and although those within them may see no way of escape, none are eternally binding on those who enter them. They are part of the one universe in which we travel. 'Distinguish between the man and his present state,' Blake said. His belief that none need remain eternally in hell is more Buddhist than Christian. Yet this same belief is surely implicit—though not explicit—in Dante's poem; for he himself made the journey to be reborn through that narrow opening, thereby showing that there is a way.

Dante's journey is of course everyone's journey; but the poet is the explorer, the opener of the way, who ventures, in a state of inspiration, into regions of consciousness which in most of us remain dark and unexplored. The honour in which poets and prophets were formerly held was in virtue of this 'inspiration' from the 'other' mind.

DANTE'S POEM HOLDS before us images of an inner world all share; of an eternal order, nor of time or place which is the measure of our humanity, the pattern, the scale (using the word in its musical sense) to which we are attuned. In those works of art which are true to the archetype we discover our own laws, our own inner order. We speak of 'beauty' because 'the beautiful' is what is true to the archetype and true to the cosmic order that upholds the world. What we call beauty brings us back to the archetype, harmonizes us with ourselves and indeed with others since it is by virtue of this inner order that we are alike. Without such works human society must suffer the kind of moral and spiritual sickness so prevalent at the present time. The necessary food of the spirit is missing; and instead of healing us and restoring us to our humanity much modern art and music is (whether deliberately or in ignorance) Satanic, destructive in an almost physical sense; dislocating the psyche, as sound-waves will bring down a building. The housing in which people live, the music to which the populace listens, the visual images presented to us by a commercial society are calculated to destroy rather than to harmonize the soul. There are of course exceptions in every art, but all too few, and these against the spirit of the established values of the time.

Plato taught that all knowledge comes from memory—recollection; but not memory of our own experience of a few years of mortal life. Plato's memory is a cosmic memory, not memory as the behaviourists would define it, something gathered from the experience of the senses, but instead a memory of the universal mind from which we are, from the confined nature of perception, shut off. Have we not all the sense of some knowledge lost, or just out of reach? To those who believe with the behaviourists that all knowledge comes through the senses, what meaning have Wordsworth's lines,

> Our birth is but a sleep and a forgetting:
> The Soul that rises with us, our life's star,
>   Hath had elsewhere its setting,
>   And cometh from afar:
> Not in entire forgetfulness . . .

For the behaviourists (as for the eighteenth-century philosopher Locke), the new-born come trailing no clouds of glory, bring with them no memories. But for the Platonic tradition, which makes not matter but mind its starting-point, Wordsworth's lines are not figuratively bur literally true; they are after all but a paraphrase of the teaching of Plotinus.

The Platonic philosophers held that we, in our natural state, are 'asleep'. Our relationship with the timeless is expressed in a number of myths of sleep and waking, remembering and forgetting. A similar view is taken by Jungian psychology, but with an important difference. Whereas the Greeks held that the 'other' mind is wakeful and conscious, is the omniscient mind of the immortal gods, and the mortal condition a 'sleep' and a 'forgetting', the terms of modern psychology are at best ambiguous.

The very term 'unconscious', though descriptive of our empirical situation in our relation to the transpersonal mind, is misleading because it suggests that conscious knowledge is in some respects more perfect; that the knowledge of the unconscious is in some sort of rudimentary state, merely potential. This is not the teaching of the ancients, nor is it of the Indian philosophers, nor of the Christian theologians who taught the omniscience of God and the relative ignorance of man.

Plato attributes our forgetfulness to the limitations of a physical body. The myth in the Tenth Book of the *Republic* to which Wordsworth's lines finally refer tells how the souls about to enter generation 'descend', like shooting stars, and then must cross a desert between the two worlds or states. They come to a river—the river Lethe, or forgetfulness. This river is interpreted by the late Platonists as ever-flowing matter; of which water is the universal symbol. The souls are thirsty for matter's sleepy draught: some drink so deeply that their oblivion of their former state is almost complete. Others drink less deeply, and arrive on earth 'not in entire forgetfulness'. All the Greek myths relating to knowledge and inspiration assume that we may in certain circumstances recover our lost knowledge of the universal mind. There are, according to Plato, three kinds of souls who are rememberers: the philosophers, who have knowledge; the lovers, who through their devotion to beauty come to knowledge of 'the beautiful itself'; and the 'musical souls', who are the artists. It is the function and the task of these to create in this world 'copies' of the eternal originals, or archetypes 'laid up in heaven', in stone or metal or music or dance or words, according to their skills. These copies will awaken in those who behold them—even if only momentarily—recollection of the eternal order of which all are part, and attunement to that order.

The poet's 'muse' is more than a literary convention: it is the experience of every creative person that inspiration comes from beyond our own knowledge. According to Plato there are nine Muses, each giving guidance in some one particular art. The poet is said to have the gift, when inspired (though not at other times), of flying to the Garden of the Muses, where he gathers, as bees gather honey, the sweetness of his song.

I think every poet knows what is meant by the muse or daimon who seems to give us knowledge we do not normally possess. Plato wrote of the Daimon of Socrates. The God of Israel 'spake by the prophets'. Shakespeare's Ariel is the very essence of the spirit who flies free but who will serve the poet-magician who knows how to control his inspirer. Milton invoked the 'Heavenly Muse' and so did Blake, with a difference: Blake was a modern man and knew that the muse is within; paraphrasing Milton, he summons the 'Muses who inspire the Poet's song' in a manner at once homely and sublime:

Come into my hand,
By your mild power descending down the Nerves of my
right arm
From out the Portals of my brain, where by your ministry
The Eternal Great Humanity Divine planted his Paradise.

Yeats had his 'instructors', Robert Graves his White Goddess. Often the figure of the muse is projected, as Dante projected his Beatrice or Bloch his 'beautiful lady', onto some human figure. Many still hold the old belief, inherited by Christendom from the Greeks, of the holy guardian angel who accompanies each of us throughout life. To speak for myself I cannot remember a time when I was not aware of the companioning presence of my own daimon. I never thought of this inner companion as an angel for this daimon spoke always of freedom and delight and beauty, never of such restrictive matters as religion dealt in. But if the daimon is not moral, neither is it immoral; carnal desires, or indeed any other self-interested thoughts, served only to drive away this delicate companion. Of the twin demi-gods Castor and Pollux it is said that one is incarnate, one in the other world or state; and I wonder if this myth does not describe precisely the relationship we each have with the daimon or guardian angel? Poets, in any case (Dante and Yeats were both born in the sign of Gemini), seem to be more than normally aware of this relationship with the 'other' mind. Of course there are many levels: as the aspiration, so the inspiration. Porphyry tells that the Delphic Oracle revealed that Plotinus was inspired by God himself, the universal spirit.

I attempted in a poem to express the relationship with the daimon:

Long ago I thought you young, bright daimon,
Whisperer in my ear
Of springs of water, leaves and song of birds
By all time younger
Than I, who from the day of my conception
Began to age into experience and pain;
But now life in its cycle swings out of time again
I see how old you were,
Older by eternity than I, who, my hair grey,
Eyes dim with reading books,

Can never fathom those grave deep memories
Whose messenger you are,
Day-spring to the young, and to the old, ancient of days.

The story is well known of nine daughters of Pierus who
challenged the Muses, daughters of Zeus, and who were turned
into magpies for their presumption. They would have fared better in the twentieth century; probably given prizes for their realism. For there is always an art of imitation which is not the
product of imaginative inspiration but of the human personality, uninspired. Such verse is not without its value—it may have
great wit, or political forcefulness, or it may be comic verse; but
the two kinds of verse, so Blake wrote, 'ought to be known as
two distinct things for the sake of eternal life'. For the sake of
eternal life because it is through imaginative inspiration alone
that contact is made with the eternal mind. Blake distinguished
between the 'daughters of memory' (the daughters of Pierus,
according to the myth) and the 'daughters of inspiration' as the
mortal and the divine Muses of the poet.

Of these things we can perhaps only speak in symbolic terms;
for symbol is the language of the psyche: the river of forgetfulness, the sleep of the soul, the Garden of the Muses. But is it
not a truth of experience that when we are moved deeply by
some piece of music or some other art, we have not, as it were,
to learn from the artist, as we might commit to memory some
technical process previously unknown? The symbols speak to us
more clearly than words. We accompany Dante on his journey
and know the place; we share the experience as if it were the
work not of some other mind but of our own. And in a sense
this is so; for though the personality of the artist may give colour

to his work, an individual style and stamp, supreme art comes from that mind which is common to all. The poet seems to be speaking out of our own deepest knowledge. 'Ah yes,' we say. 'But how did Shakespeare, or Hopkins, or Schubert, know this?' Works of imaginative genius seem our own creation. But while such works are often less 'difficult' to understand than works of mere talent which may need footnotes to supply the references, the demands they make on us are greater than the mere gathering of information needed for the elucidation of a difficult text: such works demand *anamnesis*, the wakening of recollection; and we might prefer to forget because sleep is easier and less demanding and sometimes less painful than wakefulness: which is, nevertheless, that to which we must grow.

Platonic recollection is not remembering the past but remembering the timeless. 'What we remember we shall known again', is the secret message of all beauty. These memories are also hopes; for Imagination tells both of the beginning and the end, 'mixing', as T. S. Eliot has written, 'memory with desire'. We desire what we recollect—we could not desire what we do not, in some sense, remember. Since in the timeless world end and beginning are one, the work of Imagination evokes not mere nostalgia, but also hope; the longing to be what we truly are. In the words of Plotinus, the soul 'makes its memories the starting-point of a new vision of essential being'. That is why Yeats made 'a new religion, almost an infallible Church of poetic tradition, of a fardel of stories, and of personages, and of emotions . . . passed on from generation to generation by poets and painters with some help from philosophers and theologians'. Only 'some help' for the inspiration of the poets is immediate, theology only a secondary elaboration. 'I wished for a world', he wrote, where I could discover this tradition perpetually, and not in pictures and in poems only, but in tiles round the chimney-piece and in the hangings that kept out the draught. I had even created a dogma: 'Because those imaginary people are created out of the deepest instinct of man, to be his measure and his norm, whatever I can imagine those mouths speaking may be the nearest I can go to truth.'

For Yeats the 'holy city of Byzantium' was both type and symbol of the city of the soul which the arts are forever building, surrounding us with images of an inner order. For him Byzantium was not only the ancient city of Constantine but that environment of the arts in which we live and discover ourselves; 'holy' because what art mirrors is the eternal world. Our modern technological environment is profane because it reflects no inner order in which the soul can recognize and discover itself. Constantine's city was itself an architectural mandala, built according to the plan of the heavenly Jerusalem, 'On earth as it is in heaven'. But although the city was Christian the inspiring philosophy was still Platonic. It was Plato who first dreamed of an earthly Republic whose laws and arts should reflect in every aspect of life a 'divine original', 'laid up in heaven'.

(1976)

On the Symbol

I T I S D I F F I C U L T for us to realise wherein our own unspoken assumptions, the foundations upon which we build our world, differ from those of others; for this assumed ground is the very thing we cannot discuss, for we may not even know what it is, still less what it might be; we cannot imagine how the world might appear if we did not possess the groundwork of knowledge which we do possess; nor can we in the nature of things imagine how reality would appear in the light of knowledge which we do not possess. Yet we continue to assume that whatever theories we may construct upon it the primary experience of the world is the same for everyone; even when in theory we should admit that this cannot be so, we continue to imagine that we all live in the same apparent world through sheer inability to imagine otherwise. From time to time we receive a shock, when we are compelled to realise the immense divergence not of deductions and conclusions, but of the premises, the basic assumptions upon which these rest; and thus even of the primary experience itself, inseparable from the attitude of the consciousness which receives it.

I had assumed, when I reached that long-vanished Cambridge of the late twenties, that others who spoke of poetry and who

wrote verse must understand it as I did; that those who claimed
to be poets, and who acclaimed one another, must know (since
they looked upon me as a naive creature) not less but more about
poetry than I. When I met these writers of my generation, some
of whom have since become famous, I assumed that when they
made pronouncements upon poetry that they and I were discussing the same thing. I did not like their poems any more than they
liked mine (and they were more right than I, even though they
would have disliked my work still more had it been better) but
those of William Empson were of a brilliance I could not but
admire; so that my own preference for Yeats (he was not fashionable at the time), for Keats and Shelley (who were despised)
and even for Walter de la Mare I attributed to my ignorance, and
kept very quiet.

Yet to me it seemed strange that a poem about love should
begin 'And now she cleans her teeth into the lake'. What I found
inappropriate in this image was its insistence upon a physical
function belonging simply to the hygiene of the human animal,
and not to the vision of the beautiful reflected in the person of
the beloved. (William Empson's description of surface-tensions
and so on which follows has an undeniable beauty, but the line
in question creates the context; whatever inhuman and scientific
beauty is introduced the 'human form divine' is, in such poetry,
disintegrated). I had not read Plato, and so supposed I must be
wrong to imagine a vision of spiritual perfection to be inseparable from the theme of love. I had not yet understood that those
who adopt the new philosophy of positivism must forgo such
lines as 'She walks in beauty, like the night', or 'Had I the heav-
en's embroidered cloths', or even 'Yes, you, my dear, have the
right human face', for these evocations rest upon foundations

of another kind altogether, even Edwin Muir's concept of 'the human face', an immaterial expression which has nothing to do with surface tensions. The new physicality was consistent with premises which were 'in the air' rather than understood and examined. Russell and Wittgenstein were names I did not at the time associate with a taste in poetry which preferred Donne to Milton, and which Empson's poetry reflected with so much originality and intelligence. He was praised, in our circle, for his resemblance to Donne, and Donne too was admired for the very 'modern' physicality of his

> For Godsake hold your tongue, and let me love,
> Or chide my palsie, or my gout,

and

> Marke but this flea, and marke in this, For Godsake hold your tongue, How little that which thou deny'st me is;

If my imagination was dashed and bruised I did not dare to say so even to myself, but tried, rather, to school myself to the new ruthless exclusion of all which belonged to a scale of values condemned as 'meaningless'—that favourite word of the logical positivists—because immaterial. These I assumed, must have been understood and rejected, after a process of comparison, in favour of those which I saw supplanting them; that the new values represented a failure of perception did not occur to me until many years later. (The ignorant do not, in the nature of things, discuss those ideas or modes of experience of which they are ignorant, and this exclusion is misleading to the young, who are as yet unaware that these closed fields of knowledge even exist.) I had not read Plato, nor Plotinus, nor the Vedantic literature, nor Berkeley, nor *A Vision*, nor Coomaraswamy; nor any of the books I needed in order to discover the first principles of the kind of poetry I instinctively recognized as such; and Shelley's Platonism, in isolation from its context, was incomprehensible to me. I have since had to undergo the double process of discovering the underlying assumptions of the *avant-garde* in which at Cambridge I found myself; of discovering that I could not accept these (and that I need not, therefore, attempt an undue admiration which I did not feel for works expressing such attitudes) and then, after years of search, discovering the discredited and neglected writings which constitute the learning of the imagination.

What William Empson, in his subtle, brilliant, and influential critical writings gave his generation was a theory of poetry consistent with the positivist philosophy which flourished in Cambridge; the Cambridge of Darwin and the Cavendish Laboratory, of Russell and Wittgenstein and their successors. His theory of ambiguity lacks nothing in conceptual subtlety but dispenses with the imagination and disregards the metaphysical roots of poetic thought. I still admire the brilliance—though the brilliance is often perverse—of his theory of ambiguity and of complex words; yet I see now what then I only felt, wherein it fails as a full description of poetry; for all the complexities and ambiguities and relationships which he discerns are upon the same plane of the real. There is one type of complexity which he fails to consider, that resonance which may be present within an image of apparent simplicity, setting into vibration planes of reality and of consciousness other than that of the sensible world: the power of the symbol and symbolic discourse. Then, I thought (as we all did) that it was our outstanding intelligence which compelled us to forgo beauty and lyricism at the bidding of intellect; but I have since come to understand that what such theories as we then held, together with the kind of poetry we were bidden to admire, precisely lacked (in comparison, that is, with Spenser or Shelley, Milton or Yeats), is, in the metaphysical sense, intellectuality.

The language of symbolic analogy is only possible upon the assumption that these multiple planes do in fact exist. Those for whom the material world is the only plane of the real are unable to understand that the symbol—and poetry in the full sense is symbolic discourse, discourse by analogy—has as its primary purpose the evocation of one plane in terms of another; they must find other uses for poetry or honestly admit that they have no use for it. The description of sense impressions or personal emotions, or the evocation of group emotions is assumed, by many writers at the present time, to be the purpose of poetry; but those who subscribe to a materialist philosophy would, were they honest, admit that in their scheme of things poetry can be dispensed with altogether (there is in fact a school of writing whose explicit purpose is to affirm the 'meaningless' nature of life); and in fact it has no place in the lives of the majority of the modern populace, who differ, in this respect, from their illiterate ancestors, in whose memories songs and ballads had their place. No phrase has been more misunderstood than Milton's statement that poetry should be simple, sensuous, and passionate. Milton would never have imagined that a generation would someday exist so ignorant as to suppose that the poet should confine himself to simple themes, sensible appearances and personal emotions. He surely had in mind rather the opposite thoughts: the themes of poetry being so high, so philosophic, it is necessary for the poet to embody them in imagery of perfect correspondence—thought and image must be one (simple), perfectly realised in the image (sensuous) and felt as living experience (passionate) and not merely conceptually apprehended. It is in this that the poet is distinguished from the philosopher; not in any difference in the nature of their themes but in the way of experiencing them: where philosophy makes distinctions, poetry brings together, creating always wholes and harmonies; the work of the poet is not analysis but synthesis. The symbol may be called the unit of poetic synthesis; as Coleridge in his famous definition implies:

> A symbol is characterized by a translucence of the special in the Individual, or the General in the Especial or of the Universal in the General. Above all by the translucence of the Eternal through and in the Temporal. It always partakes of the Reality which it renders intelligible; and while it enunciates the whole, abides itself as a living part in that Unity of which it is representative.

Thus the poem is able to create in the reader a sense of the wholeness and harmony its symbols and its rhythmic unity both realise and affirm. The language of analogy at once presupposes and establishes relations between the different orders of the real, an orientation towards a source and a centre. The idea of the metaphysical is thus implicit in the very figures of symbolic discourse.

There has been among poets of my generation and those a little younger a rejection of metaphor as a poetic figure: only direct description or at most simile is tolerated. The rejection of the characteristic poetic figures of metaphor, symbol, personification, and, at the apex, myth, is not arbitrary, it is logical and honest, for it represents a rejection of affirmations implicit in these linguistic figures. For as we ascend the scale we are asked to make increasingly animistic assumptions about the world. Those poets who allow themselves to describe only sensible appearances, or to compare these one with another (simile) have understood that this is demanded by the materialist view of reality. They could not (for example) subscribe to the demands made by Shakespeare when he writes

> Hark, hark, the lark at heaven's gate sings,
>> And Phoebus 'gins arise,
> His steeds to water at those springs
>> On chaliced flowers that lies,
> And winking Mary-buds begin
>> To ope their golden eyes.

For these metaphors make profound assertions about the nature of things which no materialist could possibly accept; and to which, even by a 'suspension of disbelief, he could never fully respond, because the world they are designed to open is one which he cannot experience by so negative an act. What the poem affirms is that the world is, in its whole and in its parts, living and conscious; it also affirms that there is a hidden source ('heaven') from whose 'gate' visible things issue from invisible. The sun is not called Phoebus, as Fred Hoyle's fiery bodies in space are called 'red giants', but because the poet's sun is really conceived as a living god. He travels on an animate vehicle (steeds) and the marigolds are likewise living and therefore open 'eyes' to greet the sun. The identity of their nature with that of the maidens whose name they bear (Mary-buds) is double—flowers are alive like maidens, girls are like flowers opening to the sun. The marigold (and by analogy the maiden) is itself a sun in microcosm, bearing the solar 'signature' and partaking of the solar (and therefore, in terms of the symbol) the divine nature.

The alchemical and magical doctrine of 'signatures' would have been as familiar to Shakespeare's audience as some scientific axiom at the present time. The new poets are quite right in dismissing such language from their own work; only fools would write in such a way and at the same time assent to the scientific materialist view of nature. Only many years later, through my study of the sources of William Blake, was I led to discover the almost obliterated traces of the mode of thought which is, implicitly or explicitly, the foundation of all supreme imaginative art, even of its most lighthearted songs.

In England it is above all the poets who have kept the knowledge of this perennial wisdom when this has been all but lost alike by churches and by philosophers; and their language has at all times been (not because these invented the truths they perceived or formulated, but because in Europe Platonism has been the mainstream of such thought) that of Plato and Plotinus and their predecessors and followers. The final authority of a perennial wisdom (in other civilisations differently expressed) rests not with those authors who discourse upon it, but in the nature of things, verified and reexperienced again and again; just as in the material order any other age whose scientists might investigate the laws of matter as exhaustively as our own have done, could verify their discoveries. So it is with the intelligible world, by whatever name we may choose to call it; all deities reside, now as always, 'in the human breast'.

Indeed a revival of the learning of the imagination, and especially of the works of Plato and the neo-Platonists, has been the inspiration not only of the Florentine renaissance and all that followed (in England as elsewhere) but of every subsequent renaissance. Spenser laid the aesthetic foundations of all English poetry since, in his four Hymns, of which one is to the earthly, another to the heavenly beauty. To speak only of the English language, the Romantic revival, the Transcendentalist movement in America, the Irish renaissance, all have followed a return to the same source. Yet as our culture as a whole has drifted farther and farther away from its old roots, both within the Christian religion and the Platonic philosophy, it has come to seem almost as though the poets speak a secret language. Their meaning is no longer understood—as we may see from the writings of contemporary critics upon such poets as Milton, Blake, Shelley and Yeats, who are read with sheer incomprehension for want of the knowledge out of which they themselves were writing. In so little respect is this knowledge held that it seems to be assumed by many critics that what the poets meant scarcely matters, and that their poetry can be read without such knowledge or in terms of some entirely different system of ideas; although why, if this were so, it should be read at all is hard to see.

Recent popular discussion by Anglican bishops of the Christian symbols has revealed the extent to which, even among professed believers in the Christian revelation, the use of the language of analogy, the capacity for thinking in symbols, has been lost. It is perhaps conceivable that materialists should believe that Christians when they speak of heaven being 'above' should imagine it to be situated in physical space, since they are themselves limited by the terms of quantitative discourse; but that there should be bishops who imagine—or who know—that this view is held by professed believers in a spiritual order is almost incredible. To a materialist such terms as 'above' and 'below' refer solely to position in physical space; a quantitative mentality Blake associated with Newtonian science, and wrote in a letter 'God keep me . . . from supposing Up and Down to be the same Thing as all experimentalists must suppose'. In symbolic discourse above and below are qualitative, not quantitative; light and darkness, the tree of life, the bird of the soul, voyage and road and river and cave and house, mirror, sword, cup and garment, rose and lotus, sun, moon and stars, are terms of symbolic discourse, the only language we have in which to express not merely the appearances but the content, the quality of experience.

Fortunately, while literalism has invaded poetry and religion, science has itself been reaching the end of its tether, and approaching the realisation that the world of appearances is itself only a kind of symbol of anterior causes. When this point is reached it is inevitable that we should again turn from physics to metaphysics. According to the metaphysician René Guénon the law of correspondence operates throughout the cosmos.

> By virtue of this law, each thing, proceeding as it does from a metaphysical principle from which it derives all its reality, translates or expresses that principle in its own fashion and in accordance with its own order of existence, so that from one order to another all things are linked together and correspond in such a way as to contribute to the universal and total harmony, which, in the multiplicity of manifestation, can be likened to a manifestation of the principial unity

itself. For this reason the laws of a lower domain can always be taken to symbolise realities of a higher order, wherein resides their own profoundest cause, which is at once their principle and their end.

Of modern naturalistic interpretations of this ancient doctrine Guénon points out that these 'purely and simply reverse the hierarchy of relationships between the different orders of reality'. This is true, obviously, in the field of natural sciences whose phenomena, he writes, 'by the very fact that they are derived from higher and transcendent principles, truly serve to symbolise those principles'. In the special field of the arts the reversal of hierarchies, by denying the dependence of the present world upon higher causes, expresses a vision of things emptied of the values and dignity which they can only possess by virtue of such dependence. We see this clearly in the modern treatment of sex, and of the human body. The most 'real' has come to mean the sordid, the carnal, the plebeian; this is not accidental, since the natural world owes any qualities of the sacramental, the noble, or the sublime which it may possess precisely to its relation to higher causes. The loss of the vision of informing beauty follows of necessity from a closing of consciousness to these causes. Since matter and material objects are informed from a mental world, a materialist art is doomed to loss of form, such as we see in abstract expressionist painting and its literary equivalent, a fragmented outpouring of physical (and often obscene) images and sense-impressions, divorced from any qualitative context. No doubt such art owes its vogue to the accuracy with which it reflects a widespread mentality; but to reflect ignorance, however accurately, is not to embody truth. Believing as I do that the purpose and justification of poetry is to embody and reflect truth—or the real—or beauty—they are all the same—I cannot admire works which flatter or reflect (however accurately) ignorance, but which lack any transforming power. Nor can it be admitted that there is a 'real' world, which such art reflects, which imaginative art disregards in order to depict another, which has no reality in physical existence; on the contrary, imagination alone sees things as they 'really' are, since it sees them in relation to their causes and qualitative natures; the imagination does not see different things, but sees things differently.

There have been attempts to reduce symbolism to the terms of a materialist philosophy. Freud, it is true, made the first step on the road of return when he proved to an astonished world that the dreaming mind thinks in images, employing these, and not words, as its language; but the symbols he discovered in dreams, and in the arts, he understood as the mere disguise of repressed and mainly sexual content. To this theory (being a logical and passionate man) he was prepared to sacrifice the values of civilisation, to see in the pearl nothing but a disease of the oyster, to reduce all art to terms of sexual fantasy, as one might reduce a picture to its component pigment and canvas. The Surrealists, inspired by Freud's theories, used their so-called symbols in a vivid and striking way; but these were not in truth symbols at all, lacking as they do Coleridge's essential mark of the symbol, 'the Translucence of the Eternal in and through the Temporal'.

They do not relate one order of reality to another, still less are they oriented to any source or principle. They are only a code-language, in which both terms of their metaphors apply to the same order of reality, and are so disguised only (as in time of war) to evade the censor. Surrealism is just as much a materialist art as is Social Realism; as its exponents, seeking recognition from the Marxists with whom they wished to make common cause (a recognition they were not accorded) explicitly claimed. Its symbols, released by 'pure psychic automatism', provide no bridge or ladder from which contemplation may pass from effect to cause, from lower to higher. In contrast with this view René Guénon defines that of tradition:

> A further consequence of this law of correspondence is the plurality of meanings contained in the symbol. Anything and everything can in fact be regarded as representing not only the metaphysical principles, but also realities of all orders higher than its own, even if still contingent, for these realities, on which it also more or less directly depends, play the part of 'secondary causes' in respect of it. . . . These multiple and hierarchically superimposed symbolic meanings are not in any way mutually exclusive. On the contrary, they are perfectly concordant, because they express the applications of one and the same principle to different orders; thus they complete and corroborate one another, while being integrated in the harmony of the total synthesis. This, moreover, is what makes symbolism a far less narrowly limited language than ordinary speech, and renders it best fitted to convey certain truths. The possibilities of conception it opens up are truly limitless, and it is for this reason that it constitutes the initiatory language *par excellence*, the indispensable vehicle of all traditional teaching.

In the ancient systems of magic and alchemy, based upon an elaborate system of 'correspondence' or 'signature' (often perhaps in an arbitrary and unimaginative sense at least in popular application) all things were symbolic; and such initiates as Jakob Boehme saw the whole world as imprinted, in its whole and in its parts, with the signature of the Source. To call this 'poetic' is to beg the question; for either this is a way of apprehending the real, or it is not poetic, but merely fanciful. It is, however, the poetic mode of thought. David Jones, whose 'sacramental' view of nature comes near to the *signatura rerum* of alchemy (even while lacking its symbolic precision), illustrates in the refinement and beauty of his depictions and descriptions of the natural world, and also of man-made (but not machine-made) objects—ships and garments and all 'the gear and tackle and trim' of craftsmen, the truth that the primary experience of perception is itself in its kind and quality, determined by what the artist believes to be the qualitative nature of the things perceived.

Jung came nearer than did Freud to the traditional doctrine, as taught by those alchemists, Gnostics and neo-Platonists whom he himself took for masters; for he realised that dreams do not so much conceal as embody meaning, and that this comes from sources within the psyche—or beyond it—normally inaccessible to the waking mind. Not all dreams come from the same level; and besides the personal elements recognised by Freud, Jung was led to believe in what he calls a 'collective unconscious' because it is so as a rule, though at times accessible to consciousness. This is the ancient *Anima Mundi*, the soul of the world, whose images at times, waking or in dreams, we behold with amazement, so beautiful and so fraught with meaning do these appear. Because this world is not personal but common to all, its symbols are intrinsically intelligible as Freud's symbols from the personal unconscious are not. To Edwin Muir that world seemed to open spontaneously, as it did to[2]; Yeats sought by magical evocation, as others have attempted by prayer and invocation, to pierce the veil. Others again have recognised these forms, as Wordsworth did (and perhaps every poet who in describing the natural order has discovered beauty and meaning) embodied in mountain or waterfall or lake or tree; or like Dante in the beauty of some beloved person; an inexplicable magical power which illuminates from within. In whatever guise they appear, in dream, waking vision, contemplation, or reflected in the forms of nature or of art, it is characteristic of these symbolic images that they seem to communicate essential meaning; they mean what they are, are what they mean, embodiments at once of truth and of beauty, since they are informed by the real which we recognise as at once and inseparably true and beautiful; this is necessarily so since it is the ground of our own being, at once answering and calling to that which we also are and embody.

The symbolic images come, of necessity, from the perceptible world; for this world is, in the nature of things, and unalterably, the 'given', inseparable from our human nature as incarnate beings; all the knowledge of the soul must come to it in terms of this world of embodiment—that is to say in symbolic form. Truly understood the entire world is one great symbol, imparting, in a sacramental manner, by outward and visible signature, an inward and spiritual essence.

Every poet and painter has some one, or some few symbolic themes which for him live in an especial way. For Milton, the Garden of Eden and the Fall; for Shelley, cave and river and boat and sea-voyage; for Yeats, not the soul's voyage but its migration,

---

2 George Russell.

under images of swan and dolphin; certain cosmic myths, the
Great Year, the Mundane egg; and not Eden (the origin), but
Byzantium, city of man's creation. For Edwin Muir it was above
all Eden (the timeless world), time and the journey through time,
with horse as symbol of the vehicle which carries the soul on
its journey; the angel, being that enters time from beyond time,
breaking the inexorable pattern by what seems a miracle but is
in fact the touching of another plane of the real. None of these,
surely, were deliberately chosen by the poets, but, rather, chose
them; they come, not as allegory in which the poet searches for
an apt symbol for some abstract idea—the sword of justice or the
scales of equity—but rather as epiphanies, awe-inspiring glimpses
that move us deeply and inexplicably. These images seem put
into our hands like clues which we are invited to follow back and
back, for they draw us irresistibly as by magic; and this is no less
so when we encounter them in nature than in dreams of vision.
By their numinous nature we recognise them; and not with academic curiosity do we pursue them to their mysterious source,
but as we follow the beloved person, unable to keep away, or
watch all night before a closed door hoping for a glimpse or a
sign. We live under the power of their compulsion: for they do
not present themselves, like academic problems, from outside,
as tasks to be taken up by willpower, to which we must drive
ourselves. They arise, rather, as living impulses, urges of our own
being and therefore compelling. We cannot rest until we have followed them to their source, or as far as our understanding allows.

These haunting symbols seldom take the form of single, separate images only; more often they come as complex themes, con-
stellated. Blake, most experienced of all English poets in these
insights, made many attempts to explain to an uncomprehending

world the nature of the archetypes. One which was vividly present to him was the Last Judgement. To Blake there was no question as to whether there ever would, or would not be, a Last
Judgement: to him it was an ever-present archetypal reality.

> The Last Judgement [he wrote] is not Fable or Allegory,
> but Vision. Fable or Allegory are a totally distinct & infe-
> rior kind of Poetry. Vision or imagination is a representa-
> tion of what Eternally Exists, Really & Unchangeably.
> Fable or Allegory is form'd by the daughters of
> Memory. Imagination is surrounded by the daughters of
> Inspiration. . . . Fable is Allegory, but what the Critics call
> The Fable, is Vision itself.

The Last Judgement, he goes on to say, 'is one of these
Stupendous Visions. I have represented it as I saw it—to different People it appears differently as everything else does'. Yet,
clothed in form however different, Kafka (for example of a modern writer on the same theme) and Blake would have recognised
the essential identity of the theme they so differently treat.

When I was young, I looked for, and constantly discovered,
the numinous in and through nature; and only in middle life
did I first experience in an overwhelming degree one of these
archetypal epiphanies. The vision was of the Tree of Life, with
many associated symbols, all suddenly and clearly and simulta-
neously presented to my mind. For a long time I lived on that
vision, to which I could return, so I discovered, not with the same
overwhelming awe as the first time, but clearly enough, at any
time, to contemplate aspects of it which I had not at first seen,
or had forgotten. Others have come since, some in dream, some
not. The place of my vision was neither more nor less paradisal

than Wordsworth's 'tree, of many, one / A single field which I have look'd upon' which to him appeared 'Apparell'd in celestial light'; but we may see, with the physical eye, without the experience being numinous; physical perception may sometimes be the vehicle of imaginative vision, but is not necessarily so, though William Blake claimed that 'To Me This World is all One continued Vision of Fancy or Imagination', as it has been for many poets. A tree, a light over the sea, a mountain or a garden or animal or bird or human face may seem to speak to us from beyond itself; yet the 'visionary gleam', as Wordsworth himself discovered, may be entirely absent from the sensible world. But it is impossible to experience some interior and archetypal vision without at the same time experiencing it qualitatively, as an epiphany of knowledge, for these images are themselves the vehicles of that knowledge; only as such do they arise and exist. Their meaning is their only reality, the only content of their forms.

A recent fashion has been to define the poem as 'the words on the page'; how that can be so I fail to see, since a word is itself no more than a sign, a meeting-point of associated ideas often of the most complex kind. A word is not, like the natural creation, intrinsically meaningful and intelligible, and cannot, like these, become an object of contemplation which will yield infinite meaning. To the symbolist the written poem is only apart—perhaps a small part—of the whole organism, the living unity of interplaying patterns as the words and images set one another vibrating to produce some chord or dissonance whose ripples travel through our thought. It continues, like the resonance of a note after the key is struck, or like the statement beyond Edwin Muir's semicolon.

A young poet who visited me to talk about his proposed work on Edwin Muir said 'I do not believe in *Anima Mundi*;

I know you do'. I assured him there was no question of belief, only of experience. Not to believe in the creatures of the mind (in their own plane of the real) is like not believing in the amphioxus; or the giant squid might be a better example, perhaps, since the little fish swim in and out of all our dreams. However, this poet had the humility to admit that he had not understood Muir and proposed to wait until he did before writing about him. The more usual academic mentality is undeterred by any such doubts, as we see in book after book in which ignorance passes judgement upon knowledge. In the academic world there are all kinds of theories of symbols, and, as in Plato's Cave, all these are given equal weight and attention.

Indeed the more wrong the first principles the more ingenious the theories have to be; an ingenuity, which commands more respect, in some quarters, than does the higher faculty of immediate perception of intelligibles. But those who know do not theorise, they merely bear witness to what they have seen and experienced.

In the past, the mythology and metaphysics of some total culture whose foundations are metaphysical and whose expression informs and orientates every aspect of life has been the foundation of all the arts, and provided its symbolic language; as even now in India the forms of the gods may be expressed equally in dance, sculpture, song and epic poem. It is not 'the words on the page' which create the god in question, but the reverse; and the same intelligible principle (an 'airy nothing' until it is embodied) can be recognised as alike in any and all these varied manifestations. Iconoclastic Protestantism largely destroyed, in England, the images which had always been, and must normally be, the natural language of spiritual knowledge; and one hears that religious symbols have 'lost their meaning'; but since the only meaning symbols can be said to possess lies in their power to evoke, all symbols, ancient or modern, religious or poetic, must be equally meaningless in a climate of positivism; since the function of orientation which they are designed to perform is precluded by the denial of all planes of the real other than the quantitative and the sensational. In the present situation, and within a society which as a whole has lost that unity of culture which belonged to Christendom (which included and perpetuated the earlier Classical tradition) symbolic discourse is inevitably (or must appear to be) a private, lyrical language; and not, as it normally has been, a shared and collective expression. Yet compared with the mythologies of any great religion our private revelations, vivid as these may be, are necessarily fragmentary. These myths, with their great ramification of interrelated symbols, have in the past constituted a body of imaginative traditional knowledge. To those alive to the order of reality which they embody, the old symbols will live again; it is not they, but we who are dead. The myths of all races are ageless, since their symbolic language is based upon the permanent and unchanging elements of the world we inhabit.

It is precisely the visionary poets who best know how to make use of the traditional language of symbols. The great gulf lies not between tradition and the visionary, but between tradition and vision on the one hand, and positivism in all its manifestations, whether academic or revolutionary. Shelley used the Aeschylean and Platonic myths, and nature was for him a vocabulary which he used with so much sensuous beauty that he has been misread as a nature-poet by critics ignorant of the exactness with which he employs such terms as sea and wind, dew and bees and reflections and shadows. Living imagination alone has the key to the meaning of traditional symbols, and the greater our imaginative insight the greater our understanding of these is likely to become; all the greatest English poets have used with majestic ease the myths of their inheritance, Classical, Christian, Hebrew and native. Visionaries are not iconoclasts. It is immediately evident, to those who are familiar with the universal language of symbolic discourse, whether a poet (writing of sea or river, wind or garden or cave or bird) is using such terms as words within the universal language, or in a personal and imaginatively unlearned way; those who know the secret language immediately recognize it, or miss its presence; while those, on the contrary, who do not know it may read even Shelley's 'Ode to the West Wind' under the impression that its images are merely descriptive of natural appearances; to such there is no difference in kind between Shelley and Swinburne. Spenser's *Faerie*, Shelley's caverns and river-journeys in light-sailed boats, Milton's Paradise and Coleridge's sea-voyage; Blake's images of Judgement and transformation; Yeats's migrant bird-souls and world gyres, all speak the same language, evoke the same unseen world, whose riches are as inexhaustible as those of nature. We shall do wrong if we think of symbols as single poetic images, used to obtain some literary effect; rather symbol is a language in each of whose parts a whole is implied, and each symbol in some measure makes known to us that whole, as a whole, and in its wholeness. Professor I. A. Richards, an instructed Platonist, in a remarkable exposition of the 'Ode to the West Wind' described the knowledge Shelley communicates, or seeks to communicate (invoking the supreme metaphysical tradition) as Vedantic. Hinduism is, besides, above all a mode of knowledge which embraces and comprises every aspect and expression of life and art: nothing is outside its informing influence, which orients all to the one centre; as does all symbolic art, within its own terms, acting at all times as a principle of unification and of orientation.

Jung in his autobiographical memoirs makes an observation which I believe most poets could endorse and which seems to throw light upon the diction of poetry as itself of a symbolic nature. Jung, who himself (so he says) very much disliked anything high-flown in speech or manner, found, to his own surprise, that when what he calls 'mana, daemons, gods or the unconscious' speaks in words, its utterances are in a high style, hieratic, often archaic, grandiose; as far removed as it is possible to be from the speech of that common man the everyday self. Willa Muir, in her book *Living with Ballads* speaks of the 'high style' in which the Scottish ballads were traditionally sung. The oral tradition of the ballads was the heritage of illiterate people, shepherds and crofters; but the singing of the ballads was by no means in common speech. It was extremely slow, dignified, and highly mannered. There are recordings of Jeannie Robertson, a tinker's daughter, singing such ballads as 'Lord Randall' in this manner. Indeed nothing seems more unnatural, in the art of poetry, than 'natural' diction, common speech, the conversational tone. It is a mark of imaginative inspiration and content to write in a high and mannered style, removed from common speech; as it is of the absence of imaginative participation to write either in a conversational tone or in a deliberately vulgar idiom. Milton's verse is no more the common speech of an upper than it is of a lower social class; it is the speech of his 'Thrones, Dominations, Princedoms, Vertues, Powers', of the celestial hierarchies. The inspiring daemons speak in voices far removed from common speech; the voice of the gods is oracular, rhythmic, sibylline. Its resonance stirs in us a response, when in poetry we find it, from that same level within ourselves. The language of that world is no more naturalistic than its images are, but awe-inspiring and mysterious, a sacred not a profane language. Above all, the voice of true imagination is never ironic; that is the mark of a divided mind, whereas the imagination is above all at one with itself, the principle of unification and harmony.

Among the misconceptions (one for which the Marxist doctrine of social realism was responsible) of my generation was the notion, that to speak to the common man it was necessary to speak the common language and employ an imagery of the commonplace. Auden and Day Lewis first introduced a whole range of such images from the grim, grey realism of the modern city: the bar in Forty-Second Street, the United Dairies, the pylons, the tramlines, the cigarette-stubs and the litter defacing even churches and sanctuaries of the countryside. Philip Larkin and others of his generation have since adopted and extended this demotic imagery, with no doubt the same commendable intention as inspired the poets of the thirties. I believe the doctrine to be false, for it confuses class-distinction with imagination. Indian dancers, whose audience is largely the illiterate population of villages, impersonate gods, royal persons, and heroes. In watching such dancers one may almost see the daimon take over from the human individuality as if the god were really present. A Bengali friend, who sang, from memory, one evening, songs written by Tagore, tells me that all over Bengal these songs are known and sung by the common people; their themes are often religious, always on a level of refinement and depth of feeling. I myself know, in Scotland, road-menders and foresters who can recite long passages from *Paradise Lost*, and whose memories are stored with heroic ballads; for the common man is not what their philosophy supposes. The imaginative world is outside time, and transcends class. For the more sublime the work of poetry or art, the more do we feel that it expresses something already and always known, something deeply familiar and intimately our own. Few feel that we could have written Dryden's *Annus Mirabilis*, or Auden's *Nones*; but Spenser's or Milton's description of Paradise, or *King Lear*, or *Songs of Innocence*, or 'The Ancient Mariner', do we not feel that we ourselves already knew? Juvenal's Rome, Dryden's Restoration, Auden's Twenties were all modern once and are all dated now, and what was written for the sake of easy comprehension is precisely that part of poetry which becomes incomprehensible within a few years. Those who look to a timeless world are least likely to fall into archaisms of style, for the world of Imagination is outside history altogether. Pope, Dryden and Auden are dated in a way that Dante, Milton, Coleridge, and Yeats, even when these embody in their imaginative world themes from history, can never be.

If it has become difficult to use Christian canonical symbolism, may it not be precisely in so far as the canonical symbols have come to participate in history, in the temporal, that they are unusable? In themselves they are inexhaustible in content, and they, no less than those given to us in dream or in vision, may be taken like buckets to an inexhaustible well. They will never be drawn up empty except by those who do not lower them to water-level.

(1964)

The Use of the Beautiful

WHAT DO WE, at the present time, ask of poetry? I may be mistaken about precisely what is asked, but I think I am not mistaken in the conclusion that the present time does not ask—or receive—enough. Much verse published seems to set itself no goal beyond description, sometimes pleasing, but just as often of displeasing things seen or felt. I doubt if anything is to be learned from such descriptions or from the self-expression of the subjective states reflected in so much current verse. Far from expanding our consciousness, we have often, on the contrary, in order to understand such states, to make ourselves smaller, like Alice, before we can get inside such mean rooms as are opened to us. Perhaps the poet gains by articulating and objectifying his neurosis (though I question whether that is the cure of souls it is said to be) but what the reader can hope to gain I fail to see. Does not the confusion at the present time come from the fact that many now writing, and writing about verse, are genuinely unaware that what they are writing and writing about, is not, properly speaking, poetry at all—not in any way related to, or comparable with, the art as practised and understood by those on whose account poets are, in all civilised societies, honoured? It would be absurd to say that there should be no such thing as satirical verse, or descriptive, narrative, or occasional verse; what is deplorable is the confusion of mind which has arisen, even among those who claim to be poets: an ignorance of the order of things to which their own work purports to belong, a forgetting, a deliberate turning away from the recognition that they share neither the ends, the means, nor the knowledge, of what I cannot but call the real poets.

There is one word for which we may look in vain in the writings of contemporary critics: the word beauty and the idea of the beautiful, has ceased to count for anything. Why is this? Has this age discovered something better or have we simply failed to understand a concept which to other civilisations has seemed inseparable from any consideration of the arts? I will not labour the obvious fact that this is a beautiless society. Does this matter? In losing beauty have we lost anything vital to our arts or indeed to our lives? No need to enumerate the material advantages of hygiene, transport, television, frozen vegetables and so on, not enjoyed by ages whose typical expressions were the sculptures and paintings, cathedrals and liturgy of the Christian religion; yet in terms of happiness, our exchange might be harder to defend, and in terms of the quality of our lives, harder still. George Russell, the Irish sage who wrote on the relation of what he called 'the politics of time' to 'the politics of eternity' observed that 'One of the very first symptoms of the loss of the soul is the loss of the sense of beauty'. Is what our society has lost perhaps its soul?

I am not calling in question the beauty, or want of it, in this or that school of modern poetry or art; the beautiful has taken, in the past, innumerable forms and styles. Dorothy Wordsworth thought some Indian sculptures she saw hideous idols, but we find no difficulty in recognizing the beauty of a dancing Shiva or Parvati, or of some work of Buddhist art. No, the question now is, whether certain fashionable schools, both of painting and of poetry, make beauty an end at all? William Empson does not consider it. For all his skill in the analysis of parts, he has no gift—and in this he is not alone—of perceiving wholes. Herbert Read, the chief apologist of the Modern Movement, as such, has said, if I remember aright, that the idea of beauty has been, for those involved in that movement, replaced by the idea of energy. It might certainly seem that revolution for its own sake, transformation as such, an instantaneous gesture which expresses finally nothing but its own instantaneity, process as such, has become the be-all and end-all of art; process so accelerated that all images have dissolved into the flux of continuous transformation, so much so that form, in such art, can no longer be said to exist.

A similar trend was introduced into literature with the 'stream of consciousness' and, again, all bounds of form seem to have been broken in some recent works. Not all the writers I have in mind are social realists; but a materialist philosophy precludes orders of reality and value other than the physical; and some sort of positivism or humanism is the inevitable tendency—the unconscious drift, if not the conscious intention—of all who, whether as a consciously held theory, or as an unconscious mental attitude, take their colour from the prevailing climate of opinion. This is the cast of mind of those who do not consciously adopt some other attitude, who do not think at all, or who feel that, because they are drifting with the tide they are active agents in the progress of evolution.

Social realism would presumably demand of any work of literature a respect for the truth of things 'as they are'. To depict the world otherwise than as it appears to the senses is to falsify and sincerity demands that we look at the worst unflinchingly; there is a kind of stoicism in this attitude, admirable perhaps in its way; because things are such, we ought to look at them. But since for positivism reality is situated (by definition) in the physical order only (a view consistent not only with Marxist economic theory but with the exclusively quantitative criteria of science), truth to the nature of things has come to mean truth to the physical order—a fact which perhaps explains the apparently inexhaustible current preoccupation with carnality. But in what are these records more 'true to life', more 'real', than the thoughts of Plato, St. Paul, Dante or Mozart?

These too are human. This question is not even asked; but if it were, it might be answered that spirituality, abstract thought, and intellectual beauty, not being quantitatively measurable or experienced by the senses, have not, in terms of the positive, any reality at all. It is a question of where, for a society, a caste, or a civilisation, reality is situated. In this respect there seems to have taken place a revolution, which has reversed the normal hierarchy of values, situating the physical and the quantitative above intellect and the spirit.

There has been talk of 'two cultures' and (leaving unasked the question as to whether the absence of culture can be called another kind of culture, ignorance another mode of knowledge) it seems impossible that the rift between them can be mended by good will, since the difference lies between two irreconcilable philosophies. The one is an expression of quantitative science and philosophic positivism; and since quantity is the proper measure only of physical phenomena, it must in its nature reduce the artist to some form of recording-apparatus. Upon the television-screen, the typical 'cultural' expression of the quantitative culture, we can see images from anywhere in space; but the difference in quality between the two sides of the screen is negligible. Viewers and viewed could change places and nothing would be altered. The kitchens of the common man, in which all kinds of ignorant persons express themselves in a language indistinguishable from what such persons would use in real life are held before the 'viewer'; and 'true to life' has come to mean true to the lowest expression of the lowest intelligence—true to the life of the *bête humaine*.

'The men who created the communism of the masses'—to quote Yeats—'believed that religion, art, philosophy, expresses economic change, that the shell secreted the fish'. But this implicit positivism is by no means confined to the Communist world: it is, and must necessarily be, the philosophy of the masses now everywhere rising to power, for whom the real is situated (as for material science, the philosophy inseparable from the ascendency of the proletariat) in the physical. But when Shakespeare wrote that poets hold a mirror up to 'nature', he used the word in another sense: not the physical 'nature' of science, but the nature of man, his soul and passions. To quote Yeats again,

> the mischief began at the end of the seventeenth century
> when man became passive before a mechanised nature;
> that lasted to our day with the exception of a brief period
> between Smart's *Song of David* and the death of Byron,
> wherein imprisoned man beat upon the door. Or I may dismiss all that ancient history and say it began when Flaubert
> described a masterpiece as 'a mirror dawdling down a lane'.

A mirror very different from Shakespeare's; the eye of the realist has become as passive as a camera-lens and the animal lusts
are often all that distinguishes the records of man from those of
his machines. On the other hand the art of 'abstract expressionism' has no ordering principle at all, and has at best the negative virtue of release from an imprisoning realism. These two
extreme forms, different in appearance are alike in that which
they lack. A true reflection of our civilisation such work may be;
but of what is that civilisation itself a reflection? Nor should we
forget that nature—human nature—mirrors the forms held up to
it, and the man who keeps company with machines will, as Blake
says, become what he beholds.

Flaubert's mirror can but reflect what is there, it is passive, it
changes nothing: what, we must ask, does such art propose as its
end? What can it do to us, or for us? How add to our knowledge
or transform our consciousness when all it does is to reflect back
to us what we can see without its assistance, which the camera
can show us as well? The story of Cinderella, which recurs in
many forms in many parts of the world is an allegory of the soul
disfigured, as all are, by the dust and ashes of this world; she
toils in just such a kitchen as those whose sinks and dustbins and
ironing-boards are images which have set their mark on a decade.
One version (given by Harold E. Bayley in *The Lost Language
of Symbolism*, a book Yeats read) tells how the kitchen-maid
found a looking glass in which she saw not her grimy self but a
princess of perfect beauty whose dress shone like the sun, moon
and stars. There are mirrors and mirrors; and a work of imagination is a magic glass in which we may discover that nature
to which actuality is barely an approximation. Fairy tales tell
always of royal and heroic (that is to say perfect or perfected)

persons, or of humbly born persons who become royal; as do the sacred dances which in Indian villages are the culture of the illiterate; not for economic, but for symbolic reasons. Yeats made of this myth a poem whose images have a beguiling and deceptive lightness:

> If I make the lashes dark
> And the eyes more bright
> And the lips more scarlet,
> And ask if all is right
> From mirror after mirror,
> No vanity's displayed:
> I'm looking for the face I had
> Before the world was made.

The woman who attempts to make herself more beautiful is an imaginative artist seeking to make her actual appearance accord with her (in the Platonic sense) real nature, to which her bodily appearance is only a rough approximation. Demotic art ('paint the warts') dwells on the blemishes which the eye sees; imaginative art reflects 'the true man', 'To which all lineaments tend and seek with love and sympathy', as Blake said. Imaginative poetry alone has a real function to perform; for the pseudo-arts of realism perform no function beyond that of endlessly reporting on the physical world; which quantitative science (whose proper function it is) can do very much better. But true poetry has the power of transforming consciousness itself by holding before us icons, images of forms only partially and superficially realised in 'ordinary life'.

This, in part at least, is the immemorial truth which underlies Keats's 'Beauty is truth, truth beauty'. The realists who hold the contrary, that beauty is false because it does not correspond with the imperfections of actuality, at once deprive poetry of any function whatsoever, and make of actuality a prison from which there is no escape.

In a story by another precursor of social realism, Tolstoy, there is a discernment of a kind of truth Flaubert's mirror cannot give. In *The Kreutzer Sonata* the hero, if hero he can be called, is a sensual brute of an ordinary man, as intensely aware of all to do with his own tortured animality as any modern could desire; but this brute has an inexplicable—to himself inexplicable—love of music; so unrelated is this love to all else in his life that the beauty of Beethoven's music comes to him as a kind of torture, outrage and fear:

> That piece had a terrible effect on me: it was as if quite
> new feelings, new possibilities, of which I had till then been
> unaware, had been revealed to me. 'That's how it is, not
> at all as I used to think and live, but that way', something
> seemed to say within me. What this new thing was that had
> been revealed to me I could not explain to myself, but the
> consciousness of this new condition was very joyous. All
> these same people, including my wife and him appeared in a
> new light.

The human beast at that moment saw something by no means reflected in the mirror of his outward life; and yet he knew it not as less but as more true; 'not at all as I used to think and live'. There is a truth, a reality, different from that of realism, which the realist has recognised as more real. What had he seen? Plato would say that the music had stirred in him a latent knowledge, the *anamnesis* the soul has of an order inherent within it,

a wholeness, a harmony to which the outer life is scarcely even
an approximation. If this order be real, then may we not call
the mundane reality less real—as the Platonic philosophers in
fact did, on the grounds that it is only a partial realisation, a
blurred copy, a faint imprint. He had experienced beauty; and
what he saw he recognised as a harmony already and forever
existing, something he already possessed, but as lying away in
the dark. Plato and Plotinus would say that this experience was
in no way inexplicable; for this harmonious order is said to be
an attribute, a possession of the soul, and not at all alien to it. If
this were not so, the more perfect the beauty, the more foreign
would it seem to us; but the contrary of this is true—the greater
the beauty, the more does it strike us not as strange but as deeply
familiar; 'that's how it is'. Seen with the eyes of realism, that is
not how it is at all; and in Tolstoy's terrible story, the glimpse
of perfection was not sufficient to transform the man's life. His
rejection of the music threw him back into the murderous fury in
which his story reached its climax. Even so we may say that his
momentary realisation was a momentary self-knowledge; for, to
quote Plotinus, 'we ourselves possess beauty when we are true to
our own being; our ugliness is going over to another order'. Our
deepest self-knowledge, that is to say, is a discovery of the beautiful. In self-ignorance we see the ugly, which is not a quality in
itself but, precisely, the absence of quality, form, unity; or, as the
philosophers say, reality. Of what use is Genet's *The Maids* or
Wesker's *The Kitchen* to working girls? With the instinct of their
sanity the Cinderellas prefer *Swan Lake*; as their young men,
with the sense of the heroic still uncorrupted, prefer 'Westerns'.
Their instinctive choice is not made from 'escapism' but is on
the contrary a search for self-knowledge, the 'know thyself' of

the Delphic Oracle. The Greek populace had Agamemnon and Achilles and the Elizabethan groundlings Shakespeare's long procession of kings; and in these the humanity they discovered was their own. Realism cannot show us what we are, but only our failures to become that to which the common man and the common woman inadequately, but continually, aspire and strive. The common people crave for the heroic and the beautiful; and when they cease to do so (under the influence of a nihilistic minority) can our civilisation long survive? The ugly and the vulgar enable us not to feel, not to think, not to live; they save us from the anguish of living. Let us admit that our society as a whole has chosen death—death in small, painless doses. Fortunes are made by selling it.

The present decadence of the arts, and all the more or less ineffectual attempts to find other foundations upon which to rebuild them than those of tradition, arises quite simply from the disappearance of the idea of an intelligible world (to use Plato's phrase) a spiritual order, a world of the soul, whose existence is not that of the fleeting images of nature. Existentialism is a serious philosophic attempt to do away with the necessity for a distinction between existence and essence, body and soul, idea and embodiment. In France the necessity is at least recognised; in England few trouble about such things, and our writers live in matters of first principles, from hand to mouth; forgetting that even the aspect of the natural world and the quality of carnality itself depend upon what we believe to be the nature of these things.

Had Tolstoy's jealousy-tormented husband allowed the music to form him to its pattern, instead of rejecting it, as he did with his whole being, as an outrage, a violation of social decorum, he might have been saved. Tolstoy had understood, in a profound intuition, that music has a function, a transforming power. It exists to bring the human beast to *anamnesis* of another order which exists in him; knowledge of what was once called the soul; if we prefer now to call it the psyche, its reality remains the same. This use of poetry and the other arts has at this time been almost universally forgotten—as must be so if that other order is held to be non-existent. If there be no such function for them to perform I cannot see why anyone should trouble with the arts at all: as mere diversion, are they worth keeping alive? By reason of this transforming power their existence becomes not merely justified but indispensable to the civilising process by which the human animal is transformed into something else; and what is man, if not the one creature in whom this possibility exists, upon whom this task falls?

Tolstoy's hero was a member of the old Russian aristocracy, a class by no means lacking in the means of living in comfort, luxury, affluence. These people had intelligence and feeling, and a terrifying insight into man's animal nature and the depths to which it may drag us down. What seems in the society Tolstoy describes to be lacking is precisely what is lacking in modern society: a culture adequate to its needs, of the kind which in some times and places has raised human societies as a whole to greater self-knowledge, a finer consciousness of what is in man. Italy has continued to produce, over many centuries (in painting and architecture especially, whose influence is enduring) a multitude of images, which in churches, cities and houses were continually before the eyes of people of all classes, and continue to this day to exert upon all who come into their presence, their transforming power. Edwin Muir, living in Rome, and finding himself everywhere surrounded by such images, found himself contrasting the Eternal City with Glasgow, where his youth had been spent. He was amazed to find everywhere emblems, icons of the divine mysteries; an environment created not only for the needs of the body, but above all for the needs of the soul. Do we not, in those cities where in architecture, sculpture and painting, the needs of the spirit are met, feel instantly at home, as if we could live there? And do we not, in such cities as Glasgow, or in the wastes of suburbia, seem as if exiles, living provisionally, but not as in our right place? Even when, in our modern cities and suburbs, the needs of the body are catered for, few are happy; for such an environment is intolerable, even to many who are unable to articulate the reasons for their profound unrest in the presence of the ugly—or to be more exact, in the absence of the beautiful. For, if Plotinus be right, 'the soul itself acts immediately, affirming the Beautiful where it finds something accordant with the ideal form within itself. . . . But let the soul fall in with the ugly and at once it shrinks within itself, denies the thing, turns away from it, not accordant, resenting it.' People may live a lifetime in beautiless cities, never losing the sense of exile, of alienation from something which they have never even known.

Yet no act of protest, or reiteration of the predicament as such, can give any release; for it does not provide the cure, but only describes the disease. Did not Dostoevsky say that our salvation can only be through the beautiful?

To the behaviourists, as to their predecessor Locke, nothing is in the mind which was not first in the senses, and consciousness is a mere tabula rasa, an empty recipient of impressions. For the Platonic philosophy, on the contrary, the soul is 'a plenitude of forms, an ever-written tablet, a vital intellectual energy'. The concept of the beautiful (from which it is inseparable) has for this philosophy a precise meaning, as what corresponds to an innate formal order. Whatever is congruent with the ground of our nature seems to us beautiful. The square, the circle, the laws of geometry and number are, in this sense, intrinsically satisfying to some sense of order which belongs to our nature. It is for this reason that Plato said that we learn by remembering; and shows us Socrates proving this by questioning an illiterate slave-boy in such a way that he 'saw' the solution of a problem of geometry; for the order of the soul, so understood, is not something 'personal' and 'subjective', but universal. Music is considered by the Platonic philosophers to be the highest of the arts because the nearest to the harmonious innate order of number, reflected in all the arts and in nature itself.

The order of which the arts have in the past been the expression does not cease to exist because it is no longer perceived; but the arts, as these are practised and understood by a newly literate, but still barbarous populace, are no longer its vehicle. That works of poetry and the other arts which have survived from more civilized times and places had intentions utterly different from those imputed to poets and artists in our own, has been so largely forgotten that a book like Edgar Wind's *Pagan Mysteries of the Renaissance* amazes us by its revelation of the intentions of the painters of pictures long familiar. Instead, the arts have become the expression of the very incoherence and ignorance from which they normally provide release. Some would defend the modern movement on the grounds that the task of the artist is to reflect any and every experience; an opinion unimaginable in any culture which recognises that not all experiences are of the same qualitative value. Tradition replies that a true work of imagination reflects not the imperfect but the perfect, not the disorder of failures and ignorance, but a perfection to which we are drawn; and if imperfection, only in the context of such perfection, which alone gives meaning to the process of becoming. When literature becomes merely a formulation of some state of ignorance or vulgarity, it is like a magnet which has lost its power and become common iron like the rest.

Plotinus, more fully than Plato himself, has given expression to the traditional philosophy of art. A statue, he said, is not beautiful as stone; Phidias modelled his sculpture of Zeus not upon things of sense but by 'apprehending what form Zeus must take if he chose to become manifest to sight'. Blake had read Plotinus on the Beautiful, and seems to be echoing his very images when he answers those critics who objected to his representation of spiritual essences with real bodies that they 'would do well to consider that the Venus, the Minerva, the Jupiter, the Apollo, which they admire in Greek statues are all of them representations of spiritual existences, of gods immortal to the mortal and perishing organ of sight. And yet they are embodied and organized in solid marble.' Plato, Plotinus and all who have followed their doctrine have known that to copy from a mental form, an idea, is to come nearer to perfection than to copy nature; which is itself only a reflection, image or imprint of an anterior pattern. The artist must look to the original, not to the copy.

This is not to say that nature is to be rejected in favour of abstract mental forms; for nature is itself informed by harmonious patternings of the same kind as the ideas of poet and artist. Since natural objects are themselves expressions of the formative principle, we must recognize that artists who work from nature, with knowledge of what these forms really are, give no bare reproduction of the thing seen, but go back to the principles from which nature itself derives. It is when the ideal forms of nature are themselves forgotten, and nature seen as mere opaque matter, that naturalism abandons the first principles of art. It is a paradox worth reflecting upon that in times and places where nature has been seen in terms of the traditional wisdom, depictions of bird, beast and flower and of the human body have been minute (though not necessarily in a visually literal way) in detail, impassioned and beautiful. In our own age, an exaltation of matter and a denial of spirit has led to a loss of the sense both of form and beauty in natural objects; a disintegration of form. Our modern realism no more refers to any principle of form than does its apparent opposite, abstract expressionism. It sees form and deformities alike, for without reference to any norm, the accidental and the malformation are just as 'true' as the ideal perfection—more so, it might be argued, because only these are to be found in the physical world. Even more is this so when man is depicted; if there is no innate moral perfection to which human conduct must tend and seek, all, again, is equal— the noble and the vile, the trivial and the significant; or rather all becomes trivial, and nothing significant, since there is no standard by which anything can be called worse or better. Blake warned us long ago of the formlessness which must inevitably result when instead of copying from the 'divine originals' artists copy accident and deformity, 'blots and blurs'. Then, he said, 'The line of the Almighty must be drawn again before man or beast can exist.'

Tolstoy's hero, listening to Beethoven's music, became dimly aware that the music meant something, represented some kind of knowledge which eluded him. 'That condition had a meaning for him [Beethoven] but for me—none at all. That is why music only agitates, doesn't lead to a conclusion.' The truth of course was that this man was too far off, too deeply sunk in sensuality to follow the music into, so to say, its own world; to such as him, beauty must perhaps always seem a kind of torture, forcing its demands beyond anything we can, in our low condition, answer to. I have often found myself wondering why the present age seems positively to shrink from beauty, to prefer the ugly, to feel safer, more at home with it; and I have come to realise that there is a reproach in the beautiful and the perfect; it passes its continual silent judgement and it requires perhaps a kind of courage to love what is perfect, since to do so is an implicit confession of our own imperfection. Can it be that the prevalence of the low and the sordid in contemporary writing is a kind of easy way, a form of sloth, an avoidance of that reproach which would call us, silently, to a self-perfection it would cost us too much to undertake? And yet it is in order to work upon us that transformation, that perfection, that works which embody the beautiful alone exist. That is their function, their justification in terms, one might almost say, of citizenship.

Strangest of all is the ease with which the vision is lost; consciousness contracts, we forget over and over again, until recollection is stirred by some icon of that beauty. Then we remember and wonder why we ever forgot. It is because of the continual downward drag of amnesia—for apathy and death are less exacting than life, they are the easy way of 'effortless barbarism'—that works of poetry and the other arts are necessary for our survival; survival, that is, as human beings; without, we tend to revert to what the Hindu philosophers called 'animal incarnations'—the *bête humaine*.

Indeed it may be said that it is because the beautiful is too troubling an experience to natural apathy that we avoid it; or one too painful to be endured in a world so out of tune with its order. It is certain that those who recollect most clearly the order of perfection find the life of the common world correspondingly painful, so far does it fall short. Yet, try as we may to come to terms with the ugly and the vulgar, they continue to shock, hurt and jar some intuitive sense of fitness of form and the truth of beauty. Images formless and deformed are continually being forced upon us, so that the shocks and 'kicks' which compel our attention, much as pain does, are even confused with the aesthetic experience itself; yet the formless and the deformed can only disintegrate and lacerate, whereas images of order unify and heal. There is implicit in any art which holds before us images of human perfection, the idea of perfectibility—again, a concept compatible only with a spiritual view of man.

The beautiful, then, is the active principle in any work of transforming power, summoning us to self-knowledge of the innate human norm to which we always tend, but from which we always deviate; and the greater the disparity between a sordid actuality, and the perfection of the beautiful, the greater, not the less, is the need for the 'truth' of beauty, to rectify and inform the formless reality—or unreality—of the everyday world. It is by images of perfection alone that poetry transforms consciousness. There are, among avant-garde writers, some who seem to use the ugly and the shocking in order to attract attention to themselves which their work could not command on its merits. Plotinus also knew that sensations of the ugly and evil impress us more violently than those of what is agreeable; but they leave, he says, less mark; whereas sanity tranquilly present explains itself better; it takes first place, it is the natural thing, it belongs to our being; illness is alien, unnatural, and thus makes itself felt by its very incongruity. But what of our age in which the sick and the unnatural have become the norm?

In a normal society the soul finds everywhere in the arts, in myths, in religious symbols, in all that people make and use, images expressive of that order. Yeats saw in Byzantine civilisation a nearly perfect expression of those ideal forms—a flowering of Plato's thought long after Athens. 'The painter, the mosaic worker, the worker in gold and silver, the illuminator of sacred books, were almost impersonal, almost perhaps without consciousness of individual design, absorbed in their subject-matter and that the vision of a whole people.' The work of many that seemed the work of one, that made building, picture, pattern, metalwork of rail or lamp, seem but a single image was, as he says, 'a proclamation of their invisible master', that most Platonic concept the Logos, 'the true man' or Imagination, according to Blake. Edwin Muir in his last series of lectures, *The Estate of Poetry*, spoke of our present world and its soul-destroying ills; but the most terrible, he said, is nothing which is there: it is, rather, what is lacking. We can no longer give a name to what we lack; it is precisely our forgetfulness, our *anamnesis*, our want of orientation which ails us. Art is the normal environment of the soul, the normal means of *anamnesis* and orientation. Lacking this environment we starve in the midst of quantitative plenty. What is worse, we are everywhere invaded by images of a destructive—literally a soul-destroying—nature.

The ugly and the abnormal make a quick and easy impact upon attention, to which mass communication has accustomed us. But there is another influential minority who are no friends to the beautiful—those academic critics whose conceptual *apparatus criticus* the beautiful transcends and eludes. Such criticism is concerned with parts, the *ars poetica* with wholes which are more than the sum of parts, which on the contrary inform and determine the parts. The recognition of the beautiful is immediate and intuitive, but it is the response of a faculty higher than the discursive reason; with the Platonic *nous*, the higher reason, not with *dianoia* the ratio. But the *hubris* of those whose profession is discursive will never admit this, perhaps do not even know it, since the higher perceives the lower, but the lower does not perceive the higher. The climate of critical opinion is indeed at this time increasingly plebeian and quantitative; for imperceptions may become articulate, may learn the terms of critical discourse, without ever discovering that those terms were never and never could have been the terms which enabled poet and artist to create those works on which they so complacently pronounce; to the satisfaction only of those (and these are inevitably a majority) who share their own limitations. They even appear to regard direct access to works of poetry as an infringement of their own territories (which some might say they have in any case usurped, as the rabble after the French Revolution parcelled out more concrete estates). The power to perceive the beautiful arises from a quality of consciousness: something for ever inaccessible to the *apparatus criticus*, which can be manipulated by persons who do not possess this quality at all. The cleansing of the doors of perception is a matter rather of culture than of education, and may be possessed by people in the academic sense unlearned; while it is possible to be a notorious critic and yet to be entirely without it.

We can learn about beauty only from beauty; and therefore Yeats called the sages of Byzantium (teachers of metaphysical and spiritual knowledge) and its artists, the 'singing-masters' of the soul; for the school in which the soul must learn self-knowledge is not that of the conceptual critics but such works as awaken self-knowledge by Platonic recollection; and therefore works of art and not works of criticism; with the exception of the few such works as are themselves (like those of Ruskin or Pater or Proust) works of art.

> Nor is there singing-school but studying
> Monuments of its own magnificence. . . .

Like calls to like. At best scholarship, by placing in our hands knowledge which we should not otherwise possess, can fit us to read the works of the poets, to decipher what they have written. Yeats, a poet of this century, can no more be understood by those who do not possess the knowledge of the 'learned school' in which he himself studied, than can poets of other periods; and to such knowledge there is no critical short-cut: we have to acquire it, or remain in ignorance.

Yet the common people (within a traditional society, that is, in which illiterate men and women may possess, as even now in India, and perhaps still in Ireland, a culture) respond to the beautiful, which speaks to an intellectual order innate no less in the ignorant than in the learned. Indeed it is easier for those not educated at all to respond immediately to such forms than it is for those who are miseducated; as all those are who are given false criteria. An aristocratic culture operates throughout society; and works made in knowledge communicate the quality of that knowledge (though not its learning) to 'the people'; and also to another group who may be called unlearned, to those in love; since these are (according to Plato's sense of the word love) oriented towards the beautiful as by a divine enchantment.

> Pythagoras planned it. Why did the people stare?
> His numbers, though they moved or seemed to move
> In marble or in bronze, lacked character.
> But boys and girls, pale from the imagined love
> Of solitary beds, knew what they were. . . .

The mathematical proportions based upon Pythagorean number speak immediately to an innate sense of harmony; and Yeats goes on to consider those more mysterious ideas which evoke in the common man a response to conceptions of the heroic:

> When Pearse summoned Cuchulain to his side,
> What stalked through the Post Office? What intellect,
> What calculation, number, measurement, replied?

Painful as it may be to remember an order of perfection with which the common world is out of tune, it is even more painful not to remember—would indeed be spiritual death were it possible. We are haunted by the presence of an inaccessible knowledge, and by a sense as of estrangement from some place or state native to us; the Paradise of all mythologies, once and for ever known, but lost. Of this Paradise all are native, for it lies within ourselves, forgotten or half forgotten. Adam, according to the Genesis myth, fell into 'a deep sleep'. Plotinus describes mankind passing, as it were from bed to bed, from sleep to sleep'. Plato tells in a fable that souls as they approach birth drink the forgetful waters of Lethe—matter. Some drink so deeply that they forget all they knew in eternity; some who drink less deeply have partial remembrance.

> The Soul that rises with us, our life's Star
> Hath elsewhere had its setting,
> And cometh from afar:
> Not in entire forgetfulness

—so Wordsworth paraphrases Plotinus. Or as Yeats wrote, those born

> must sleep, shriek, struggle to escape
> As recollection or the drug decide.

Jung is but returning to tradition in holding that beyond and behind our personal memories there lies a *terra incognita* which we have perhaps known, as Plato taught, in some former state; or which we have never known, but which, when we bring it to consciousness, has the familiarity (it being a part of ourselves) of something recollected. That is why it comes to us as something deeply familiar. It is with no sense of surprise, no shock of strangeness that we listen to a fugue by Bach or follow with our eyes the meeting and flowing of Gothic arches, or attend to those profound realisations of *King Lear*, or read Milton's or Dante's descriptions of Paradise. The greatest art seems always like our own thoughts made conscious. We recognise in some Chinese or Italian landscape, in a Samuel Palmer or a Claude, in Shelley's 'little lawny islet, with anemone and violet like mosaic paven', or in the tapestries of *La Dame à la Licorne* a world we seem always and forever to have known. To experience such art is, as when we contemplate the beauty of a Botticelli face, a figure drawn by Giotto, a homecoming, though the way from this world to that is long and we may well fear the journey.

To transmit, to raise to consciousness this hidden order which we call 'the beautiful' the arts have traditionally existed. Yeats indicted the modern movement in words both contemptuous and exact:

> Scorn the sort now growing up
> All out of shape from toe to top,
> Their unremembering hearts and heads
> Base-born products of base beds.

Baseborn and unremembering: to be base-born is to be earth-born, the *bête humaine*.

'The sort now growing up' have not forgotten what they have learned in their textbooks; they remember events of the physical order to the last sordid detail. What Yeats declares they do not remember is the order of beauty and wisdom, and the orientation of all things towards perfection. On Plotinus' 'beds' they are sunk in Blake's 'deadly sleep'. Lacking access to the ordering principle their works are 'all out of shape', and covered with warts. Art becomes formless when it becomes soulless. The Platonists spoke of the 'souls' of stones, plants and animals; the 'soul' of a crystal is the form—the mathematical formula—of the crystal; the soul of the plant, more complex, is the tendency towards a certain form of which time as well as space is a dimension. Soul, far from being a vague concept was, on the contrary, the principle of form and the formative principle; which in man is the imagination. According to Coomaraswamy 'Art is expression *informed* by ideal beauty'; 'My shaping spirit of imagination,' Coleridge wrote; and Yeats

indicts the modern movement for its 'spawning formless fury'—
the quantitative proliferation of anything and everything in the
absence of a controlling formal principle; a kind of cultural
cancer.

Spenser beautifully defines, in what amounts almost to a
paraphrase of the Platonic doctrine, the poet's philosophy of the
beautiful:

What time this worlds great workmaister did cast
To make al things, such as we now behold,
It seems that he before his eyes had plast
A goodly Patterne, to whose perfect mould
He fashioned them as comely as he could;
That now so faire and seemly they appeare,
As nought may be amended any wheare.

That wondrous Patterne, wheresoere it bee,
Whether in earth layd vp in secret store,
Or else in heauen, that no man may it see
With sinfull eyes, for fear it to deflore,
Is perfect Beautie, which all men adore.
Whose face and feature doth so much excell
All mortal sence, that none the same may tell.

Thereof as euery earthly thing partakes,
Or more or lesse by influence diuine,
So it more faire accordingly it makes,
And the grosse matter of this earthly myne,
Which clostheth it, thereafter doth refyne,
Doing away the drosse which dims the light
Of that faire beam, which therein is empight.

The same philosophy runs through Shakespeare; but he, enchanted, like Plato's lovers, by a particular beauty, as it were plays with the doctrine, pretending that the mortal exemplar is really the heavenly original; by this inversion he pours out at the feet of the one beloved all the riches of the immortal treasuries:

Describe Adonis and the counterfeit
Is poorly imitated after you;
On Helen's cheek all art of beauty set,
And you in Grecian tires are painted new:
Speak of the spring and foison of the year,
The one doth shadow of your beauty show,
The other as your bounty doth appear;
And you in every blessed shape we know.

Shakespeare could not have written so if these originals had not, for him, kept their place of honour in the order of perfect forms; only because these divine originals may be invoked can he delight in the play of hyperbole in praise of the beloved.

Spenser, Shakespeare, Milton, Herbert, Blake, Vaughan, Coleridge, Keats, Shelley, Yeats, all these poets are strung upon a single thread, all echo one another and the doctrine of poetry in all is the same; so that examples might be multiplied endlessly, as if a single mind spoke in all.

Shelley in 'The Sensitive Plant' describes the presence of beauty in this world in the form of an allegory, of a lady who tends a garden, bringing to their perfection all its flowers; the theme is an old one—Venus in Spenser's Garden of Adonis is the same figure, the 'goddess nature'. When Shelley's divine lady dies, the garden decays, and weeds, rankness and death alone

are left. Yet the truth is the reverse of that which appears; the
garden is

> this life
> Of error, ignorance, and strife,
> Where nothing is, but all things seem,

but truly understood

> That garden sweet, that lady fair,
> And all sweet shapes and odours there,
> In truth have never passed away:
> 'Tis we, 'tis ours, are changed; not they,

> For love, and beauty, and delight
> There is no death nor change; their might
> Exceeds our organs, which endure
> No light, being themselves obscure.

Since the beautiful is an order of wholes, and of wholeness,
a mark of its informing presence is the symmetry and pattern
of verse. It is impossible to speak of beauty without speaking
of form. Beauty is a unity, a unification; and lyric form, as all
poets know, comes from something 'given', precisely when
imaginative inspiration is strongest. Such forms can, of course,
be imitated, but that is quite another matter; although it may
be that such dead imitations for a time brought lyric form into
disfavour. However, a deeper reason for the disappearance of
lyric form between the two wars, and the use of a disjointed and
broken 'free verse' had probably much more to do with precisely
that loss of access to the 'other' mind which both occasioned and
characterised the mood of 'the world of *l'entre deux guerres*', as
Eliot himself called it. It is wholly consistent with his Platonic

view of poetry that Yeats should adhere to formal verse; and with the nature of life that lyricism should have risen up with a rush in the poetry of Dylan Thomas.

Contemporary critics have little to say of lyric form, just because it is impossible to discourse about it, to analyse its whole into parts. Is not Yeats the greatest poet of his time because, together with the learning of the imagination he possessed this natural gift, which no learning can command? James Joyce, with his natural ear for verbal music, singled out as supremely beautiful the poem which begins

> Who will go drive with Fergus now,
> And pierce the deep wood's woven shade,
> And dance upon the level shore?
> Young man, lift up your russet brow,
> And lift your tender eyelids, maid,
> And brood on hopes and fears no more.

Paraphrased into discursive terms there is nothing there at all, nor in the verse that follows; which haunts like a phrase of music, and, like music, communicates a meaning and a knowledge not of fact but of quality. Why is it that those very poets who held to the Platonic doctrine can write perfect lyrics, whereas those who do not can produce only imitations of such forms, working by rules of prosody which are themselves merely deduced from spontaneous rhapsodic speech? Lyric form is itself the supreme embodiment of archetypal order, the nearest to music and number; it is beauty itself informing words in themselves ordinary; and it cannot, as Plato wrote in the *Ion*, be achieved by the poet writing from his mundane consciousness, but only in that divine madness in which he is possessed by the 'other' mind.

AE (George Russell) objected to the unfitness of marrying such forms to prosaic content, instancing Robert Graves, who with his great talent has no difficulty in producing any verse-form he likes. He instances a letter supposedly from a British officer, written in iambics; and goes on to say

> the heart of love, in imagination, in meditation mounts at times to an ecstasy where its being becomes musical . . . the pattern of sound, the recurrent beat of verse echo that inner music. In all languages where poetry has been written there has been pattern, rhythm, echo, measure or recurrent beat, and what would be unreal if it was merely speech of lip or brain becomes most sincere when we feel it of intense spiritual or emotional life. We need not discuss the psychology of this, whether when the inner nature subdues the outer nature, whenever flesh is melted into soul, the soul imposes upon the body some image or echo of itself, as a ray of the logos, of the Mind which made music and harmony in the universe. We need not enter upon difficult or unprovable speculation. It is certain that metrics as a mode of speech correspond to something in the soul. But if we say this we are impelled to deny the fitness of verse as utterance of any feeling, imagination, or reverie which has not originated in the magic fountain.

(1966)

III

THE WITNESS
OF POETRY

Innocence and Experience

B EFORE WE LOOK more closely at Blake's *Songs of Innocence and of Experience* it would be well to ask why he wrote them. Already in the answers to this question we shall discover that, as in all Blake's writings, wherever we find apparent simplicity there are deeper issues involved than we had thought. Historically the answer could be simple enough; during the late eighteenth century poems were for the first time being written for children by those concerned with education. The hymn-writer Isaac Watts, for example, had published *Divine Songs for Children*, and *Moral Songs*, whose 'language and Measures should be easy and flowing with Cheerfulness, and without the Solemnities of Religion . . . that the Children might find Delight and Profit together.' These poems remained popular for a century and more; my father knew most or many of them by heart (having been taught them in school) and indeed I learned some of them myself as a child. To Watts we shall return, for Blake had evidently read his Songs with attention, and much indignation.

But Watts himself—and there were others—were themselves products of their time. Childhood was for the first time being considered by philosophers in relation to theories of knowledge; and this in its turn produced a prolific crop of theories of education.

Locke had much to say on the nature of knowledge. His view was that all knowledge comes to us through the senses. A new-born child is like a blank page on which nothing has yet been written, and on which anything can be written that the educators choose; there was much talk among followers of Locke about the 'forming' of the infant mind—a process of conditioning that could not begin too soon. According to Locke there are no innate ideas:

> If we will attentively consider new-born Children we shall
> have little Reason, to think that they bring many Ideas into
> the World With them. For, bating, perhaps, some faint
> Idea's, of Hunger, and Thirst, and Warmth, and some Pains,
> which they may *have* felt in the Womb, there is *not* the least
> appearance of any settled Idea's at all in them. . . . One may
> perceive how, that they get no more, nor no other, than
> what Experience and the Observation of things, that come
> in their way, furnish them with; which might be enough to
> satisfie us, that they are not Original Characters, stamped
> on the Mind.

This is a view much like modern Behaviourism, which sees life as a matter of reflexes conditioned in beings themselves to be regarded as mechanisms. The brain is considered as if it were the mind which controls it, and described as a highly receptive computer 'programmed' by education. This evil view is false because it considers man in merely quantitative terms and denies all levels of being except the physical. Indeed Blake from the beginning to the end of his writing life strove to answer and expose the falla-cious teaching of Locke, regarding Locke's materialism as a view of humanity as destructive as it is false. He had already given much thought to Locke before he wrote *Songs of Innocence*, his radiantly inspired answer to a false philosophy prevalent in his day, and still clung to by a majority in our own: the materialist view of man and his mental processes accepted as axiomatic by the framers of programmes for the mass media, and, if ques-tioned by some of the best scientists, never questioned by the less well-informed multitude for whom science is a religion.

The first of those beautiful illuminated books in which Blake published his prophetic writings (works no less sacred and inspired than those Missals and Books of Hours which they resemble) was a little tractate entitled *There is No Natural Religion*. This is Blake's carefully argued answer to Locke and his view of human knowledge as given in the first book of his *Essay Concerning Human Understanding*. Blake summarises Locke's argument in his own words: 'Man has no notion of moral fitness but from Education. Naturally he is only a natural organ sub-ject to Sense.' This view many would still accept as self-evident. Blake then takes Locke's premise and exposes its fallacy step by step. Since it is granted that 'Man cannot naturally Perceive but through his natural or bodily organs'—as Locke had argued—he can only compare and judge what he has so perceived, collecting more and more sense-data, as a computer might by programmed with information, without becoming any the wiser. 'If the many become the same as the few when possess'd. More! More! is the cry of a mistaken soul; less than All cannot satisfy Man.'

It is Locke and the scientists who cry 'More! More!' and ransack nature from the solar system to the minute structure of cells to add information to information. But their universe is merely quantitative. Like that of 'science fiction', it is, inevitably, claustrophobic because it lacks any vertical dimension in regions of experience other than that of the sensible order. Whether expanded or contracted, by change of scale or the postulation of additional senses, man becomes wearied of 'the same dull round, even of a universe' when that universe is only the 'mill with complicated wheels' of Newtonian science in which we are still, more or less, living to this day.

But because we are not computors programmed with sense-data, 'the desire of Man being Infinite, the possession is Infinite & himself Infinite.' The 'true man' is not the mortal body but the life, the consciousness that informs it, the imagination that experiences, not the senses that transmit information. 'The true faculty of knowing must be the faculty that experiences', Blake declares, cutting through all Locke's irrelevances about senses finer or more acute) more or less numerous. 'This faculty I treat of ', and indeed throughout his writings he is seeking to communicate his understanding that the 'true man' is the 'Poetic Genius' or 'Imagination', the God within. 'The Poetic Genius is the True Man', and 'As all men are alike in outward form so (and with the same infinite variety) all are alike in the Poetic Genius.' He was seeking for a term to describe the living Self which experiences and understands and creates life.

Blake's tractates against Locke were engraved in 1788; at that time he had not come to use the word Imagination for the indwelling living Self; later he wrote always of 'Jesus, the Imagination'. As 'God made man' he identifies Jesus with the Imagination and in his view Jesus is the Self in all men, fully realised, no doubt in the historical person of the founder of Christianity.

Thomas Taylor the Platonist, the first translator of Plato into English was himself another impassioned opponent of the mechanical philosophy and equalled Blake in his contempt for Locke. He contrasts with Plato's view of ideas as 'eternal and immaterial beings, the originals of all sensible forms,' Locke's opinion that 'ideas are formed from sensible particulars, by a kind of mechanical operation':

> According to Mr. Locke, the soul is a mere *rasa tabula*, an empty recipient, a mechanical blank. According to Plato, she is an ever-written tablet, a plenitude of forms, a vital and intellectual energy. On the former system she is on a level with the most degraded natures, the receptable of material species, and the spectator of delusion and non-entity.

How different, therefore, is Blake's conception of a new-born child from that of Locke and the Behaviourists. For Blake every child is a divine child, a manifestation of the Imagination of God in the human world. The birth of Jesus Christ is reflected in every birth. The one God is reflected 'multitudinous' in all the many births which bring the divine Self into human existence. In every child born there lives the indivisible universal 'spirit that knoweth all things'. This is the 'All' that can, in Blake's words, alone satisfy man. The many belongs to the temporal world; in the spiritual world each being experiences the One, not a part of the One (for God is indivisible) but the everywhere presence of the All.

Near the end of his life Blake wrote annotations in his copy of Berkeley's *Siris*; Berkeley the philosopher who had himself answered Locke, and from whom in all likelihood Blake had borrowed some of his own arguments. Blake's marginalia are radiant affirmations of all that he had proclaimed thirty years before in his early tractate: 'Imagination is the Divine Body in Every Man'; 'The Four Senses are the Four Faces of Man & the Four Rivers of the Water of Life.'; and he is still speaking of the Imagination when he writes 'Knowledge is not by deduction, but Immediate by Perception or Sense at once. Christ addresses himself to the Man, not to his Reason.' 'Jesus supposes every Thing to be Evident to the Child & to the Poor & Unlearned.' And Blake quotes from the Gospel the text in which it is said that 'the Spiritual Body or Angel as little Children always behold the Face of the Heavenly Father.'

And with a final thrust at Locke, 'The Natural Body is an Obstruction to the Soul or Spiritual Body.' 'What Jesus came to Remove was the Heathen or Platonic Philosophy which blinds the Eye of Imagination, The Real Man' 'Sense is the Eye of Imagination'; and to Blake it was clear that a window does not see; Locke had mistaken the window for the dweller in the house of the body. But Blake wrote, 'I question not my Corporeal or Vegetative Eye any more than I would Question a Window concerning a Sight. I look thro' it & not with it.' And in verse,

> We are led to Believe a Lie
> When we see With not Thro' the Eye
> Which was Born in a Night to perish in a Night

Such is the background of the profound issue which for Blake underlay the writing of *Songs of Innocence*. The newborn child is not the poor unformed dough that it seemed to Locke but an immortal spirit alighting on the threshold of this world, in full possession of a spiritual identity, no less fully human than a

mature man. In 'Infant Joy', (a poem he illustrated most beautifully with a crimson flower opening to show a new-born infant
in the care of a little female spirit of vegetation) Blake, as nearly
as it is possible for any poet, defines the nature, the essence of
being itself:

> 'I have no name:
> I am but two days old.'
> What shall I call thee?
> 'I happy am,
> 'Joy is my name.'
> Sweet joy befall thee!

Being—consciousness—bliss; *sat-chit-ananda*; such was
Blake's understanding of the essence of life. Joy is not something
that happens to the soul, it is the essential nature of every soul.

In the beautiful *Book of Thel* the virgin Thel, who is the
ungenerated soul looking down into the world of generation,
sees 'the worm upon its dewy bed', an 'image of weakness'. In
astonishment she says,

> Art thou but a Worm? Image of weakness, art thou but a
> Worm? I see thee like an infant wrapped in the Lilly's leaf.

But that worm is the *multum in parvule* of the Christian
Nativity. There were other influences besides Locke who played
their part in causing Blake to write *Songs of Innocence*. One of
his friends was Johnson, a radical publisher and bookseller in St
Paul's Churchyard, for whom Blake worked from time to time
as an engraver. Johnson's French editorial assistant was Mary
Wollstonecraft who had come under the influence of Rousseau;
whom Blake had also read. Rousseau had a view of childhood

very different from that of Locke. He believed in the innate goodness of all creatures, according to their nature. No one is born with a bad nature, and Rousseau held the humane and reasonable view that the innate qualities of every child, various as these are, can all be developed in such a way that they will flower of their own accord; just as a flower will develop from its seed if it is given conditions to suit it. This enlightened and kind psychology seems at this time almost self-evident; but this was far from being so in a world where on the one hand Locke and his followers saw a child as a mechanism to be programmed, and on the other the Calvinists taught the terrible doctrine of Predestination.

This virtually means that some people are born bad, and destined to damnation. This was the doctrine taught by the Presbyterian Church of Scotland, and there were plenty of Calvinists in England also and in other Protestant countries of Europe.

But infancy, as Blake understood long before Freud, is amoral, governed by the 'pleasure principle':

Infancy! fearless, lustful, happy, nestling for delight
In laps of pleasure: Innocence! honest, open, seeking
The vigorous joys of morning light; open to virgin bliss.
Who taught thee modesty, subtil modesty, child of night
   & sleep?

Blake wrote no more terrible indictment of the tyranny of morality over the innocent pleasure-principle of childhood than 'A Little Boy Lost,' in *Songs of Experience*. Calvin's Geneva had appalled Shakespeare; but the spirit which had burned a little boy for disrespect towards his father still, Blake reminds us, continues; if not physically, children may still be mentally and spiritually seared and destroyed. People seldom do harm to children from conscious and deliberate sadism, but most often in the name of some false ideology, believing that faults must be corrected and virtues instilled.

W. B. Yeats, in 'A Prayer for my Daughter,' writes of how the soul recovers 'radical innocence':

> And learns that it is self-delighting
> Self-appeasing, self-affrighting,
> And that is own sweet will is Heaven's will.

He is following Blake, who wrote *A Little Boy Lost*.

> Nought loves another as itself
> Nor venerates another so,
> Nor is it possible for Thought
> A greater than itself to know:

> And Father, how can I love you
> Or any of my brothers more?
> I love you like the little bird
> That picks up crumbs around the door.

> The Priest sat by and heard the child,
> In trembling zeal he seiz'd his hair:
> He led him by his little coat,
> And all admir'd the Priestly care.

> And standing on the altar high,
> "Lo! what a fiend is here!" said he,
> "One who sets reason up for judge
> Of our most holy Mystery."

The weeping child could not be heard,
The weeping parents wept in vain;
They strip'd him to his little shirt,
And bound him in an iron chain;

And burn'd him in a holy place
Where many had been burn'd before;
The weeping parents wept in vain.
Are such things done on Albion shore?

Rousseau's novel ideas on natural goodness were adopted with enthusiasm by Mary Wollstonecraft, and also by Blake, even though the Rousseaunian conception of freedom, being atheist, is only in certain respects comparable with Blake's. Rousseau too believed in an innate principle, and so far the two are alike; but he assigned its operation to the natural and not to the spiritual man. While seeing sympathetically the generosity of impulse which prompted the Swiss reformer, Blake points to the fallacy contained in the use of the word 'liberty' by the ideologists of the French revolution:

Many Persons, such as Paine & Voltaire, with some of the Ancient Greeks, say: 'we will not converse concerning Good & Evil; we will live in Paradise & Liberty.' You may do so in Spirit, but not in the Mortal Body as you pretend.

Mary interested herself in questions of education. She translated a charming book entitled *Elements of Morality for the Use of Parents and Children*, by Saltzmann; kindly stories with a great number of illustrations of which Blake made some of the engravings. Mary wrote a book of her own, *Original Stories from Real Life*, for which Blake was both illustrator and engraver. At the time he must have known Mary Wollstonecraft well. *Visions of the Daughters of Albion*, whose theme is the situation of women under restrictive marriage-laws, may also have been inspired by Mary, who as well as publishing her *Vindication of the Rights of Women* adopted Rousseau's views on free love and courageously and disastrously put those ideas into practice. She was abandoned by her lover, the American explorer Imlay, the father of her first daughter, Fanny. Mary afterwards married Godwin, who was also an acquaintance of Blake's, and Shelley's second wife, (Mary also) was the child of this marriage. Shelley was thus in a sense a spiritual heir to Blake's views on love and marriage also.

Blake's *Songs of Innocence* may well have been directly or indirectly suggested to him by Mary Wollstonecraft; they were his contribution to the current conflict of ideas in the field of education at the end of the eighteenth century, and to the new thought of which Rousseau was the moving spirit. His poem 'The Schoolboy' well describes the restrictive kind of education practised by those who, believing that all knowledge comes from without, set themselves, to form the infant mind by cramming it with facts. Blake's poem puts forward the view he shared with Mary and with Rousseau that every child will develop by the light of its own nature if given freedom to follow its innate bent. Blake's poem challenges the practice of 'forming' the young mind by loading it with information, envisaging just such a childhood as Wordsworth had been living only a few years earlier, and about which he too, in *The Prelude*, was to write under the influence of Rousseau.

> I love to rise in a summer morn
> When the birds sing on every tree;

The distant huntsman winds his horn,
And the sky-lark sings with me.
Oh! what sweet company.

But to go to school on a summer morn,
O! it drives all joy away;
Under a cruel eye outworn
The little ones spend the day
In sighing and dismay.

Ah! then at times I drooping sit,
And spend many an anxious hour,
Nor sit in learning's bower,
Worn thro' with the dreary shower.

How can the bird that is born for joy
Sit in a cage and sing?
How can a child, when fears annoy,
But droop his tender wing,
And forget his youthful spring?

O! father & mother, if buds are nip'd
And blossoms blown away,
And if the tender plants are strip'd
Of their joy in the springing day,
By sorrow and care's dismay,

How shall the summer arise in joy,
Or the summer fruits appear?
Or how shall we gather what griefs destroy,
Or bless the mellowing year,
When the blasts of winter appear?

In *Tiriel*, engraved in the same year as *Songs of Innocence*, Blake describes with indignation the results of the kind of education he rejects in 'The Schoolboy'. Tiriel is the victim of the cruel training and forming of a child until he loses his humanity and becomes in turn the blind tyrant of his own children, passing on the evil he had himself suffered. Blake describes the results in bitter anger. The speaker is the old and dying Tiriel, who sees too late that his humanity had been destroyed:

> The child springs from the womb; the father ready stands to
> form
> The infant head, while the mother idle plays with her dog
> on her couch:
> The young bosom is cold for lack of mother's nourishment,
> & milk,
> Is cut off from the weeping mouth: with difficulty & pain
> The little lids are lifted & the little nostrils open'd:
> The father forms a whip to rouze the sluggish senses to act
> And scourges off all youthful fancies from the new-born
> man.
> Then walks the weak infant in sorrow, compell'd to number
> footsteps
> Upon the sand.

It is in *Tiriel* that Blake first asked 'Why is one law given to the lion & the patient ox?' The 'one law' is the law of the world of Locke and the materialists, which denies the innate disposition of every creature. In contrast with this 'one law' might stand one of Blake's 'Proverbs of Hell', 'No bird soars too high, if he soars with his own wings.'

Songs of Innocence can be called poems for children and were presumably written as such, although they are also much more. But for Blake children are themselves fully human, capable of understanding at as great a depth as can adults. Certainly children are unaware of many facts, but they can feel, discern qualities of goodness and beauty or evil and ugliness perhaps even better than adults can. In *Jerusalem*, his longest and last Prophetic poem, Blake writes of

> the Wonders Divine
> Of Human Imagination throughout all the Three Regions
>   immense
> Of Childhood, Manhood & Old Age.

These are but 'regions' within a single experience, a single lifetime, none more or less valuable than the other.

Believing as he did that our world is a mental world Blake understood that dreams are also regions of the soul's reality, places of the Imagination. Thus the dream of Tom the chimney-sweeper in *Songs of Innocence* is just as real—perhaps more so—than the drab world of his daily labours. The inner freedom of his dream-world enables Tom to face the day happy and inwardly warm as the poor boys get to work with their bags and brushes.

> When my mother died I was very young,
> And my father sold me while yet my tongue
> Could scarcely cry ' 'weep! 'weep! 'weep! 'weep!'
> So your chimneys I sweep, & in soot I sleep.
>
> There's little Tom Dacre, who cried when his head,
> That curl'd like a lamb's back, was shav'd: so I said

Hush, Tom! never mind it, for when your head's bare
You know that the soot cannot spoil your white hair.

And so he was quiet, & that very night,
As Tom was a-sleeping, he had such a sight!
That thousands of sweepers, Dick, Joe, Ned, & Jack,
Were all of them lock'd up in coffins of black.

And by came an Angel who had a bright key,
And he open'd the coffins & set them all free;
And down a green plain leaping, laughing, they run
And wash in a river, and shine in the Sun.

Then naked & white, all their bags left behind,
They rise upon clouds and sport in the wind,
And the Angel told Tom, if he'd be a good boy,
He'd have God for his father, & never want joy.

And so Tom awoke; and we rose in the dark,
And got with our bags & our brushes to work.
Tho' the morning was cold, Tom was happy & warm;
So if all do their duty they need not fear harm.

It is destructive rationalism that deprives many of the comfort their dreams seek to bring them; as in another poem (which he did not include in *Songs of Innocence and of Experience*) Blake pathetically describes how to the child the Land of Dreams where he meets his dead mother is 'better far' than 'this Land of unbelief and fear'; while his father 'could not get to the other side' where he could have been with her also, had he accepted the reality of his experience.

O, what Land is the Land of Dreams?
What are its Mountains & what are its Streams?
O Father, I saw my Mother there,
Among the Lillies by waters fair.

Among the Lambs, clothed in white,
She walk'd with her Thomas in sweet delight,
I wept for joy, like a dove I mourn;
O when shall I again return?

Dear Child, I also by pleasant Streams
Have wander'd all Night in the Land of Dreams,
But tho' calm & warm the waters wide,
I could not get to the other side.

Father, O Father! what do we here
In this Land of unbelief & fear?
The Land of Dreams is better far,
Above the light of the Morning Star.

Two poems first included in *Songs of Innocence* but later transferred to *Songs of Experience* are strange narratives, evidently belonging to some world of myth or fairy-tale that yet does not seem to be drawn from any familiar tradition. 'The Little Girl Lost' tells of a girl-child who falls asleep beneath a tree in a 'desart wild'; she is found by the lion-king, who carries her to his cavern where she continues to live safely among leopards and tigers; in a plate which accompanies this poem a young woman is shown among her children; so that we must conclude that the Little Girl descended into the 'world of generation', where in the 'animal' existence of the embodied soul she gave birth to children. In the second poem, 'The

Little Girl Found', her parents, grief-stricken, seek for their daughter. The mother in turn meets the Lion-king, and recognises the king of the 'caverns deep' of the underworld of generation as 'a spirit arm'd in gold'. He leads the mother to her child, whom she finds living in safety among the creatures of the natural creation. The stories are based on the Greater and Lesser Mysteries of Eleusis; doubtless based on Thomas Taylor the Platonist's *Dissertation on the Mysteries of Eleusis and Dionysus*. The poems stand appropriately among his songs of childhood, as an affirmation of his belief that the soul that enters the world of generation is already complete in humanity, existing in an eternal world from which it descends and to which it will return. To Wordsworth's friend Crabb Robinson Blake declared his belief that it is nonsensical to talk (as many Christians do) of an immortality after death if there is no immortality before birth.

It seems virtually certain that Blake did believe in Neoplatonic doctrine of reincarnation. The time-world—the 'cave' of those who enter mortal bodies—he saw as an interruption of the eternal mode of existence and experience which is native to our humanity. The body he speaks of always as a 'garment' put on by 'the weary man' when he 'enters his cave'; using the very terms of the Neoplatonists who saw this world as the true Hades, the grave of those who have 'died' from eternity. The 'true man' or Imagination is bodiless and immaterial, no less so here and now than hereafter. Blake understood that we are already spiritual beings, and therefore immeasurable, boundless, and not (except through our bodies) confined by times and places.

I spoke earlier of the influence on Blake of the hymn-writer Isaac Watts. Blake may well have liked the simple metre and language of Watts's *Divine Songs* and agreed that they were suitable for children, for he uses similar metres in some of his own Songs; although he also uses far more subtle and lovely lyric forms, more reminiscent of Shakespeare than of Watts, and highly characteristic of his own genius. But he did not like the conventional morals the clergyman sought to inculcate, and saw in Watts one of those instructors who were seeking to 'form' the infant mind according to the wisdom of this world. Blake saw the current religious mentality of his day as no less materialist than Locke and Newton. Deism, or 'natural religion', was Blake's abomination. He saw the Deists as really accepting current scientific opinion on the nature of the world, and merely adorning a materialist ideology with morality and meaningless promises of immortality. Blake understood that eternity and immortality are not for the mortal body, but belong to the spirit. Man is eternal and beyond time and space here and now, in the spirit, or not at all. But conventional religion had become such a profane mixture of materialism and credulity that it had nothing to offer those deprived of a truly spiritual religion which, far from being other-worldly, can enable those who understand the true nature of things to live, as Blake did, here and now 'in eternity's sunrise.' There were plenty of other issues on which Blake differed from Watts, and a number of Blake's songs are in answer to Watts's. There is for example a poem entitled 'Praise for the Gospel' which no doubt many people in all good faith found acceptable.

Indeed it is only recently that the assumption that because Christianity is a true religion all others are therefore false began to be questioned within either the Catholic or the Protestant churches. Watts wrote:

Lord, I ascribe it to thy Grace
And not to Chance, as others do,
That I was born of *Christian* race
And not a *Heathen or a Jew.*

Blake, who believed that all religions are one, replied to Watts in a glorious poem which would not have been acceptable in the churches of his own time, 'The Divine Image'.

And all must love the human form,
In heathen, turk, or jew;
Where Mercy, Love, & Pity dwell
There God is dwelling too.

One of Watts's most popular pieces is 'The Sluggard', (*Moral Songs* No. 1) a poem intended to inculcate the moral virtuousness of hard work. Watts's sluggard refuses to work and asks for

A little more Sleep, and a little more Slumber,
Thus he wastes half his Days, and his Hours without Number.

But in Blake it is the false nurse of the world of Experience who preaches to her charges the morality of Watts, 'Your spring & your day are wasted in play'. The nurse of *Innocence*, on the contrary, loves to hear her children's laughing voices as they play on the hill until the last moment of the day. Watts's sluggard, because he is not industrious, has his garden full of weeds:

I passed by his Garden, and saw the wild Bryar,
The Thorn and the Thistle grow broader and higher;

but Blake's Garden of Love becomes full of thorns because joyless moralists kill the flowers of delight:

And Priests in black gowns were walking their rounds,
And binding with briars my joys & desires.

Watts's sluggard is a character after Blake's own heart;

He told me his Dreams, talk'd of Eating and Drinking
But he scarce reads his Bible, and never loves Thinking.
Said I then to my Heart, *Here's a Lesson for me*,
That Man's but a Picture of what I might be.
But thanks to my Friends for their Care in my Breeding
Who taught me betimes to love Working and Reading.

As for those friends who teach the child 'betimes to love working and reading', to Blake these are not as Watts supposed, improving, but destroying the young life. If the buds of life have been nipped and the joys stripped from childhood there will be no harvest. Blake's innocents tell their dreams, like Tom the chimney-sweeper; his schoolboy would rather play than work; indeed there is nothing whatever about work in *Songs of Innocence*, only life itself, with its everlasting play.

Eating and drinking too are among the delights of innocence, from 'the table where cherries and nuts are spread'. Watts would surely have reproved the levity of Blake's 'Laughing Song', whose children are as thoughtless as the proverbial grasshopper.

When the green woods laugh with the voice of joy,
And the dimpling stream runs laughing by;
When the air does laugh with our merry wit,
And the green hill laughs with the noise of it;

When the meadows laugh with lively green,
And the grasshopper laughs in the merry scene,

When Mary and Susan and Emily
With their sweet round mouths sing 'Ha, Ha, He!'

When the painted birds laugh in the shade,
Where our table with cherries and nuts is spread,
Come live & be merry, and join with me,
To sing the sweet chorus of 'Ha, Ha, He!'

One of Blake's most beautiful images is of that idle creature the grasshopper, conventionally contrasted with the parsimonious ant. Blake, who believed that eternity is ever-present, does not condemn the grasshopper for living in it:

the Grasshopper that sings & laughs & drinks:
Winter comes, he folds his slender bones without a murmur

And how different is Blake's ant from Watts's models of toiling industry. The hymn-writer cannot have read Jesus's words about taking no thought for the morrow when he praised the ants:

They don't wear their time out in sleeping and play
But gather up corn in a sun-shiny day,
    And for winter they lay up their stores:
They manage their work in such regular forms
One would think they foresaw all the frost and the storms.

But Blake saw in these anxious ants, unable to enjoy the sunshine because they are for ever taking thought for the morrow only pathos. He wrote his poem 'A Dream' to comfort the anxious with the knowledge that there is a 'watchman of the night' who cares for them.

Once a dream did weave a shade
O'er my Angel-guarded bed,
That an Emmet lost its way
Where on grass methought I lay.

Troubled, wilder'd, and forlorn,
Dark, benighted, travel-worn,
Over many a tangled spray,
All heart-broke I heard her say:

'O, my children! do they cry
Do they hear their father sigh?
Now they look abroad to see:
Now return and weep for me.'

Pitying, I drop'd a tear;
But I saw a glow-worm near,
Who replied: 'What wailing wight
Calls the watchman of the night?

I am set to light the ground
While the beetle goes his round;
Follow now the beetle's hum,
Little wanderer, hie thee home.'

Many have supposed that the state of Innocence is a state of
illusion; that the ignorance of childhood must give place to a more
'realistic' view of life which comes with Experience. Some Blake
commentators have tried to fit Blake's Innocence and Experience
into this preconceived pattern, even suggesting that Blake
encountered the stern 'realities' of the world for the first time
between the writing of Songs of Innocence and of Experience;

a most ridiculous notion, incomparable with his most central teaching on the truth of Imagination and the 'error' of 'creation'. Those who think so have failed to understand that Blake held the paradisal vision to be a vision of reality, while 'Experience' is a false view of the world resulting from the materialist illusion. Experience is not what we learn it is what happens to us when we forget. It is what befalls us when we lose the imaginative vision; or a world of values created by those who do not possess it. This Blake throughout his life tried to make us understand, for he knew that to the majority, in the modern West, the material world is all, and seems the reality, imagination a foolish fancy. But Blake understood that Imagination knows the eternal world; reason, building upon Locke's theory that knowledge comes to us only through the senses, creates its bitter world not by opening but by closing our minds. Blake did not believe, as Wordsworth did, that the 'visionary gleam' belongs only to youth; it is something to be won back, as he had himself kept his vision through a lifetime hard enough by the standards of this world. But to those who knew Blake, the poor engraver, living with his wife in one room, in Fountain Court, off the Strand, seemed like one of the ancient Prophets, walking always with God.

Songs of Experience, then, are all describing states of tragic error and illusion. On the title-page of the book are shown sleepers on a tomb, with mourning figures. The meaning is that those in the world or state of Experience are sleepers, or spiritually dead. The poems are not all about childhood, and few—except 'The Tyger' and one or two others—suitable poems for children or written for children. All are concerned with the hells, with the life-destroying results of the world materialism creates in its own image, and which it imposes upon innocence.

These states of the human soul are expressed in many situations in the poems. In 'Introduction' and 'Earth's Answer' Blake goes to the heart of much human misery, the enslavement of sexual love. Selfish and selfless love are contrasted in 'The Clod and the Pebble', the theme of sexual guilt and repression runs through 'Nurse's Song', 'The Sick Rose', 'The Angel', 'The Garden of Love', and 'A Little Girl Lost'. Some of the poems are paired with others of the same title or theme in *Songs of Innocence*. To the eyes of Innocence it is a lovely sight to see the orphan children, 'their innocent faces clean' singing in St Paul's on Maundy Thursday; 'Seated in companies they sit with radiance all their own.' But without the light of paradise that shines in them they are

> Babes reduc'd to misery
> Fed with a cold and usurous hand.

Tom the chimney sweeper is warmed by his dream; but in this world he is 'A little black thing among the snow', treated not as an immortal soul but as a commodity by some master-sweep. 'The Little Vagabond' attacks the loveless morality of the churches; 'London' is a dark picture of a city whose inhabitants, then as now, come and go, for the most part, unlit by the light of eternity, where the poet can only

> mark in every face I meet
> Marks of weakness, marks of woe.

'Infant Sorrow' is the lot of countless unloved babes who never are allowed to know 'infant joy'; and 'A Little Boy Lost' is sacrificed to parental egoism sheltering itself within the mask of religious virtue. No moral law could be justified that reduced

'Babes to misery'. Blake must have shocked his contemporaries by reminding the religious that 'The Little Vagabond' preferred the 'pleasant and warm' ale house to the cold church, and suggested that 'if at the church they would give us some Ale' things might go better:

And God, like a father rejoicing to see
His children as pleasant and happy as he,
Would have no more quarrel with the Devil or the Barrel,
But kiss him, & give him both drink and apparel.

It seems that Blake preferred, even for children, any intemperance to temperance sermons. Whereas 'the true man' wears the human face of 'Love, mercy, pity, peace', there is a more terrible image in the world cut off from the 'God within'. This poem Blake entitles 'A Divine Image': for when man does not bear in his soul the signature of God, then he himself invents an image of God in the likeness of his own selfhood:

Cruelty has a Human Heart,
And Jealousy a Human Face;
Terror the Human Form Divine,
And Secrecy the Human Dress.

The Human Dress is forged Iron,
The Human Form a fiery Forge,
The Human Face a Furnace seal'd,
The Human Heart its hungry Gorge.

This is the terrible image of the God of 'Natural Religion' worshipped by great numbers of human beings who have no experience of the 'God Within'.

There is in *The Four Zoas* a terrible but magnificent description of the state Blake calls 'experience'; the aspect of this world for those who can discern no other; it is the earth-mother who speaks:

> I am made to sow the thistle for wheat, the nettle for a
>   nourishing dainty.
> I have planted a false oath in the earth; it has brought forth
>   a poison tree.
> I have chosen the serpent for a councillor, & the dog
> For a schoolmaster to my children,
> I have blotted out from light & living the dove & nightingale,
> And I have caused the earth worm[3] to beg from door to door.
> I have taught the thief a secret path into the house of the just,
> I have taught pale artifice to spread his nets upon the
>   morning.
> My heavens are brass, my earth is iron, my moon a clod
>   of clay,
> My sun a pestilence burning at noon & a vapour of death
>   in night.
> What is the price of Experience? do men buy it for a song?
> Or wisdom for a dance in the street? No, it is bought with
>   the price
> Of all that a man hath, his house, his wife, his children.
> Wisdom is sold in the desolate market where none come
>   to buy,
> And in the wither'd field where the farmer plows for bread
>   in vain.

---

3 The 'earth worm' is man seen as the 'mortal worm'.

Blake is not here writing against Political & Social 'Conditions': this is the world into which Adam and Eve are driven, to learn wisdom in the barren land of 'error or creation'. The passage continues with a bitter description of the conditions of poverty and labour to which the Man and Woman were condemned by their fatal choice. But yet, realistic as are his descriptions of the 'conditions' of society in his own city of London, that dark world of experience is called a 'deadly dream' into which mankind has fallen; an illusion of those who live not from the 'divine humanity' within, but from the ego, 'the God of this world' of the five senses.

That is why *Songs of Experience* opens and Innocence closes with 'the voice of the Bard'—the poetic genius who speaks from, and to, the Imagination, 'the true man', calling to the fallen soul of the world to return to the Imagination and to awaken from her 'deadly dream'. The voice of the Bard is the voice of Imagination:

> Hear the voice of the Bard!
> Who Present, Past, & Future, sees;
> Whose ears have heard
> The Holy Word
> That walk'd among the ancient trees,
>
> Calling the lapsed Soul,
> And weeping in the evening dew;
> That might controll
> The starry pole,
> And fallen, fallen light renew!

There could be no clearer answer to those who imagine that Blake thought we could learn anything from what he calls

'experience' than the last poem of *Songs of Innocence*; 'The
Voice of the Ancient Bard':

> Youth of delight, come hither,
> And see the opening morn, Image of truth new born.
> Doubt is fled, & clouds of reason,
> Dark disputes & artful teazing.
> Folly is an endless maze,
> Tangled roots perplex her ways.
> How many have fallen there!
> They stumble all night over bones of the dead,
> And feel they know not what but care,
> And wish to lead others, when they should be led.

(1977)

Wordsworth:
A Remembered Experience

I WAS BORN IN 1908 and as I come to write of my childhood find myself thinking of Edwin Muir's line, 'My youth
to myself grown fabulous', so different was that long-ago
world from that of even country children today. Both my parents were born in 1880; my father a schoolmaster—the son of
a coal-miner, of the Industrial Revolution—and my mother the
daughter of a Scots country schoolmaster who had moved across
the Border and taught a school in the remote moors of Kielder.
I remember my grandparents' house and its garden bright with
flowers—now it is under the waters of Kielder reservoir, and the
open heather moors dense plantations of conifers. My parents
had met as students at the Armstrong College in Newcastle, my
father having risen through the old apprenticeship of becoming
a 'pupil teacher', then taking his B.A. degree, and his M.Litt., for
which his thesis was on Wordsworth.

Thus in several ways I grew up in Wordsworth's world; but
my parents experienced that world very differently. My mother
had grown up in the wilds among places and people not unlike
those Wordsworth had known in adjacent Cumberland and
Westmorland and has made for ever a part of the landscape of

the English imagination. All my father's school holidays were spent in Northumberland, and during the First World War I was sent to live with my mother's family in a place I already loved; and there between the ages of eight and ten I lived the life of a Wordsworthian country child. My schoolfellows were the children of farmers and shepherds living on the farms they had most likely inherited from generations bearing their names, and who would certainly have been at some time to Newcastle but never to London—indeed Edinburgh seemed nearer, culturally speaking, in our Presbyterian world.

My father had never been in this sense a country child and seemed always alien in that world which was to me 'the real world', permanent and secure. His Wordsworth, I now surmise, was the Wordsworth of left-wing political idealism, for I remember his often quoting those lines about the French Revolution,

Bliss was it in that dawn to be alive,
But to be young was very Heaven.

My father still lived in the light of that new dawn; and his belief in mankind's innate goodness, once freed from whoever the 'tyrants' may have been, was unshakeable. I have in my own lifetime seen revolutions come and go—in Spain, in Russia—and seen how one day's glorious freedom becomes the next day's tyranny, and I find it hard to imagine that Wordsworth's youthful political enthusiasms can carry conviction any longer. But to many like my father the political idealism of the early nineteenth century—shared by Blake and Shelley as well as by the young Wordsworth—was an inspiration from which no doubt many excellent political reforms followed. But I cannot help but feel that the 'politics of time' (to use a phrase of the Irish mystical

poet[4]) is a secondary matter to 'the politics of eternity' which
is the real concern of those unacknowledged legislators of the
world, the poets.

My mother was indifferent to politics, and *The Rights of
Man* and the rest, Rousseau's heady wine that had so intoxicated
Wordsworth's generation—and which through his poetry continued to inspire young idealists still hoping for a better world
as the outcome of glorious revolution—she never drank. But she
never failed to notice the violet by a mossy stone, the primrose
by a river's brim, the murmuring sound of a swift burn with its
pools and waterfalls, inhabiting the world of nature's inviolate
places with no less love than did Dorothy Wordsworth herself;
and it was my mother's world, not my father's, that I inhabited,
that seemed to me the 'real world', in which the slag heaps and
the machinery that were part of my father's people's mining village in County Durham—and indeed the rough lives of the min-
ers and their families in their mean homes—seemed an outrage
against the integrity and beauty of the earth, against what ought
to be. I could not understand why slag heaps should be, all that
seemed an appalling mistake, an outrage against the beauty of
nature. I participated in the lives of my country schoolfellows,
and that seemed the only natural way of life. The London suburb
where my father taught the sons of city commuters who travelled
to 'the city' in third-class carriages in the morning to return in
the evening; and the defilement of industrial villages and towns
seemed a tragic and inexplicable mistake. As did whatever is
ugly or vulgar—nature is never without some beauty to which
the soul can turn for solace; and country people might be poor

---

4 George Russell.

and were certainly ignorant of many things that civilisation has bequeathed, but were not vulgar.

In such beliefs Wordsworth's poetry, as I received it from both my parents, confirmed me; and if to his ideas I paid little heed, the people and places of the Lyrical Ballads and all those poems dealing with country life and ways and places corresponded so completely with the world as I knew it and loved it that the poetry seemed no less part of the natural order of things than did the hills and the clouds and the snow and the winds themselves. Like the young Wordsworth I roamed free in the rocky hills and open moors as he had done as a child. My young heart assented to his vision of 'nature' in its dignity and grandeur and in its lovely close-at-hand, the lesser celandine, the sparrow's nest, the owls at night; to the drama of weather, storm, snow-bound winter, in a world where men and women still lived and died in the farms and cottages where they had been born. Their culture did not come from newspapers and 'the media'; the men had their rural skills, the women baked their weekly batches of loaves and pasties, churning butter, embroidering, making their own clothes, skills surely more rewarding than the 'freedom' to leave home for the city, like Michael's son Luke, type of all those prodigals who never return.

Because undistracted by world-news real events carried with us their full weight and significance—births and deaths and weddings, or some story of lives going wrong, people had their full stature and dignity, and we heard the words of the Bible read Sunday by Sunday in our dignified seventeenth-century Presbyterian kirk; stories of country people of other lands but whose 'seed-time and harvest, summer and winter, day and night' were like our own, as were the storms and the mountains that inspired awe and lifted our eyes to the hills whence came divine help, through those age-old natural correspondences to the soul's moods and intuitions.

Or can one say that world was already over when I knew it by reason of the very causes that had doomed it: the First World War, the Industrial Revolution, the population explosion that drove people to the towns and the exile of London suburbs, without memory, without beauty? And was it not already doomed when Wordsworth described what was already threatened, is not his own story that of the Prodigal who seeks to return only to find that we cannot re-enter the past? For all he returned to the loved places after his adventure in the worlds of London and of revolutionary France, these were no longer the places he remembered for he was no longer the child who was 'father to the man', who returned. Wordsworth's story tells of Paradise Lost unwillingly, a loss perhaps never to be fully accepted by the poet; who, for all he returned to his beloved Westmorland never again reentered the living experience of 'nature' he had known. For he himself had undergone education at Cambridge, undergone history, undergone the first shocks of a revolution which was not to realise those high hopes of his for mankind, but rather to sweep away that rural culture which from time immemorial had been the norm of human life on earth: not for the Promised Land but for the exile of modern industrial cities. Already when he set out so joyfully for Cambridge he had left that primordial world and its timeless ways to become a stranger in a strange land, however seductive the pleasures of exile may at times have been. And for all the 'bliss' of the French Revolution, that revolution was the way of no return for Western civilisation.

❋

YET WHAT I WOULD call the 'Wordsworth experience' has
seemed to those of us who lived within it an affirmation of the
timeless, the permanent, to be a celebration of the enduring grass
roots of life, in harmony with the cosmos itself, whose children
we are. But how many children now, even among those living
not in cities but in what is still called I suppose 'the country'
can experience that sense of nature's protective embrace and the
wisdom of her teaching that Wordsworth celebrates? How much
of his poetry is 'relevant' to times and places so different? Roads
and railways, trains and motor cars and buses have penetrated
the remote places, shrinking the scale of the great hills and empty
spaces. So even more have telephones and radio and television
brought the distant places within the same network of experience as our inner cities. The manse at Bavington where I lived in
the far-off years had neither water-closet, taps nor electric light.

Instead we had a well of spring water and a water barrel
to collect the rain, candles and oil lamps and the *Northern
Presbyter* once a week (or was it once a month?) by way of news
of the outside world. Like Wordsworth and Dorothy, when we
visited our friends on distant farms we walked. The local farmers and their wives drove to church on Sundays in traps; farmers
and their sons rode on horseback and I seem to remember there
were donkeys too. But the natural scale, so to say, of the world
yielded rich joys, the plants and the birds of the roadsides were
close to us, and the hills kept their dignity of distance, as we
moved in, not through, our world. The weather made drama
enough of these comings and goings. Lost lambs on ledges, a
bull loose from the bull field, the fidelity of a sheepdog were

realities of our lives, and all that happened within a community of neighbours, who had known one another for better and worse for years, had the significance of the Border Ballads whose descendants still bore proudly the old names. Now the television set brings into the remotest kitchens, be these in the Outer Hebrides, Indian villages in the Deccan or native American reservations in Southern Arizona, instantaneous news of the whole planet; every solitude has become permeable. In my own remote hamlet weekenders occupy the cottages abandoned by the country people, farmers' daughters spend their honeymoon in the Caribbean or on travelling round the world. The world Wordsworth describes has receded from those hills and valleys, dear to tourists, where speedboats tear the silence of Ullswater and Windermere and holiday caravans line their shores. Yet it is in search of lost paradise that tourists themselves come, and perhaps for a moment we may be blessed by the ever-presence of nature. And yet each modern improvement, each labour-saving invention of mass production, our souls experience as a loss, a deprivation, an alienation—such is the paradox. And what, I wonder as I re-read poems that once seemed to have grown out of the very world I inhabited, does the modern urban reader discover in those celebrations of a vanished world?

Much, I believe; for it is in my own lifetime that the motor car, the telephone and the television have transformed us from children of nature to children of the cities. And what are two or three generations to us, who from time immemorial have been children of the living earth, companioned by the hills and the stars, clouds, birds and animals, summer and winter, day and night? I believe we are still what heaven and earth have made us, the elements, and the ever-changing never-changing epiphany of nature that Wordsworth celebrated, even now more native and familiar to us than our technological environment can ever be. Do we not live in exile from our real selves, in a sort of second self, a self without memory, which we construct in order to survive in that exile? But that second nature which with such ease adapts to all those modern inventions with which we insulate ourselves, is only a superstructure. We discover in the abiding world of nature our older, truer selves. I do not believe that such as I, who remember that vanished world, are alone in the grass-roots rural world of people, and in the natural world Wordsworth experienced with so much love, and that his poetry has bequeathed us a human norm. In our marvellous cities we live as exiles. From Hesiod to Virgil to Robert Frost and Rabindranath Tagore men and women have lived in the embrace of nature since Adam delved and Eve span. And does not Wordsworth's greatness lie in his bearing witness, as we were about to lose it, to that age-old norm which in this century we have so largely destroyed, to our great loss and indeed to our great peril? But if we forget our cosmic ancestry are we not still

> Rolled round in earth's diurnal course,
> With rocks, and stones, and trees [?]

There have of course always been cities, of whose rise and fall great civilisations have left the records. Epic poems have told of the great and outstanding events and achievements of tribe and nation. In the personae of Hamlet and Lear and Prospero, Iago and Macbeth, Shakespeare has explored the bounds and limits of human experience, as have the writings of Plato and the sacred literature of India and Arabia. The religious and epic literature of all civilisations has told of the exceptional, of the farthest reaches of the human spirit. The grass roots were always there and perhaps seemed to need no telling. Was Wordsworth's decision to 'choose incidents and situations from common life, and to relate or describe them throughout, as far as possible, in a selection of language really used by men' a response to the coming change which already threatened that age-old norm? Had this choice of material been no more than a political response to a changing society moving from an aristocratic to a democratic structure its interest would have been historical only. But that speech, that language Wordsworth bequeathed to us is in itself an inestimable treasure. Modern demotic speech of our post-industrial world may be 'really used by men', but it is a rootless language reflecting not so much humankind's immemorial experience over generations as our modern forgetfulness of these. It is an instant language fit for the communication of matters of fact rather than our deeper and more permanent experiences. But this was not the 'language really used' by the men and women of Wordsworth's Cumberland and Westmorland, to whose speech he had listened from childhood. Being unlettered, theirs was a spoken language inherited from an ancestral past, a regional speech which, like every oral tradition, was attuned to the ear, not a soundless language of 'the words on the page' as critics a few years ago used to say was the language of poetry. Indeed the language Wordsworth would have known—in common with all oral traditions—possessed many virtues already lost to written language, and still more to the modern media.

Free from the adulteration of external influences, words come, in any traditional society, from generation to generation laden with the experience and memories of family and tribe, wedding language to certain places, wedding people to the land itself, as

indeed did the Border Ballads which constituted the oral tradition of Cumberland and Northumberland and adjacent Scotland.
So the reality of memories and language was self-perpetuating,
enhancing the collective and individual dignity of those who
shared both language and culture. Such stable societies are now
rare and in England no longer to be found. It is still possible
to find—or to find those who still remember—in the Western
Highlands of Scotland or in Ireland a living regional speech and
culture. Fast vanishing as in every kitchen in the remotest croft
or cabin the television set usurps the place of the bard and the
storyteller who kept alive the language and the stories. English is
now a world language, but with the acquisition of information
gleaned from the entire planet speech has lost the resonance of
ancestral memories of people inheriting words from their ancestors, and ancestral sanctities. In the Hebrides I have been told that
Gaelic is 'the language of Eden'. That surely is not to be taken
as a fact of philology, but in a symbolic sense as an affirmation
of the primordiality of ancestral speech from time immemorial,
with the continuity of memory before it became permeable by
the new rootless tongue. Surely Wordsworth's 'language really
spoken by men' would have been a variant of this immemorial
'language of Eden'. Such a language has been the expression of
basic human experiences deeply undergone because no anodynes
of our modern 'distraction from distraction by distraction' had
anaesthetized hearts broken by guilt and sorrow, poverty, solitude, sickness, old age and death, those unchanging inescapable
human griefs; and joy too comes simply, and love is for the near
and known. Wordsworth's language common to men—at best a
poetic diction capable of Biblical dignity and immemorial simplicity—he understood as a language common to men because

it is the bearer of those universal deep experiences of life and death. He came near, surely, in seeking a language 'really spoken by men' not to a shared mediocrity but to the universal language of Eden. There is no anonymity in Milton's exalted speech, nor in Shelley's eloquence of the world of the soul, nor in Tennyson's smooth, nor in Browning's rough idiomatic speech. At best Wordsworth renders speech transparent in a common tongue commensurate with the dignity of unfallen Man. Perhaps one must go to America to find the like—Whitman, or even Robert Frost, heirs to no hampering poetic conventions; and dare I venture to use also the comparison with the simplicity and depth of language of the African American spirituals and the 'blues'—for the 'language of Eden', in this sense, is universal.

Few English poets have attained a language which to the same degree crosses barriers of class and education, a language deeply satisfying as such, even in the most diffuse passages of *The Prelude* and *The Excursion*. It carries us in its flow, the ordinary and the unusual inextricably mingled; it has the sustaining quality of ever-present reality, carrying us on over hidden depths and rare illuminations, which would suffer by isolation from that whole texture, seamless, like life itself.

The grass roots of life had, when Wordsworth wrote, hitherto always survived the rise and fall of civilisations, in men and women whose lives were simple, but not mean or corrupted, whose skills of husbandman and shepherd satisfied the needs not only of material survival, but also the instinctive need to beautify life with music and dance, with flower gardens such as Dorothy Wordsworth planted round Dove Cottage, the arts of embroidery and wood-carving, the furnishings of farm and cottage. And in many poems Wordsworth speaks of the courteous and thoughtful speech of the old huntsman Simon Lee, or the lonely leech-gatherer, village children, even vagrants on the road. Nor should we forget that the King James Bible and the Book of Common Prayer raised, from the sixteenth to the end of the nineteenth century, the level of culture for all classes in England, for whom those books formed perhaps their only reading, or who at least habitually heard that simple and noble language weekly in parish churches; a structure of minimal culture no longer available to the 'ordinary men' of the end of the twentieth century. The demotic speech of our modern cities carries no memories of Eden nor current of sacred wisdom from the Christian religion; rather it is the speech of a world that has ceased to remember.

BUT NONE OF this is surely in itself sufficient to account for the profound transformative effect on the soul of the English nation of which I am but one of the many who experienced its power. At the time of his writing no doubt Wordsworth's political enthusiasms found an echo which had more to do with history than with poetry, and are in their nature transient however transformative in the world of outer events. Milton too had strong political affiliations, but who cares now, as we read *Lycidas* or 'Il Penseroso'—or indeed *Paradise Lost*—what these were? Or who cares whether Dante supported the Guelphs or the Ghibellines? Whereas the moon setting over Lucy's cottage, or an old shepherd in a fold of the hills who went 'many and many a day' to the never to be finished sheepfold that years before he had planned with his son who had departed never to return 'And never lifted up a single stone'; or a schoolboy who 'blew mimic hootings to the silent owls' until they answered him; or that two boys rescued a lamb carried away in a flooded beck, are no less real to us than they were to Wordsworth. True, the pastoral Golden Age is an archetypal reality of the Imagination that never dies and Wordsworth's poetry is a retelling of that myth in terms of his time and place. But he was also the voice of a revolution of consciousness of a more profound kind, a reorientation of the national soul, hitherto sustained by the Christian religion within a framework of theological terms no longer adequate. Wordsworth's profound insight into nature was rather cosmological than theological. For better or worse Western Christianity has always been deeply suspicious of 'pantheism', preferring to keep creator and creation apart; never more so than in nineteenth century Deism, that 'natural religion' that acknowledged the creator of a universe that thereafter operated according to natural laws, which themselves were in due course to eliminate the divine life from the universe to give place to atheist materialism. But Wordsworth's living experience went beyond creed or reason in his 'Lines written a few miles above Tintern Abbey':

> a sense sublime
> Of something far more deeply interfused,
> Whose dwelling is the light of setting suns,
> And the round ocean, and the living air,
> And the blue sky, and in the mind of man,
> A motion and a spirit, that impels
> All thinking things, all objects of all thought,
> And rolls through all things. . . .

The experience of the mystic—and surely Wordsworth's was no less—went beyond those structures available to his time and place: for him 'nature' was alive, sometimes fearfully so, as for the boy who one evening loosed the chain of a little boat and pushed it out from the shore of Ullswater; and pleasure gave place to fear—

> When from behind that craggy Steep, till then
> The bound of the horizon, a huge Cliff
> Upreared its head. I struck and struck again
> And, growing still in stature, the huge Cliff,
> For so it seemed, with purpose of its own,
> Rose up between me and the stars, and still,
> With measured motion, like a living thing
> Strode after me . . .
> and after I had seen
> That spectacle, for many days, my brain
> Worked with a dim and undetermined sense
> Of unknown modes of being. . . .

Again we remember those lines from *The Prelude* in which Wordsworth describes the Simplon pass:

> Black drizzling crags that spake by the way-side
> As if a voice were in them, the sick sight
> And giddy prospect of the raging stream,
> The unfettered clouds and region of the heavens,
> Tumult and peace, the darkness and the light
> Were all like workings of one mind, the features
> Of the same face, blossoms upon one tree
> Characters of the great Apocalypse,
> The types and symbols of Eternity,
> Of first and last, and midst, and without end.

The gods of India would have been at home here!

Janet Adam Smith and other mountaineers have rightly compared this passage with Turner's great painting of the pass of St Gothard, as an expression for the vogue of the Sublime which had characterised painting for some time. While natural genius is not to be explained in terms of 'influences' one undercurrent of the time which played a part in Wordsworth's imaginative experience was surely the Greek revival, of which Thomas Taylor's translations of Plato, Plotinus and the greater part of the Neoplatonic literature into English for the first time is an important but neglected aspect. Doubtless some scholar might be able to establish evidence of the extent to which Wordsworth was indebted to the Platonic writers. Certainly the preexistence of the soul so clearly affirmed in the 'Ode: Intimations of Immortality' witnessed in early childhood is taken directly from Plato:

> Our birth is but a sleep and a forgetting:
> The Soul that rises with us, our life's Star,
>   Hath had elsewhere its setting,
>   And cometh from afar:
>   Not in entire forgetfulness,
> But trailing clouds of glory do we come
>   From God, who is our home.

Plato in the Tenth Book of the *Republic* describes the descent of souls about to be generated on earth, who on their way cross 'the plain of oblivion' and 'the river of forgetfulness' of which all must drink. Some souls drink so deeply of this river as to forget entirely the heavenly world; others who drink less deeply reach this world 'not in entire forgetfulness'. And last of all, the souls are wafted to their birth 'like shooting stars'—every image in Wordsworth's memorable lines is taken from this famous passage. Throughout the writings of Plotinus also we find the image of the 'sleep' and forgetting of generated souls—forgetfulness of the eternal world, 'Of God who is our home'. Such statements are purely Platonic: the preexistence of the soul has no part in Christian theology.

Blake too declared that to believe in the immortality of the soul after death is not possible if not also before birth. Blake actually knew Thomas Taylor, and his Arlington Court Tempera is an illustration of Taylor's translation of Porphyry's *De Antro Nympharum*, a treatise on the descent and return of souls through the world of generation. Shelley, deeply imbued as he was with the Platonic philosophy, held the same belief in the soul's preexistence:

> Is it that in some brighter sphere,
>   We part from those we meet with here?
> Or do we see the future pass
>   Across the present's clouded glass?

Wordsworth was not, like Shelley, a committed Platonist and increasingly in his later years reverted to Christianity; but in his famous 'Ode' he echoes Plato's words which re-echo through the Greek philosophers and poets, 'Who knows whether to live be not to die, and to die to live?' Life is the soul's 'death' or forgetfulness, yet 'haunted for ever by the eternal mind'. In this world there remain

> those obstinate questionings
> Of sense and outward things,
> Fallings from us, vanishings;
> Blank misgivings of a Creature

Moving about in worlds not realised,
High instincts, before which our mortal Nature
Did tremble like a guilty thing surprised:
    But for those first affections,
    Those shadowy recollections,
    Which, be they what they may,
Are yet the fountain-light of all our day.

Wordsworth describes the fall of the soul of which philosophers have written, not as a 'belief' but, according to the greatness of his genius, as a living experience

    Though inland far we be,
Our souls have sight of that immortal sea
    Which brought us hither.

Another, and recurring, Platonic—or rather Plotinian—theme is the one life that 'rolls through all things' in nature, from rock and star to the so-called living world. I believe that 'Lines written in Early Spring' derives directly from Plotinus, *Ennead* 1:4, as translated by Thomas Taylor. Wordsworth's lines have the spontaneous simplicity of an immediate thought which had come to the poet from the 'grove' in which he 'heard a thousand blended notes', which inspired in him the conviction that even the very plants enjoyed pleasure:

Through primrose-tufts, in that sweet bower,
The periwinkle trailed its wreathes;
And 'tis my faith that every flower
Enjoys the air it breathes.

The birds around me hopped and played:
Their thoughts I cannot measure,
But the least motion which they made,
It seemed a thrill of pleasure.

The budding twigs spread out their fan,
To catch the breezy air;
And I must think, do all I can,
That there was pleasure there.

Plotinus' theme is 'True Happiness' [the author quotes from
the MacKenna translation]—or 'felicity' as Taylor translates the
word. Plotinus begins, as does Wordsworth, with 'such living
beings as have the gift of music'—birds in other words—who
'finding themselves well off in other ways, they sing, too, as their
nature is, and so their day is pleasant to them'. Plotinus goes
on to say that felicity lies in attaining the fulfilment of 'some
ultimate Term pursued by inborn tendency', and then 'nature
in them comes to a halt, having fulfilled its vital course from a
beginning to an end'. He then says that not only is happiness, in
this sense, attributable to the animal world, but 'not withholding
it even from the plants, living they too and having a life unfolding to a Term'. So whatever creature unfolds to the completion
of its nature, says Plotinus, must be allowed to be happy: 'If
pleasure be the Term, if here be the good of life, it is impossible
to deny the good of life' to any order of living things.

Even Wordsworth's phrase 'do all I can'—which might seem
to be an unnecessary phrase whose only purpose is to fill in a
rhyme—may well reflect Plotinus' own reservations: 'It may be
a distasteful notion' he writes 'this bringing-down of happiness

so low as to the animal world—making it over, as then we must, even to the vilest of them and not withholding it even from the plants'. It seems that Plotinus also had 'done all he could' to avoid the conclusion that plants and the very lowest forms of life enjoy felicity. Had Blake too, who wrote that 'every particle of dust breathes forth its joy', read Plotinus's words?

Blake, who never lost 'the divine vision' as Wordsworth declares he did, to the day of his death, comments on the Preface to the 1815 edition of Wordsworth's poems, that 'Wordsworth must know that what he Writes Valuable is Not to be found in Nature'. It lies, according to Blake, in the Imagination. In this Blake was in accord with what one may call the orthodoxy of the Perennial Philosophy, as taught by the Platonists, and by Plotinus especially, and also by the Oriental philosophies, for whom mind is primary, and 'nature', *māyā*, a world of appearances.

According to Plotinus Nature images and reflects the soul; as Coleridge also understood.

No political liberation from external 'tyranny' can effect that transmutation of mortal life; Coleridge, philosopher that he was, understood that the alchemy can be transformative of nature with such feeling and fullness as did Wordsworth. Blake wrote that 'everything that lives is holy'. Wordsworth, in his greatest poetry, famously communicates that reality; and has so far communicated that vision as to make for many the Lake District a national shrine to this day, a holy land. Yeats has written that the imagination of a nation must be 'wedded' to the mountains and rivers and places of our native land, that a remote 'holy land'—as is the land of Israel for Christians—fails to achieve the consecration of our own 'holy places', a dimension without which the soul suffers perpetual exile. Surely no other English poet has in a comparable degree thus 'wedded' the Imagination to his native place, and in a lesser degree to the natural world wherever he found it.

Blake objected to lines from *The Excursion*

How exquisitely the individual Mind
    . . . to the external World
Is fitted:—& how exquisitely, too,
Theme this but little heard of among Men,
The external World is fitted to the Mind.

One can see why Blake objected since for him 'Nature is Imagination Itself ' and the 'external world' is a deadly illusion. But Wordsworth was surely expressing a truth, described in our own time by the French phenomenologist Gaston Bachelard in his remarkable books on the four Elements and the poetic Imagination, which continually discovers in nature its 'objective correlative'. No poet knew better than Wordsworth how the mind is raised to elevated thoughts by mountain heights, calmed by the contemplation of still lakes, finds its correspondences in both the minute and in the vast, the violet and the star, as Imagination continually discovers its fitting symbols in the epiphanic flow of the world of nature daily opening before our eyes. The experience of this marriage between Imagination and the natural world is one to which Wordsworth continually returns; to a living experience of nature as *meaning*—not emblematic and arbitrary as in allegory, but a continual invitation to the beholder to communion with the great cosmic mystery and the microcosm of Man. His culture—the culture of his age, provided him with no adequate context for these profound experiences within Christian orthodoxy with its strange dread of 'pantheism'. His living experience did not accord with that creed, to which in his later years he attempted to conform his vision. Better had he had the courage of his own insights, and affirmed with Blake that the universe is 'all alive' and 'every particle of dust breathes forth its joy'. A belief more in accordance with our own 'New Age' than with the confident assurance of nineteenth-century materialism.

I believe those who assent to the description of Wordsworth's art as 'the egotistical sublime' have failed to understand that he was not recording his individual experiences because they were unique but because they were universal. He assumed the role of Everyman, because it is through the uniqueness of the individual self through whose mediation alone we perceive the world, singular to each yet common to all. This role he took on, in this sense, to explore his own particular ego, in the name of anonymity. The eye of universal consciousness receives only in the particular life what is our universal heritage. Byron surely was interested in his own story in a way that Wordsworth was not, otherwise than as a window on the world. And is it not when he is most personal—as in the Lucy poems—and in his solitary communings with Nature that Wordsworth is most universal, offering us images through which we can enter the world as he experienced it? I find no such egoism in the *Prelude*, or in his greatest poems, only in those afterthoughts of his later life in which, as David Jones puts it, the poet gives place to what the world tells us we 'ought to think' and should 'try to feel'. I have never been able to work my way through the Ecclesiastical Sonnets; but when Wordsworth trusted the experience he was unerring. Is not the sense of the sacred more perfectly conveyed in those lines describing his sister Dorothy *experiencing* the sparrow's nest than in all the sonnets?

She looked at it and seemed to fear it;
Dreading, tho' wishing, to be near it.

The sparrow's nest is a *temenos*, a sacred sanctuary of life, the thing itself, not an emblem or an allegory; Coleridge's 'translucence of the eternal in and through the temporal' which 'always partakes of the Reality which it renders intelligible'. Because he so fully experienced himself as 'sole heir of the whole world' Wordsworth was 'more than so, because men are in it who are everyone sole heirs' as well as he. Nature, as Wordsworth experienced her inexhaustible epiphany of wonders, is indeed everyman's heritage, whether born in the country or in the city; nor, even in the city, is Nature inaccessible to us; Wordsworth found it even on Westminster Bridge, and in a tree at the corner of Wood Street; and

To me the meanest flower that glows can give
Thoughts that do often lie too deep for tears.

(2000)

Shelley as a Mythological Poet

T HE TURN OF the eighteenth century saw a flowering of the imagination in English poetry as brief as it was marvellous. This flowering has left its heritage, unvalued by the materialist culture of the past two hundred years, but awaiting its rediscovery as (in Yeats's words) 'wisdom and poetry return', as he believed they must. This will come about as it is realised that not reason but Imagination is the supreme faculty: is, in Blake's words, 'the human existence itself'. Two centuries of materialism in the English-speaking West have brought us to a point at which, for a majority, 'the real world' is the solid measurable world of 'matter' which in its nature has no place for immeasurable realities of mind and imagination. Coleridge called Imagination 'a repetition in the finite mind of the infinite I AM', the creative power by whose agency we build our world 'on earth as it is in heaven', in the likeness of our innate vision. Whereas for the Abrahamic religions man is a creature other than and external to 'God', for the Oriental religions as for the Platonic tradition—and especially for Plotinus and the Neoplatonists—there is a divine presence innate in man and in all creation. Our world is real because it is the creation of the human imagination. Shelley himself defines poetry as 'the expression of the imagination' and continues:

> It awakens and enlarges the mind itself by rendering it the receptacle of a thousand unapprehended combinations of thought. Poetry lifts the veil from the hidden beauty of the world, and makes familiar objects be as if they were not familiar. . . . Poetry enlarges the circumference of the imagination by replenishing it with thoughts of ever new delight. . . .

Imagination is a mental world, a world of which 'nature' is a language rather than an object to be described by language; and Shelley's world is above all a world of thought. One can say that all civilisations before our own have been concerned with thought and its values: indeed is not mind the human kingdom itself? The great works of the world's wisdom have been concerned with meanings and values, not with measurement of a material order. But does it, one may ask, make any great difference, since we all see and experience the World, whether we hold it to be an object external to us or an experience of the Imagination?

There is one great and all-important difference: to the materialist the world is a lifeless object, to the man of Imagination the world is a living being, 'full of gods'. For the materialist the question is 'what' is nature, 'what' are its rocks and stones and trees, earth, air, fire and water, whereas for Imagination the question might more properly be 'who'. Who is the West Wind, spirit of inspiration, who the skylark, the cloud, the moon, who the rivers and the trees? So it was for all the great romantic poets: Blake saw nature as 'One Continued Vision of Fancy or Imagination' where 'The morning stars sang together and all the Sons of God shouted for joy', as in the Book of Job. For Wordsworth there is 'a motion and a spirit' that 'moves through all things' and for Shelley all lives with the life of the mind. There are 'subtle and fair spirits' whose homes are the dim caves of human thought. The language of Imagination is symbolic, that is to say nature is a language in which ideas, moods, meanings, find their correspondence, while at the same time the forms of nature take on meanings. Henry Corbin, taking his thought from the Persian Sufi philosopher-poets, has introduced the term *imaginal* to describe the world of Imagination, as distinct from the word 'imaginary' which in modern parlance means simply unreal, nonexistent.

But although all thought is symbolic, not all symbolic thought is mythological. Thus Wordsworth sees nature as a great epiphany of the one 'motion and spirit' that is everywhere present. Conversely, mythological themes may be treated in an historical and biographical manner as fictions as Tennyson's Idylls of King Arthur and the Holy Grail are treated as literal fact. Delightful as these narratives may be they are not mythological in Tennyson's treatment of them, nor are they in T. H. White's *The Sword in the Stone*, though they again become so in David Jones's 'The Hunt' and 'The Sleeping Lord'. But Shelley's 'subtle and fair spirits' which inhabit the human mind live and move and have their being in the world of the Imagination; and are, for Shelley, redemptive and inspiring:

> From unremembered ages we
> Gentle guides and guardians be
> Of heaven-oppressed mortality;
> And we breathe, and sicken not,

The atmosphere of human thought:
Be it dim, and dank, and grey,
Like a storm-extinguished day,
Travelled o'er by dying gleams;
   Be it bright as all between
Cloudless skies and windless streams,
   Silent, liquid, and serene;
As the birds within the wind,
   As the fish within the wave,
As the thoughts of man's own mind
Float thro' all above the grave;
We make there our liquid lair
Voyaging cloudlike and unpent
Thro' the boundless element.

In terms of materialist definitions, invisible spirits by whatever
name simply do not exist—they are imaginary. But if Imagination
is the 'boundless element' in which we and our world exist, this
world is reality itself. It is not nature that includes mind, but
mind which includes the vision of the universe we call 'nature'.
To many this is simply unthinkable, but from the standpoint of
every spiritually grounded civilisation it is the world of materialism that is limiting, imprisoning and mutilating to the living
spirit, preventing the caged bird from flying in its proper element. To the materialist mentality imaginative awakening seems
illusion and self-deception, and denial thus becomes the highest
wisdom for those who

Charge Visionaries with deceiving
And call Men wise for not Believing.

Shelley's *Prometheus Unbound* is a celebration of the return to life and joy of a world freed from the fetters of denial by the affirmation of love. One might describe it as a poem of transfiguration through love—to use a word from Christian theology—for Shelley—as indeed for the Christian theologians—'transfiguration' reveals things as they really are, not less but more than they seem to the common daily mind, the world as it really and for ever is. As the spirits sing

> We come from the mind
> Of human kind
> Which was late so dusk, and obscene and blind,
> Now 'tis an ocean
> Of clear emotion,
> A heaven of serene and mighty motion.
>
> From that deep abyss
> Of wonder and bliss,
> Whose caverns are crystal palaces;
> From those skiey towers
> Where Thought's crowned powers
> Sit watching your dance, ye happy Hours!
> . . .
> And, beyond our eyes,
> The human love lies
> Which makes all it gazes on Paradise.

Yeats, for whom Shelley is the supreme poet, recalls that image, and Shelley had his towers; thought's crowned powers he called them once. What for the materialist is illusion, for the Imagination is reality itself. Thus all in Shelley's world lives with the life of the mind itself; of Imagination that creates it. Sky-lark and Cloud, Sensitive-Plant, the charmed boat of the Witch of Atlas, are all living with the one life of the universe. Yeats in his essay 'The Philosophy of Shelley's Poetry' writes that he is 'certain that the imagination has some way of lighting on the truth that the reason has not, and that its commandments, delivered when the body is still and the reason silent, are the most binding we can ever know.' And he continues that he has re-read *Prometheus Unbound* 'and it seems to me to have an even more certain place than I had thought among the sacred books of the world'. Yeats goes on to say that Shelley, in *A Defence of Poetry*, 'will have it that the poet and the lawgiver hold their station by right of the same faculty, the one uttering in words and the other in the forms of society his vision of the divine order, the Intellectual Beauty' for (in Shelley's words) poetry is 'the creation of actions according to the unchangeable process of human nature as existing in the mind of the creator, which is itself the image of all other minds'. This image of the mind of the creator is Imagination, which Shelley calls 'intellectual beauty'— as did Plato, who was himself Shelley's supreme teacher. Shelley has been called an 'atheist' and indeed he rejected the Judaeo-Christian God of the Ten Commandments as a tyrannous demi-urge—as had Blake before him. But in the *Defence of Poetry* he speaks of 'the divine order' and of 'the mind of the creator', and in *Prometheus Unbound* makes the distinction very clear between the Creator and the moral tyrant. Asia, the bride of Prometheus, puts to Demogorgon the question:

> *Asia.* Who made the living world?
> *Demogorgon.*   God.
> *Asia.*   Who made all

That it contains? thought, passion, reason, will,
Imagination?

    Demogorgon. God: Almighty God.

    Asia. Who made that sense which, when the winds of
spring In rarest visitation, or the voice
Of one beloved heard by youth alone,
Fills the faint eyes with falling tears which dim
The radiant looks of unbewailing flowers,
And leaves this peopled earth a solitude
When it returns no more?

    Demogorgon.   Merciful God.

    Asia. And who made terror, madness, crime, remorse,
Which from the links of the great chain of things,
To every thought within the mind of man
Sway and drag heavily, and each one reels
Under the load towards the pit of death;
Abandoned hope, and love that turns to hate;
And self-contempt, bitterer to drink than blood;
Pain, whose unheeded and familiar speech
Is howling, and keen shrieks, day after day;
And Hell, or the sharp fear of Hell?

    Demogorgon.   He reigns.

    Asia. Utter his name: a world pining in pain
Asks but his name: curses shall drag him down

    Demogorgon. He reigns.

There follows a praise of Prometheus, friend of man, and denunciation of his enemy, ending with the question:

Asia.   Declare
Who is his master? Is he too a slave?
Demogorgon. All spirits are enslaved which serve things evil:
Thou knowest if Jupiter be such or no.
Asia. Whom called'st thou God?
Demogorgon.   I spoke but as ye speak;
For love is the supreme of living things.
Asia. Who is the master of the slave?
Demogorgon.   If the abysm
Could vomit forth its secrets. But a voice
Is wanting, the deep truth is imageless;
For what would it avail to bid thee gaze
On the revolving world? What to bid speak
Fate, Time, Occasion, Chance, and Change? To these
All things are subject but eternal Love.
Asia. So much I asked before, and my heart gave
The response thou hast given; and of such truths
Each to itself must be the oracle.

For the eighteenth and much of the nineteenth century there
was no recognised alternative to Christianity except scepticism.
One can only describe the English at that time (and even now)
as spiritually, metaphysically and imaginatively illiterate. There
was, however, another current, of which the Romantic poets are
each in a different way a product: this was a revival of Platonism.
At the turn of the century Thomas Taylor the Platonist—called
'the English Pagan' made the first complete translation of Plato's
works into English, besides Aristotle, most of Plotinus, Proclus
and the other Alexandrian Neoplatonists.

Shelley was himself a proficient Greek scholar but he cannot fail to have been aware of Taylor's challenge to Christianity in the name of the Platonic theology—for it was as a religious (or metaphysical) alternative to Christianity that Taylor saw the canon of the Platonic writings. Taylor's contribution to a revival of Platonism was deeply resented by the Academic establishment, but was seminal among those engaged in imaginative thought, and especially the poets. Coleridge absorbed his writings as a schoolboy; he was an early friend of Blake, gave a series of lectures on the Platonic theology at the house of Blake's friend Flaxman the sculptor, appears in one of the novels of Shelley's friend Thomas Love Peacock, and Mary Wollstonecraft, mother of Mary Shelley, was at one time his lodger. Shelley's rejection of Christianity was that of a deeply versed Platonist, not that of a sceptic. Like Taylor he had no respect for Christian theology, and saw (as did Blake also) the moral law-giver of the Bible as a tyrannous illusion. Shelley's vision was a larger, more philosophically subtle, more metaphysically traditional alternative to Christianity, but one not likely to be understood by his contemporaries, whether the Anglican clergy who held absolute control of the Universities, or the emerging figures of science and technology whose material success in promoting the Industrial Revolution was to prevail. Shelley was in reality more deeply committed to a vision of man as a spiritual being than the Deist clergy of his time and place. Not in the Christian doctrine of the resurrection of the body but in the traditional Platonic and Vedic doctrine of the immortality of the soul he certainly believed. Plato's affirmation 'for who knows whether to live be not to die, and to die to live?', repeated from one to another poet and philosopher of the Hellenic world, lies at the heart of 'Adonais',

Shelley's great celebration of Keats. Heraclitus' teaching the 'mortals are immortals, and immortals, mortals' is not fancy (as it can only seem to the ignorant modern West) but is an integral part of the Platonic theology. The generating soul 'dies' from eternity into the time world, to resume its native immortality at death, and it is this doctrine, not some fancy of his own, that Shelley affirms in those burning lines familiar to us all:

> The One remains, the many change and pass;
> Heaven's light forever shines, Earth's shadows fly;
> Life, like a dome of many-coloured glass,
> Stains the white radiance of Eternity,
> Until Death tramples it to fragments.—Die,
> If thou wouldst be with that which thou dost seek!
> Follow where all is fled!—Rome's azure sky,
> Flowers, ruins, statues, music, words are weak
> The glory they transfuse with fitting truth to speak.

The time-world—Plato's 'moving image of eternity'—is a pale and imperfect image of the eternal world it reflects. Furthermore (in common with Blake and perhaps with Wordsworth also) Shelley clearly held the belief, common to the Hellenic world, the Jewish mystical tradition and India to this day, in reincarnation. Lines which most of Shelley's readers can only take as poetic fancy, he certainly did not intend as such:

> Is it that in some brighter sphere
> We part with friends we meet with here?
> Or do we see the future pass
> Across the Present's dusky glass?
> Or what is it that that makes us seem

To patch up fragments of a dream,
Part of which comes true, and part
Beats and trembles in the heart?

For Shelley we are 'pilgrims of eternity'.

Symbolic images are not arbitrary signs—light and dark-ness, sun and moon, wind and cloud, mountain peaks and underground caverns, dove and swan and albatross—all these correspond in the nature of things to the meanings from time immemorial associated with them; as do some human creations, towers, palaces, or Shelley's magic boats on magic journeys. Myth carries symbolic discourse a stage further, it personifies, it enacts, and its actors are what Yeats calls the eternal 'moods', the 'gods' of all pantheons, who correspond, as it seems, to (in Shelley's words) 'the unchangeable process of human nature as existing in the mind of the creator'. All myths relate parts of what Edwin Muir called the 'fable' of which every individual human story is an approximation and partial enactment. What the fable is we do not know, only certain parts of it, Imagination is ever at work weaving and revealing. In that timeless world, as in the 'once upon a time' of fairy-tales, as in our dreams, the 'laws of nature' give place to the 'laws of the Imagination' where thoughts are causes and effects magical. The bleak factuality of materialist scientific doctrine is once again called into question by the Imagination. In that dimension Shelley moved habitually and with ease. Mythological discourse, in Shelley, unites what is in its own right imagery of the natural world of perfect pre-cision and beauty, with meanings on another level, that of the Imagination. 'Ode to the West Wind' is at once a marvellous description of the wind and storm blowing over Italian skies, the behaviour of clouds charged with electricity about to discharge itself; and 'wind' as an age-old symbol of inspiration. Shelley can never be faulted in those beautiful 'correspondences' he always finds for the language of the soul. The lark is at once the bird and the soaring impulse of joy; cloud and moon, all the scale of nature on which he played as a musician upon a keyboard, form that texture of beauty by which he knew so well how to transport us on to another plane, seldom realised in daily life, yet never remote or inaccessible. In *Hellas*, Shelley takes the figure of Ahasuerus from the medieval legend of the 'wandering Jew' who is the deathless possessor of cosmic knowledge, the archetypal figure Jung calls 'the wise old man' who in different guises is to be found in all mythologies, and visits our dreams imparting wisdom beyond the reach of individual experience and the daily mind.

How like a dream is this passage of myth:

> He who would question him
> Must sail alone at sunset, where the stream
> Of Ocean sleeps around those foamless isles,
> When the young moon is westering as now,
> And when the pines of that bee-pasturing isle,
> And evening airs wander upon the wave;
> Green Erebinthus, quench the fiery shadow
> Of the gilt prow within the sapphire water.
> Then must the lonely helmsman cry aloud
> Ahasuerus! and the caverns round
> Will answer Ahasuerus! If his prayer
> Be granted, a faint meteor will arise
> Lighting him over Marmora, and a wind

Will rush out of the sighing pine-forest,
And with the wind a storm of harmony
Unutterably sweet. . . .

It is not hard to understand from such passages why, for Yeats, Shelley is the supreme poet, uniting in his symbolic virtuosity images of the visible world with resonances of meaning and beauty of the immeasurable worlds of Imagination. What, as natural description, could surpass the fiery shadow of a gilt prow in sapphire water? The 'faint meteor', the wind that will 'rush out of the pine forest' with 'a storm of harmony'? The sunset where

> the stream
> Of Ocean sleeps around those foamless isles
> When the young moon is westering as now.

With what virtuosity does the poet use these images as a language of 'correspondence'—as metaphors for soul's country. As in our dreams each image is charged with meaning and feeling. No detail is added which does not serve—again as in our dreams—to communicate realities of another order. The time is twilight, between the light of common day and the mystery of darkness, 'between the sleeping and the waking mind', as Yeats has described the place of imaginative inspiration. The summoner of a secret wisdom must go alone, for his is an inner journey none can share. The 'sea-cavern' doubtless signifies for Shelley the Homeric Cave of the Nymphs, sacred shrine where life itself issues from a source hidden in impenetrable darkness.

That mysterious cave where Ahasuerus dwells is the place of the 'demonesi', daimons, spirit-messengers between worlds,

intelligences known in other traditions as 'angels'—and indeed
Shelley does so name them in the 'Ode to the West Wind',
the same who on Jacob's Ladder ascend and descend between
heaven and earth, the higher and lower worlds. Ahasuerus,
archetype of cosmic knowledge, is to be summoned from
the inner realms of soul itself—as in *Prometheus Unbound*
Demogorgon makes Asia understand, 'of such truths/Each to
itself must be the oracle'. Ahasuerus advises the Sultan who has
come to consult him to

> commune with
> That portion of thyself which was ere thou
> Didst start for this brief race whose crown is death.

None can approach that frontier without awe, without the
sense of the numinous which can be experienced but not defined.
The inspired voice speaks of a mystery which is in its nature
beyond the comprehension of reason. This is the realm of mythology, at once strange and familiar. Our remote ancestors moved
within that world with ease, their records are their myths. We
ourselves experience that world in our dreams; indeed we should
read symbolic poetry and myth as we would interpret dreams
and read our dreams as if they were poetry. That world is no
less native to us than is the world of common day, and it is the
art of imaginative poetry to open to us its frontier. Shelley also
understood that this imaginative dimension is in reality present
as a dimension in every life, and it is for the poet to reveal its
presence. In *Epipsychidion*, the great love poem addressed to
Emilia Viviani, Shelley's passionate indignation at the thought
of this beautiful young woman taking the veil arose from his
vision of the sacredness of the erotic; he sees the divine beauty in

the woman of flesh and blood, and in the particular woman the presence of the goddess:

> the brightness
> Of her divinest presence trembles through
> Her limbs, as underneath a cloud of dew
> Embodied in the windless Heaven of June
> Amid the splendour-winged stars, the Moon
> Burns, inextinguishably beautiful:
> And from her lips, as from a hyacinth full
> Of honey-dew, a liquid murmur drops,
> Killing the sense with passion; sweet as stops
> Of planetary music heard in trance.
> In her mild lights the starry spirits dance,
> The sun-beams of those wells which ever leap
> Under the lightnings of the soul—too deep
> For the brief fathom-line of thought or sense.
> The glory of her being, issuing thence
> Stains the dead, blank, cold air with a warm shade
> Of unentangled intermixture, made
> By Love.

Paradoxically poets are the 'legislators of the world' not because they attend to those outer events that are the concern of politicians and journalists, but because they perceive inner realities, these being the spiritual causes of natural effects. Blake's great mythological narratives are concerned with the inner condition of England's national life at the time of the French, American and Industrial Revolutions. As a mythologist concerned with the world of causes, no poet has effected more in the world of history than did Shelley. It was Shelley who formulated the principle of non-violence as a power more potent than arms, and it was Shelley's *The Mask of Anarchy* that inspired Gandhi, who carried Shelley's seemingly impracticable dream into effect in a way that has changed the conscience of the world. But greater still I believe is the importance of Shelley's proclamation of the sacred nature of erotic love. In the Christian tradition sexual love was the cause of the 'fall' of man. With Shelley on the contrary Eros is redemptive. Rousseau had, in his *Confessions*, first made his plea for 'free love', and Mary Wollstonecraft, follower of Rousseau, had in her tragic life put into practice Rousseau's revolutionary principle. Shelley's second wife, Mary, was the daughter of this first feminist and of Godwin, the political theorist, whom she married, to die giving birth to Shelley's Mary. Shelley's older contemporary, Blake, had known and much admired Mary Wollstonecraft, two of whose books he had illustrated, and Blake's poem, *Visions of the Daughters of Albion*, an eloquent plea for free love, is clearly inspired by Mary. It seems likely that Blake would have given a copy of this poem to Mary, who had inspired it, and if so Shelley could have seen it in Godwin's house. Christianity, which exalts virginity and motherhood in the Blessed Virgin Mary, never at any time allowed a place for the erotic. For the first time, with Shelley (and to a lesser degree with Keats, whom Shelley passionately admired) the erotic was to enter English poetry not as the cause of the Fall of man but as a sacred and numinous reality. In his choice of Prometheus as the friend of man, Shelley was to transform Aeschylus' drama on the theme of Prometheus into a celebration of the power of love.

Prometheus, benefactor of mankind, because he stole fire from the gods and gave it to men, was punished by Zeus, chained to a rock in the Caucasus, where the eagle, bird of Zeus, tore his liver, a torment daily renewed. In the version of Aeschylus Prometheus was freed because he held the secret of a prophecy that Thetis, a daughter of Poseidon, would bear a son greater than his father. By revealing this secret to Zeus, Prometheus prevented his union with Thetis who was married to Peleus, a mortal, and fathered Achilles—but Shelley was unwilling to allow the great friend of man to surrender to his enemy 'the tyrant of mankind'—indeed he had at one time thought of Milton's Satan as the heroic rebel. He changed the story, introducing Demogorgon as the son of Zeus by Thetis, greater than his father who was to lead in a new age in which love would be the supreme power and rule the world. Shelley understood that the world of myth—of Imagination—is a living, self-creating world and to be bound by history is not in its nature. Thus, while Prometheus and Jupiter are taken from Aeschylus, Demogorgon and Asia are of Shelley's creation, in accordance with what he himself discerned of the inner changes taking place behind the history of his own age. Blake too had proclaimed a 'New Age', and Wordsworth saw in the French Revolution a dawn of freedom.

There is in Aeschylus' drama no feminine figure, except Io, turned by jealous Hera into a cow, who in her wanderings visits Prometheus. Perhaps Io is vestigially present in Shelley's *Prometheus Unbound* in the form of Ione, who with Asia and Panthea (which simply means all-goddess) are the 'daughters of Ocean'. In a note by Mrs Shelley Asia is said to represent Venus, or Nature: why then is she named Asia? Shelley sets the scene of Prometheus' torment in 'a Ravine of icy rocks in the Indian Caucasus'. Now the Caucasus range is not in India, as Shelley must have known. The location belongs not to the geography of the planet but to the geography of the Imagination: the region of Prometheus' redemption is located on the border of the India of the Imagination for symbolic reasons. His beloved, his *Shakti*, Shelley names 'Asia' as if to say that the Promethean Western mind needs for its completion the feminine soul of the Orient.

Asia can only be, in this context, 'India'; for the scene of the reunion of the liberated Prometheus with Asia is in 'that far Indian vale', 'a lovely vale in the Indian Caucasus'. The temple of Prometheus was formerly built

> beyond the peak
> Of Bacchic Nysa, Maenad-haunted mountain
> And beyond Indus with its tribute rivers.

The mention here of Bacchus and his Maenads is, again, geography of the Imagination, for Dionysus was the god of Inspiration, and the Maenads are invoked in the 'Ode to the West Wind' in this context. Doubtless it would be possible to find 'sources' for Shelley's 'lovely Indian vale' in travellers' tales of the forests of Kashmir, but no accuracy or inaccuracy of description is needed to account for the rich imaginative landscape of symbolic correspondence:

> a cave
> All overgrown with trailing odorous plants
> Which curtain out the day with leaves and flowers,
> And paved with veined emerald, and a fountain
> Leaps in the midst with an awakening sound.
> From its curved roof the mountain's frozen tears
> Like snow or silver, or long diamond spires,
> Hang downward raining forth a doubtful light;
> And there is heard the ever-moving air

Whispering without from tree to tree, and birds,
And bees; and all around are mossy seats,
And the rough walls are clothed with long soft grass;
A simple dwelling, that shall be our own.

Rama and Sita built their bower in those same woods where all lovers dwell in their paradisal dream. The Ramayana is full of lovely luxurious descriptions of incense-bearing trees and lotus lakes; for the poetry of erotic love demands and itself creates those forest glades of unspoiled nature where 'The Champak odours fall/Like sweet thoughts in a dream' (Where did Shelley come to know the scent of Champak?)

But Shelley would never have created a character so central to his greatest work from vague impressions of exotic beauty gathered from travellers' tales. What could Shelley have known of Indian poetry? Charles Wilkins, friend and colleague of Sir William Jones (and friend of Dr Johnson) had published the first translation of the *Bhagavad Gītā* into English in 1785. Blake knew this work, and Shelley, with his interest in things Indian, would certainly have done so; but although this great poem is spoken by the Lord Krishna to his cousin Arjuna on the battle-field of Kurukshetra, there is no mention in it of erotic love.

There are two works which Shelley is likely to have known, both translated by Sir William Jones himself. One is Kalidasa's *Shakuntala*, the story of a half-divine daughter of an Apsara who was found in the forest and married by the king of Bharat; this work was popular and widely read. Goethe is said to have admired it. The other is the *Gītā Govinda*, written in the twelfth century by Jayadeva, celebrating the loves of the Lord Krishna and Radha one of the Gopis of Brindavan. The worship of the god Krishna throughout India is associated with Radha, his beloved, with Krishna as the divine flute-player who enchants and seduces the milkmaids of Brindavan. Jones's translation appeared in the *Proceedings of the Calcutta Society* in 1792 and although there is no record of Shelley having read it, it seems very unlikely that he had not. Would not the poet, his mind engaged in the theme of the sacredness of erotic love, in naming his goddess-figure 'Asia', and situating her home in India, have had better evidence than vague exoticism for choosing India, the home of the great cult of sacred erotic love? The *Gītā Govinda* is the source of the widespread Bhakti cult of India, of numberless paintings of the love of Radha and Krishna, of the famous Circle dance performed in Brindavan to this day, and the most widely performed theme of the Indian classical dance. The supreme love theme of India is the love between Krishna, the divine lover and Radha. The erotic images are understood on several levels as the mystical union of the soul with God, but also as a celebration of the sacred nature of sexual love itself. The Krishna of the *Bhagavad Gītā* may have existed as a king in Northern India, but Radha is an invention of poetry, yet has become a goddess, whose myth is danced, painted, enacted and celebrated throughout India, with temples dedicated to Radha and her divine lover. Indeed I found myself, not so many years ago, at the very heart of Radha's festival celebrated on the feast of Holi at Brindavan where the child Krishna grew up among the gopis.

There is of course much in common between the Platonic and the Vedic tradition; but there are passages whose cosmic sweep seems to take their inspiration from the song of the Lord Krishna, the *Bhagavad Gītā*. In *Hellas* these words of Ahasuarus:

> this Whole
> Of sun, and worlds, and men, and beasts, and flowers,
> With all the silent or tempestuous workings
> By which they have been, are, or cease to be,
> Is but a vision—all that it inherits
> Are motes of a sick eye, bubbles and dreams;
> Thought is its cradle and its grave, nor less
> The future and the past are idle shadows
> Of thought's eternal flight—they have no being:
> Nought is but that which feels itself to be.

The Shakespearean reference notwithstanding ('all that it inherits') 'thought's eternal flight' seems closer to India than to Plato. Be that as it may India has always had a deep love for the poetry of Shelley, at least until secularisation and Westernisation of Indian education began to destroy their great traditional culture. Shelley has been the most loved of the English poets; India has for Shelley a greater sense of affinity than he has ever enjoyed in his own country save from those who, like Yeats, were themselves seekers for spiritual knowledge. Indian friends have quoted to me, as an example of Shelley's closeness to Indian symbolic thought the penultimate stanza from *Adonais*:

> That Light whose smile kindles the Universe,
> That Beauty in which all things work and move,
> That Benediction which the eclipsing Curse
> Of birth can quench not, that sustaining Love
> Which through the web of being blindly wove
> By man and beast and earth and air and sea,
> Burns bright or dim, as each are mirrors of

The fire for which all thirst; now beams on me,
Consuming the last clouds of cold morality.

Blake in his old age wrote his own reflection on those who live on earth as if it were already that other timeless world of mind or spirit, which to Imagination is more real than the shadow world of 'cold mortality'; he was surely remembering, besides Thomas Paine, those young revolutionary idealists who used to meet weekly at Johnson's bookshop in St Paul's Churchyard, when they were all young, among them Godwin and Mary Wollstonecraft; and his words apply no less to Shelley, child of that revolution:

> Many persons, such as Paine & Voltaire, with some of the Ancient Greeks, say: 'we will not converse concerning Good & Evil; we will live in Paradise & Liberty'. You may do so in Spirit, but not in the Mortal Body, as you pretend, till after the Last Judgment; for in Paradise they have no Corporeal & Mortal Body.

Shelley affirmed the sacred nature of sexual love, and in his attempt to live by that vision bruised himself and has ever since been condemned by those who live in 'the real world'. But to Shelley the vision was more real than the world of 'cold mortality' that has judged him, and he believed that, some day, the world will live according to the truth of the Imagination, under the rule of love. In his great poem, which Yeats names among 'the sacred books of the world', he gave that vision its vesture of poetry, as a reality of the human spirit already realized.

(1997)

The Chamber of Maiden Thought

WHILE I WAS still at school Keats was for me the supreme poet, in whose vision I felt I could wholly participate, an experience I am sure many of us have shared; for his poetry perfectly expresses youth's vision—it is 'a vision in the form of Youth', as he himself phrases it. But that is not at all to say that this vision is in any way partial or immature: rather that Keats had retained for long enough to embody it in his poetry that paradisal recollection of the radiant beauty of the world whose loss is called experience. Moneta, or Mnemosyne, Keats's own figure of Platonic recollection of some anterior perfection, is the goddess who in *Hyperion* initiates Apollo, the lyre-bearer, symbolic image of Keats's own poetic genius. I do not share the view that Keats had not yet found the range of that genius or that, had he lived, he would have written greater poetry. He might indeed have developed in ways unforeseen; but that he failed to give complete expression to the young poet's dream I do not believe. True, life teaches us more about imperfection, but do we ever see perfection more clearly than we do at the outset?' I believe that those who seek to defend Keats by speaking not of his achievement but of his promise do him a disservice. Some have sought to defend him on the grounds that

he would, had he lived, have abandoned the 'deliberate happiness' of his imagination to write about the sufferings of the
world; as in his life he did indeed assume his share of human
responsibility, in caring for his dying brother, his younger sister, and generously concerning himself with the problems of his
friends. But such pleas could never reconcile social realist critics
to the poetry he actually wrote. When I was at Cambridge in the
early thirties Keats was rated low by the school of I. A. Richards,
F. R. Leavis, and William Empson. That so-called 'scientific
criticism' was grounded in the positivist ideologies then current;
the very terms of such criticism discounted the Imagination.
Speaking as his poetry does immediately to the imagination and
not at all to the discursive reason, Keats was easily demolished
by standards that left out of account all that was valuable in
his work. By such standards he became invisible, like the magic
palace of his Lamia. Keats himself knew that mentality; and his
aged Apollonius is Blake's Urizen to the life, 'Aged Ignorance'
whose wisdom of experience clips the visionary wings of youth:

> Do not all charms fly
> At the mere touch of cold philosophy?
> There was an awful rainbow once in heaven:
> We know her woof, her texture; she is given
> In the dull catalogue of common things.
> Philosophy will clip an Angel's wings,
> Conquer all mysteries by rule and line,
> Empty the haunted air, and gnomed mine—
> Unweave a rainbow. . . .

There has been much clipping of wings and unweaving of rain-
bows in our time, and soul's butterfly with her deep-damasked

wings—Keats's goddess Psyche—taught to know itself a pre-sumptuous caterpillar. Imagination reverses the unweaving operation by means of an alchemy which transmutes common things into gold. It depends on which we choose to consider as more 'real', the perfection we lack, and fail, in greater or less degree, to realise; or the archetype of that never-realised inner reality by whose measure we see and feel and know the actuality of common things always to fall short. No social improvement—and this Keats knew only too well, young as he was—can change the nature of the mutable world:

> Here, where men sit and hear each other groan;
> Where palsy shakes a few, sad, last grey hairs,
>   Where youth grows pale, and spectre-thin, and dies;
>   Where but to think is to be full of sorrow
>   And leaden-eyed despairs;
> Where Beauty cannot keep her lustrous eyes,
>   Or new Love pine at them beyond to-morrow.)

Sickness, old age, and death; Keats had seen them, and looked elsewhere than to natural life for Psyche's house; he found it—and built it—in art. Indeed, for what else does poetry exist but to create for us these 'gardens where the soul's at ease' (so Yeats, who understood Keats so well, phrased it), a 'rest for the people of God', not to be found in the world of generation and death. And if poor flesh and blood will always cry out that 'The fancy cannot cheat so well/As she is fam'd to do', yet Keats also knew that his Grecian Urn is 'a friend to man' just because it stands as an affirmation—an epiphany—of a perfection unattainable in natural terms, but real in the world of Imagination.

Throughout European history every reaffirmation of the truth and value of the soul and her universe, the Imagination, the *mundus imaginalis*, has been accompanied by a revival of the Platonic philosophy, whose ground is not, as for modern materialism, matter, but mind. The Romantic Revival is no exception. All the English Romantic poets were, in their various ways, Platonists. Coleridge and Shelley studied their Plato in the original Greek, Blake in Thomas Taylor's translations of Plato and the neo-Platonists into English. And what of Keats? Is the Platonic caste of his thought only a reflection of ideas 'in the air' at the time of the Greek revival, between 1780 and 1821 (the year of Keats's death), or was he something more than a poet whose aesthetic sense was acute to the point of recreating his imagined Greece from the Elgin Marbles and the Portland Vase? The Greek revival was at one time considered chiefly in terms of the visual arts—Flaxman and the Wedgwood replicas, the housing of the Parthenon Frieze in the British Museum built for its reception, the publication of Stuart and Revett's *Antiquities of Athens*, and so on. What has until recently tended to be overlooked—I would even put it more strongly, and say deliberately dismissed—by a critical school that reflects current secular materialism is the accompanying revival of the Platonic theology. I say theology rather than philosophy because an early essay by Thomas Taylor—an essay that is at once a manifesto and a programme—is entitled 'A History of the Platonic Theology by the Late Platonists'. In that essay (included in the second volume of his translation of Proclus's *Commentaries on Euclid*) Taylor pours scorn alike on Deist Christianity and materialist science as lacking philosophic grounds and unworthy of serious consideration by a true philosopher. Taylor called for a new restoration of that great Western formulation of the *sophia perennis* to replace the vapid Deism of the day, and the no less naive materialism which was already its successful rival. Fighting as he did on two fronts, Taylor found few supporters; but his call to the young men of the new age to enlist themselves under the banner of Plotinus and Plato was certainly heard by the poets. From Taylor's translations and commentaries came that great influx of Platonic thought which transformed English poetry from the rationalist mode of the Augustans to the imaginative flowering of the Romantic movement. Taylor was an acquaintance of Blake, to whom he even gave some lessons on Euclid; and he had given a course on the Platonic theology in the house of Blake's friend 'Flaxman the statuary': probably the basis of the essay already mentioned. Coleridge was reading the works of 'the English Pagan' at school. It seems unlikely that Shelley's misadventure in Oxford only coincidentally took the form of a rejection of the Christian in the name of the Platonic theology; and Shelley may well have met Taylor through their mutual friend Thomas Love Peacock who put Taylor in his novel *Melincourt* as 'Mr. Mystic'. Could Keats, anticlerical as he was (yet believing in the soul's immortality), and in love with all things Greek, have failed to discover Taylor, whose translations and commentaries were the only ones at that time available?

It is true that Keats nourished his imagination above all on the visual arts. In his book *Keats and the Mirror of Art* Dr Ian Jack has shown us many of the actual paintings Keats had seen (often in the form of engravings) in the collections of his friends Leigh Hunt and Benjamin Robert Haydon. Most of these, certainly, were the Greek myths as transmitted and transmuted through Ovid into Renaissance Italian painting, and so to

Claude, Poussin, Canova and the rest. Dr Jack also paints for us the picture of Keats, in Haydon's company, strolling by candle-light among the Elgin marbles, nor yet on view to the public but stored in a shed in Park Lane. The closeness of Keats's visual descriptions to these pictorial and sculptural originals is abundantly demonstrated in that fascinating book. Although Keats's Greece is at many removes from classical Greece, we may see his genius at work, penetrating through so many intervening veils, to the imaginative essence of that great seminal tradition within which he himself stands in a manner no less authentic than do the Italian and French painters of themes from Greek mythology, all alike inspired by the Platonic philosophy of the beautiful.

Bernard Blackstone, whose book *The Consecrated Urn* is the best critical and scholarly assessment of Keats's poetry known to me, believes that Keats read Taylor's translation of the *Timaeus* in 1817, at the time he was writing *Endymion* during his stay at Magdalen College, Oxford, with William Bailey. Which if any of Taylor's other books Keats had read we can only surmise. Professor Blackstone thinks possibly Porphyry's treatise *On the Cave of the Nymphs*, which is included in Taylor's essay on the restoration of the Platonic Theology. It is possible that he knew Taylor's *Mystical Hymns of Orpheus*, which include a hymn to Demeter listing many of the symbolic attributes of his own goddess of Autumn, and an essay on the Orphic theogonies which might have suggested some elements of *Hyperion*; though from internal evidence this is no more than conjectural.

The *Timaeus* is a dialogue on the theme of nature; with which Keats was doubly concerned as a student of medicine and as a poet for whom nature was a mirror of imaginative life and meaning, 'full of gods' as for the Greeks. Professor Blackstone has perceptively written that of all the Romantic poets Keats stands closest to Blake—a view by no means self-evident in style or temperament, but certainly so in the view they shared of the natural world as a living being and not, as the experimental scientists and their Deist followers held, as a material mechanism.

> I'll . . . shew you all alive
> The world, where every particle of dust breathes forth its joy

Blake wrote. And so with Keats, whose oreads and nymphs and spirits of the elements are not at all (as for the Augustan Poets, or as for that interesting nature-poet Erasmus Darwin) natural substances personified by the simple device of a capital letter. As for Blake, so for Keats, Nature is living:

> A thousand Powers keep religious state,
> In water, fiery realm, and airy bourne.

If both poets were familiar with the *Timaeus*, where Plato calls the world 'a blessed god', informed with life from a divine source; and also perhaps with the tradition, which preserved in Alchemical and Rosicrucian writings, the lovely living figure of the soul of the world, the *anima mundi* (as she appears, for example, in Robert Fludd's *Mosaicall Philosophy*), the resemblance between Keats and Blake in this respect is not coincidental. Not indeed that Keats resembles Blake as a poet who fought a lifelong battle with Bacon, Newton and Locke, using all the weapons and arguments of powerful discursive thought: rather, perhaps, he was fortunate in never having lost the experience native to childhood of a living earth. He perhaps discovered in time, in the *Timaeus*, a philosophic vindication of something we all, in childhood, know without the assistance of philosophy.

The 'four elements' as described by Plato have little to do with the elements of matter as analysed and defined by chemists. These states of matter have indeed more to do with poetry than with the scientific way of speculating about our world. This has been revealingly demonstrated in the writings of the French phenomenologist, Gaston Bachelard. Bachelard, as a scientific historian, set out to purge the language of science from all such animistic implications as gender, or of such phrases as acids 'attacking' bases, and the like. But in so doing he perceived, as in a flash of revelation, that the very terms he was seeking to eliminate from pure scientific discourse constituted no mere residue of inaccuracy but a whole poetic vocabulary expressing our living experience of nature. And basic in this poetic, qualitative experience—no less a mode of knowing our world than is scientific measurement—he discovered earth, air, fire and water to be elements not of material science but of poetic experience. He later wrote his famous books on the poetics of the four elements—of Shelley's use of the element of air; of the sombre stagnant water-imagery in which Edgar Allen Poe discovered the objective correlative of his dark vision; or Blake's mythological characters seeking to break out of the constrictions of a world of 'rocks and solids'. In Keats's *Endymion*, had he known this poem, Bachelard would have found in their poetic purity the four elemental worlds of imaginative experience through which Endymion travels: the jewelled caverns of the earth; the land-under-wave of Glaucus and Scylla; the airy ascent of the hero to attain immortality in his union with the divine beloved, as ' into her face there came/Light, as reflected from a silver flame.' As in the *Timaeas* the ascent from the lowest to the highest of the four elemental worlds is at the same time a qualitative ascent.

Endymion must 'by some unlook'd for change/Be spiritualiz'd', as in an alchemical transmutation.

In *Song of Four Fairies* the elements are charmingly personified (as so often they are throughout the whole European alchemical tradition) in a play of love; while in *Hyperion* we see them at strife:

> earth, water, air, and fire,—
> At war, at peace, or inter-quarreling
> One against one, or two, or three, or all
> Each several one against the other three,
> As fire with air loud warring when rain-floods
> Drown both, and press them both against earth's face,
> Where, finding sulphur, a quadruple wrath
> Unhinges the poor world.

From that elemental world the poet may learn 'strange lore, and read it deep', Keats writes. As against our scientifically oriented knowledge of nature, he knew nature imaginatively, yet in a detailed and intimate manner in which nature is not merely cognized but experienced; not observed, but lived.

There are indeed poets who observe and describe natural appearances as an external object of knowledge, as it is to science. Keats uneasily felt that this was true of Wordsworth and refused to be 'bullied into a certain philosophy' by the great elder Poet. Nature was for Keats much nearer to Blake's definition of body as 'a portion of Soul discern'd by the five Senses'. Keats is the 'chameleon poet', 'continually informing and filling some other Body—The Sun, the Moon, the Sea and Men and Women'. He pours himself into whatever he beholds—'if a Sparrow come before my Window I take part in its existence and pick about the Gravel'. This imaginative apprehension, this flowing out of the soul into nature, sets Keats apart from the descriptive school of English poetry. Indeed we might say that for him the natural world does not belong to the physical order at all, but is, rather, his experience of that 'great dream' of which he wrote in *Endymion*

> I have clung
> To nothing, lov'd a nothing, nothing seen
> Or felt but a great dream!

In a letter to Bailey he wrote more explicitly, more Platonically, of the *mundus imaginalis*, 'The Imagination may be compared to Adam's dream—he awoke and found it truth.' The archetypes of that world of Imagination (in the words of Coleridge) 'already and for ever exist', in mind, which discovers in the panorama of nature the correspondences of an inner world.

Like Spenser, whose work he loved, Keats had the gift of entering imaginative times and spaces which open into a boundless inner universe, which he adorns with all the minute particulars of the sensible world that eye has observed. We do not enter Endymion's forests as we set foot on Wordworth's dales and fells by looking outwards but by opening the eye of Imagination into a spacious and changeless world within the mind, of which external nature serves as a mirror which reflects back to the poet those archetypal forms which already and for ever exist not in physical nature but in the Imagination itself; without which, indeed, we would be unable to recognise and distinguish them; or (to use Keats's own image of Adam's dream) to 'name' them, and know what they signify.

This is a quality of all mythological stories, all fairy tales from time immemorial to Tolkien; and what are *Lamia*, and 'The Eve of St Agnes' and 'La Belle Dame Sans Merci' and *Endymion* but fairy-tales?—and so is that light-hearted satirical fairy-tale *The Cap and Bells*. In this scope and spaciousness Keats saw the very essence of poetic imagination. He liked poems to be long, and wrote (of *Endymion*): 'I must make 4,000 lines of one bare circumstance and fill them with Poetry'—and he adds,

> God forbid that I should be without such a task! I have heard Hunt say and may be asked—why endeavour after a long Poem? To which I should answer—Do not the Lovers of Poetry like to have a little Region to wander in where they may pick and choose, and in which the images are so numerous that many are forgotten and found new in a second Reading: which may be food for a Week's stroll in the Summer?

He understood Imagination as a region to be entered—the 'realms of Gold' with its many states and goodly kingdoms, Plato's 'Garden of the Muses', which is Psyche's inner kingdom:

> Now it appears to me that almost any Man may like the Spider spin from his own inwards his own airy Citadel—the points of the leaves and twigs on which the spider begins her work are few, and she fills the air with a beautiful circuiting: man should be content with as few points to tip with the fine Web of his Soul, and weave a tapestry empyrean—full of Symbols for his spiritual eye, of softness for his spiritual touch, of space for his wandering of distinctness for his Luxury.

He held 'that if Poetry comes not as naturally as the Leaves to a tree it had better not come at all'; a statement that may be compared with Blake's words that 'He who does not imagine in stronger and better lineaments, and in stronger and better light than his perishing mortal eye can see, does not imagine at all'. Both poets knew the way to Plato's Garden of the Muses which can be reached only by flying there—'on the viewless wings of poesy', in Keats's words. That Garden is Adam's Paradise, the soul's native country. In his poetry Keats transports us there, and how familiar, how native to us it seems. For it resembles earth in all but its imperfection and mutability, the weight of body and years and distances.

KEATS KNEW VERY well the regions of his own inner universe, and wrote of this in one of his wonderful letters:

> I compare human life to a large Mansion of Many
> Apartments, two of which I can only describe, the doors of
> the rest being as yet shut upon me—The first we step into
> we call the infant or thoughtless Chamber, in which we
> remain as long as we do not think [. . .] we no sooner get
> into the second Chamber, which I shall call the Chamber of
> Maiden-Thought, than we become intoxicated with the light
> and the atmosphere, we see nothing but pleasant wonders,
> and think of delaying there for ever in delight . . .

But beyond that point the poet perceives

> that the World is full of Misery and Heartbreak, Pain,
> Sickness and oppression—whereby This Chamber of
> Maiden Thought becomes gradually darken'd and at the
> same time on all sides of it many doors are set open—but all
> dark—all leading to dark passages—We see not the balance

of good and evil. We are in a Mist—*We* are now in that state—We feel 'the burden of the Mystery'.

To this point, Keats goes on to say, Wordsworth had come; and we remember Wordsworth's sense of the fading of the Paradisal vision. We may think also of Blake's Thel, the virgin soul, who is shown the 'grave-plot' of the earthly life that awaits her. She sees, as Keats saw those dark passages,

> the secrets of the land unknown.
> She saw the couches of the dead, & where the fibrous roots
> Of every heart on earth infixes deep its restless twists:
> A land of sorrows & of tears where never smile was seen.

Keat's soul, like Thel, was never destined to make that descent; rather his genius was to give expression to the light and the atmosphere of the Chamber of Maiden Thought; not, as for Wordsworth, the world of childhood, but that dream of beauty and love that unveils itself to adolescence and ends with the descent into sexuality. Yet it is not true that Keats as a poet did not reach his prime: his prime *was* his youth, '"a Vision in the form of Youth", a Shadow of reality to come'. Endymion is the lover not of mortal woman but of the archetype, the virgin goddess within the soul. Although he tries to argue that in loving the goddess Endymion had deprived his natural love (the Indian girl) of her due, and that it is necessary to discover the immortal love in and through the mortal, he fails to convince us. The passages on natural and sensual love are (to use his own words) 'mawkish' and uninspired. They lie outside that universe of Adam's dream in which the poet beholds the vision of the goddess, in an unfallen world, over whose dream-landscape there hangs 'An orbed drop of light, and that is love'. John Keats the man was to experience the bitterness and anguish of the 'descent' of Adam from Paradise, from the dream of the beloved to the reality of a very different relationship with 'the girl next door'. The poet sought to discover the image of his soul in Fanny Brawne; who could never be that goddess, not because she was the wrong woman but because the soul-image inhabits the Imagination, not this world. Let us not make moral judgements about the necessity of 'coming to terms' with this world's reality: let us rather be grateful to the poet who holds before us the soul's first vision of love in all its intensity and purity. In a letter to his Platonic friend Bailey, Keats declares his faith in that ideal vision: 'That the Prototype must be here after-that delicious face you will see'. For the prototype dwelling in the recesses of the soul is the reality of which no earthly love is more than the shadow. The moon-goddess is ever virgin, though she kisses the lips of Endymion in dreams.

Lamia too, with her house built of lovers' dreams, is a fairy-bride whose rainbow fades in 'the dull catalogue of common things'. And the enchantment of those exquisite poems of first love, 'The Eve of St Agnes' and *Isabella*, distilled from the world of Romeo and Juliet, depict a love that is total, in which each sees in the beloved not (as in mortal life—how all too well Byron understood this) one among many possibilities, but the only beloved, the one and all. 'The Eve of St Agnes' celebrates the dreamed-of consummation of the first embrace; and although the lovers depart towards a future of which the narrative seems to imply that they 'lived happily ever after', what the symbolism of the images themselves tells us is quite otherwise. As they depart the magic has faded; the arras

Fluttered in the besieging wind's uproar;
And the long carpets rose along the gusty floor.

The lovers have no future:

And they are gone: aye, ages long ago
Those lovers fled away into the storm.

As long ago as Eden; and the poem ends as the lovers go out into the storm through an 'iron porch' whose 'door upon its hinges groans', more suggestive of Adam and Eve's departure from Eden than of a happy future. The castle that had held the lovers' jewelled chamber is now 'be-nightmared' with forms of woe and mortality—'Of witch, and demon, and large coffin-worm'. The future of the young lovers is foreshadowed in the images of old age and death with which the poem ends. Angela the nurse 'died palsy-twitch'd, with meagre face deform' and

The Beadsman, after thousand aves told,
For aye unsought for slept among his ashes cold.

Dust and ashes; and how significant that the ballad Porphyro sings to Madeleine as he is about to bestow on her that mortal kiss in which the Paradisal dream enters corporeality is 'La Belle Dame sans Merci', telling of a world of post-coital sadness where 'The sedge is withered from the lake,/And no birds sing.' Only in the archetypal world does beauty abide in her own universe; and it is of this inner world that music speaks, and poetry, and the imagined figures on the Grecian urn; itself virginal, the 'still unravished bride of quietness'. And it was this *imaginal* world inaccessible to flesh and blood, that Keats chose:

Fair youth, beneath the trees, thou canst not leave
   Thy song, nor ever can those trees be bare;
     Bold Lover, never, never canst thou kiss,
   Though winning near the goal—yet, do not grieve;
She cannot fade, though thou hast not thy bliss,
   For ever wilt thou love, and she be fair!

Body cannot enter that native country of the soul,

   All breathing human passion far above,
     That leaves a heart high-sorrowful and cloyed,
   A burning forehead, and a parching tongue.

But for Keats Paradise was nor unreality but reality itself. He asks his friend Bailey:

Have you never by being surprised with an old Melody—in a delicious place—by a delicious voice, felt over again your very Speculations and Surmises at the rime it first operated on your Soul—do you not remember forming to yourself the singer's face more beautiful than it was possible and yet with the elevation of the Moment you did not think so— even then you were mounted on the Wings of Imagination so high—that the Prototype must be here after—that delicious face you will see.

In the story of Cupid and Psyche Keats discerned something more than a fable of sexual love; for Psyche is the soul itself, and Keats, addressing her (in his 'Ode to Psyche') as 'goddess', did so of intent, for he believed the soul to be immortal. She is winged, too, wings being symbolic of her spiritual nature. His very voluptuousness is of the Imagination. In Canova's statue of the embracing lovers (known to Keats, according to Dr Jack) the sculptor has caught that timeless moment between dream and carnality, whose atmosphere is reflected in Keat's poem:

> They lay, calm-breathing on the bedded grass;
>> Their arms embraced, and their pinions too:
>> Their lips touched not, but had not bade adieu. . . .

The poet vows to be the priest of Psyche and her love:

> Yes, I will be thy priest, and build a fane
> In some untrodden region of my mind.

Psyche's house will be raised into being by the same magic that built Lamia's palace:

> A rosy sanctuary will I dress
> With the wreathed trellis of a working brain,
>> With buds and bells and stars without a name,
> With all the gardener Fancy e'er could feign,
>> Who breeding flowers, will never breed the same;
> And there shall be for thee all soft delight
>> That shadowy thought can win,
> A bright torch, and a casement ope at night,
>> To let the warm Love in!

It is the country of the soul, not that of the body, which is 'holy land'. Madeleine in her chamber too is depicted as a being of that world:

> Rose-bloom fell on her hands, together pressed,
> And on her silver cross soft amethyst,
> And on her hair a glory, like a saint:

She seemed a splendid angel, newly drest,
Save wings, for Heaven. . . .

And we remember how the anti-clerical Keats took a love-letter
from Fanny Brawne into Winchester Cathedral in order to read
in a holy place words that for him were sacred.

ALTHOUGH IT IS impossible to say with certainty which, if
any, of Thomas Taylor's Platonic writings Keats had read, there
is one which I would venture to guess that he knew. Taylor's
paraphrase translation of Plotinus's *Concerning the Beautiful*,
which in 1792 you could have bought for half-a-crown, was one
of the most widely read of Taylor's works, going into a second
edition. Did this little volume play a part in the formation of
Keats's religion of the beautiful—the authentic religion, so he
must have believed, of the ancient Greeks of whom his own consecrated urn is the symbol? Keats's declaration of faith, 'beauty
is truth, truth beauty', signifies in terms of the Platonic philosophy infinitely more than to the unphilosophic reader; and in
the concluding section of this paper I shall try to bring the light
of Plotinus's thought to bear on Keats's words and what they
meant for him.

Plotinus in his Tractate equates the beautiful not with 'truth'
but with 'the Good'; but in Platonic terms the Good signifies
the real, or what is, source of being, the creative and ordering
principle rather than moral goodness in the modern sense of
the word as the contrary of 'evil'; a fact which may have determined Keats's identification of beauty with truth rather than 'the
good'. On the title-page of Proclus's *Commentaries on Euclid*
Taylor has himself inscribed a phrase from Plotinus, 'There is

nothing higher than the truth'; and in this sense there is no difference between the Good, the Truth, and real being. We need
not, therefore, make any distinction between the Good (in the
Platonic sense) and Truth (in Keats's sense). Taylor in a footnote
to his annotated paraphrase translation says:

> It is necessary to inform the Platonical reader, that the
> Beautiful, in the present discourse, is considered accord-
> ing to its most general acceptation, as the same with the
> Good: though, according to a more accurate distinction, as
> Plotinus himself informs us, the Good is considered as the
> fountain and principle of the Beautiful.

In Keats's letter to his Platonic friend Bailey, already quoted,
in which we find the poet's fullest affirmation of his thought on
'the authenticity of the Imagination' he also wrote: 'What the
Imagination seizes as Beauty must be truth—whether it existed
before or not—for I have the same Idea of all our Passions as of
Love they are all in their sublime, creative of essential Beauty.'
The whole context of the letter is Platonic, and seems to be taking up themes the two young men had already discussed in terms
that are here assumed rather than argued.

Some may here object that, far from speaking of a Platonic
ideal world, Keats here goes on to proclaim his faith in sensations and his scepticism about philosophizing; such readers
would like to present Keats as a thoroughly down-to-earth poet;
for he writes: 'I have never yet been able to perceive how any
thing can be known for truth by consequitive reasoning . . . O
for a Life of Sensations rather than of Thoughts! It is "a Vision
in the form of Youth" . . .'. Yet the sentence continues in specifically Platonic terms, for this life of sensations is

a Shadow of reality to come—and this consideration has
further convinced me for it has come as auxiliary to another
favourite Speculation of mine, that we shall enjoy ourselves
here after by having what we called happiness on Earth
repeated in a finer tone and so repeated—And yet such a
fate can only befall those who delight in sensation rather
than hunger as you do after Truth—Adam's dream will do
here and seems to be a conviction that Imagination and its
empyreal reflection is the same as human Life and its spiritual repetition.

'Beauty *is* truth' could well be Keats's clinching of this run-
ning argument with Bailey, the abstract thinker for whom truth
was an abstraction. What then are we to make of the apparent
paradox of this poet who delights in sensation yet relates the
experience of the senses to an empyrean and spiritual order?
We may compare Keats here again with Blake, who wrote
that sense is 'the Eye of Imagination'. Commenting on a passage from Berkeley's *Siris* in which the philosopher argues that
'all beings are in the soul' and that it is 'the soul that impar-
teth forms to matter', Blake wrote in the margin: 'This is my
Opinion, but Forms must be apprehended by Sense or the Eye
of Imagination.' Blake then goes on to write of 'the Heathen or
Platonic Philosophy, which blinds the Eye of Imagination, The
Real Man'. Unjust as Blake's words are to the Platonists, we
catch an echo here of Keats's disagreement with Bailey, who
tried (as Blake implies the philosophers also tried) to reach truth
by abstract thought. Elsewhere Blake wrote that the inspired
poets (Homer, Virgil, Milton and the Bible) addressed their
writings to the Imagination, 'which is Spiritual Sensation &

but mediately to the Understanding or Reason'. For Keats, as for Blake, this sensible world is 'one continued vision of the Imagination', and 'Nature is Imagination itself '. The parallel is so striking that we are inclined to look for some common source; which was, I believe, Plotinus, who argues that the Perception of the beautiful is unmediate through sense. Such is the opening theme of his Tractate:

> Beauty, for the most part, consists in objects of sight: but it is also received through the ears, by the skilful composition of words, and the consonant proportions of sounds; for in every species of harmony, beauty is to be found. And if we rise from sense into the regions of soul, we shall there perceive studies and offices, actions and habits, sciences and virtues, invested with a much larger proportion of beauty. But whether there is, above these, a still higher beauty, will appear as we advance in its investigation.

And Plotinus goes on to consider 'What is it then, which causes bodies to appear fair to the sight, sounds beautiful to the ear, and science and virtue lovely to the mind? May we not enquire after what manner they all partake of beauty?' Keats wrote of sensation 'repeated in a finer tone'; and Blake wrote on the same theme—the Imagination: 'There Exist in that Eternal World the Permanent Realities of Every Thing which we see reflected in this Vegetable Glass of Nature.' Blake, for all his denunciation of the Heathen Philosophers is here writing pure Platonism; and so is Keats when he speaks of his 'speculation'. Keats wrote in playful mood of this archetypal paradise of the Platonic 'eternal forms' whose imperfect reflections we meet in nature; there the poets are

Seated on Elysian lawns
Brows'd by none but Dian's fawns;
Underneath large blue-bells tented,
Where the daisies are rose-scented,
And the rose herself has got
Perfume which on earth is not;
Where the nightingale doth sing
Not a senseless, tranced thing,
But divine melodious truth;
Philosophic numbers smooth;
Tales and golden histories
Of heaven and its mysteries.

But that the poet could play with the idea is not to say that 'happiness on Earth repeated in a finer tone' was not therefore an idea to which he had given more serious thought; in 'Ode to a Nightingale' the bird does indeed sing 'divine melodious truth'; it sings with the voice of Imagination itself. And for his speculation Keats can claim the support of Plotinus himself. It is not reason but sense that perceives the beautiful; about which indeed reason can tell us nothing, as Keats and Blake both understood. So far from placing him among the down-to-earth poets we see that Keats's words 'O for a life of Sensation rather than thoughts!' place him among the Platonic lovers, whom Plato in the *Phaedo* describes as proceeding from the love of earthly to the love of heavenly beauty. Sense, not thought, is the organ which first perceives that beauty 'repeated in a finer tone'. How important this idea was to Keats we know from those lines in his 'Ode on a Grecian Urn':

Heard melodies are sweet, but those unheard
   Are sweeter; therefore, ye soft pipes, play on;
Not to the sensual ear, but, more endeared,
   Pipe to the spirit ditties of no tone.

The unheard melody is not a faint overtone of sense but, as Plotinus taught, the higher reality of which the lower is an echo or reflection inviting the lover of beauty to ascend:

      He ne'er is crowned
With immortality, who fears to follow
Where airy voices lead.

And we remember also the singer of the 'old melody' that awakened in the poet the imaginative certainty 'that the Prototype must be here after—that delicious face you will see'.

Plato has written in the *Phaedrus* of the three ways to knowledge, that of the philosophers, of the musical souls, and of the lovers. Keats was, surely, of all English poets the one who most closely conforms to the type of the lover who, from the adoration of mortal beauty, ascends to the discernment of 'the beautiful itself'. For beauty is perceptible only by love; it is the object of love; and Plotinus is true to Plato's teaching when he writes of the awakening of the affections which 'ought to be excited about true beauty, as admiration and sweet astonishment; desire, also; and love, and a pleasant trepidation.' So it was with Keats; and it ill becomes those less sensitive to the divine essence of beauty to reproach him with the excess of his love for Fanny Brawne. All souls, Plotinus says (in Taylor's paraphrase), are indeed affected by beauty, 'but those the most who have the strongest propensity to their love; as it likewise happens about corporeal beauty: for all equally perceive beautiful corporeal forms, yet all are not equally excited, but lovers in the greatest degree.' A religion of beauty is alien alike to Christian puritanism and positivist materialism; but Keats had in this respect rediscovered the very essence of the Greek vision of the holy quality inherent in beauty; the religion that made Helen the daughter of Zeus a goddess, on account of her beauty alone.

For Keats, as for the Greeks, the lover's vision of the beauty of the beloved is a mode of spiritual knowledge and leads to the perception of 'the good itself'.

Plotinus seeks to penetrate to the mystery of sensible beauty, asking the question 'What is the beauty of bodies?', and he answers:

> It is something which, at first view, presents itself to sense; and which the soul familiarly apprehends, and eagerly embraces, as if it were allied to itself. But when it meets with the deformed, it hastily starts from the view, and retires abhorrent from its discordant nature.

Those who insist that we ought to look squarely at the far from beautiful 'reality' of the world of sickness, old age and death, who in nature see above all conflict and decay, seek to make the doctrine of beauty seem trivial. These ideologies deny the soul and its universe, the *mundus imaginalis*. But the Platonists see beauty otherwise, as the principle which leads the soul to self-knowledge by discovering through sense, the eye of Imagination, its own nature, and the nature of the Good. In the words of Plotinus since the soul in its proper state ranks according to the most excellent essence in the order of things, when it perceives any object related to itself, or the mere vestige of a relation, it congratulates itself on the pleasing event, and astonished with the striking resemblance, enters deep into its essence, and, by rousing its dormant powers, at length perfectly recollects its kindred and allies.

Psyche was for the Greeks, as for Keats, a divine being. Because body, as Plotinus writes, 'becomes beautiful through the communion supernally proceeding from divinity', he supports with his authority Keats's leap in the dark, his trust in the immediate perception of sensation; for

the soul, by her innate power, than which nothing is more powerful, in judging its proper concerns . . . acknowledges the beauty of forms. And, perhaps, its knowledge in this case arises from its accommodating its internal ray of beauty to form, and trusting to this in its judgment. . . .

No rational process is required, only the immediate discernment of beauty.

Keats's lovers, too perfect in every feature for the warty world—lovers thrice distilled, as Dr Jack has shown us, through the world of art—do nevertheless conform to his 'Vision in the form of Youth'; and here again Plotinus is with Keats in praising the beauty of youth. Against those who in youth have seen only its transience, Keats, with Plotinus, saw in the beauty of youth an image of soul's immortal lineaments; writing that 'virtue shining forth in youth is lovely, because consonant to the true virtue, which lies deep in the soul.' Why else do we love fairy-tales, those archetypal stories of the soul, let the proponents of anti-heroes and anti-art say what they will?

Yeats, whose own writings are so full of echoes of Keats—and of Plotinus also—understood that a beautiful body is the likeness of the soul:

> All thought becomes an image and the soul
> Becomes a body: that body and that soul
> Too perfect at the full to lie in a cradle,
> Too lonely for the traffic of the world:
> Body and soul cast out and cast away
> Beyond the visible world.

Plotinus concludes of the beauties of sense that they 'like images and shadows flowing into matter, adorn with spectacles of beauty its formless being, and strike the respective senses with wonder and delight'. How much more philosophical, how much more profoundly true to our human nature, is Keats, poet of sensible beauty, than are those arrogant detractors who have never looked so high.

For the soul is, according to the Platonic tradition, in its nature beautiful, belonging as it does to the order of forms, of which bodies are more or less perfect copies or imprints. It is immersion in matter that obscures the inherent beauty of its lovely forms:

> And as the gold is deformed by the adherence of earthly
> clods, which are no sooner removed than on a sudden the
> gold shines forth with its native purity; and then becomes
> beautiful when separated from natures foreign from its own

—so the soul, when separated from the 'base stains' of its immersion in a material world will 'shine forth with its native beauty'. The soul, according to Plotinus, in its true nature, 'wholly participates of that divine nature which is the fountain of loveliness, and of whatever is allied to the beautiful and fair' and 'the beautiful itself is that which is called beings; and turpitude is of a different nature, and participates more in nonentity than being'. Of what value is an art that shows us only the absence of the unifying and illuminating life of the soul of whom Spenser wrote 'For soul is form and doth the body make'? What young girl, reading the story of Cinderella, identifies herself with the ugly sisters?

But every Platonic school of art, whether the sculptors of Parthenon Frieze Keats with his friend Haydon studied in such detail, or the Renaissance painters, or the English Romantic poets and painters—Keats and Shelley and Blake, Calvert and Samuel Palmer—show the soul its own obscured features. And what higher function has art than to show us our deepest reality?

> Thou, silent form, dost tease us out of thought
> As doth eternity: Cold Pastoral!
> When old age shall this generation waste,
> Thou shalt remain, in midst of other woe
> Than ours, a friend to man, to whom thou say'st,
> 'Beauty is truth, truth beauty,—that is all
> Ye know on earth, and all ye need to know.'

Plotinus's Tractate ends with an eloquent passage describing how the divine principle, the 'fountain of Good', 'every where widely diffusing around the streams of beauty', is called 'the beautiful itself; because, beauty is its immediate offspring'. Therefore it is not either necessary or possible to separate beauty from its principle, and 'you may place the first beautiful and the good in the same principle'. The aspect—beauty—is inseparable from its principle—the Good. If Keats had not read Plotinus's *Concerning the Beautiful* the conformity of his own view of the supreme character of the beautiful to the philosophy of Plotinus would be nothing short of miraculous; and I therefore believe that he had both read and loved this book.

Taylor adds a long footnote in which he attacks 'material-ism and its attendant sensuality 'as the philosophy in vogue, then as now. Keats, who proclaimed the truth of beauty, was not ignorant of the alternative ideologies; he had, on the con-trary, too much reason to know the discrepancy between the archetypal perfection and the so-called 'reality' of the world. For many reasons—and among them, I believe, the specific charac-ter of his own genius—Keats was to die young. But, whatever he might have become, it remains true that he gave perfect and complete expression to his 'Vision in the form of Youth', in all its scope and depth. His work lacks nothing of completeness; to what he knew of the *imaginal* and its beauty experience could have added nothing—could only have misted and obscured that bright Chamber of Maiden Thought. For, as Yeats writes,

> What portion of the world can the artist have
> Who has awakened from the common dream
> But dissipation and despair?

—and Yeats goes on to write of Keats, whose work he had so deeply loved and so well understood:

Hic   And yet
    No one denies to Keats love of the world;
    Remember his deliberate happiness.

Ille His art is happy, but who knows his mind?
    I see a schoolboy when I think of him,
    With face and nose pressed to a sweet-shop window,
    For certainly he sank into his grave
    His senses and his heart unsatisfied,
    And made—being poor, ailing and ignorant,
    Shut out from all the luxury of the world,
    The coarse-bred son of a livery-stable keeper—
    Luxuriant song

(1981)

Hopkins:
Nature and Human Nature

F EW POETS CARRIED to fame, as Hopkins was, on a tide of fashion, speak, as he does, no less immediately to the present generation than to my own in the 1920s. Political and religious ideologies come and go, as do literary fashions; but Hopkins meets us in the one world all share—Catholic and Communist, Imagist and Existentialist, sacramentalist and positivist—the world of the senses, the natural world. Out of our common treasury of sensible nature Hopkins brings 'things both new and old'; the song of the lark, woods carpeted with bluebells in spring, leaf and shadow and cloud moving in the wind; the scents, sounds and feel of things. In 'God's Grandeur' he speaks of our cities where

> Generations have trod, have trod, have trod;
>   And all is seared with trade; bleared, smeared with toil;
>   And wears man's smudge and shares man's smell: the soil
> Is bare now, nor can foot feel, being shod.

> And for all this, nature is never spent;'
>   There lives the dearest freshness deep down things'.

It is this immaculate freshness of the earthly Paradise his poetry gives back to us. Never has the word 'nature' been so richly complex in fullness of meaning as for the Victorians. To the Victorian scientist nature was still something he could, like the painter and the poet, observe with his senses. Yet, from Galileo to Newton, vistas of space had opened; with Darwin, vistas of time. Wordsworth's *Prelude* became the sacred book of a new 'natural religion', whose universe seemed infinitely grander in its mystery than the cosmology of the Churches. History, not nature, had long been the context of Christian theology; and scholars could still in the eighteenth century argue that the earth was created in 4004 BC. Hopkins had learned from Ruskin that scientific structural minuteness of observation which makes his 'inscapes' live for us with such truth and realism. The Lake Poets he thought 'faithful but not rich observers of nature'. But through them, and no less through the paintings of Constable, Turner and their successors—for Hopkins might have been a painter, like some other members of his family, had he not been a poet—he was heir to the richest inheritance any nature poet ever received from his immediate predecessors.

But Hopkins did more than enrich, extend, particularise, the Wordsworthian 'nature' of the Victorians. If Wordsworth re-situated human kind in nature, as prodigals welcomed back to our native country, it remained for Hopkins to re-situate nature in the context of man, and both man and nature within the Christian context which sees man, if not as the be-all, at all events as the end-all of creation. We cannot go 'back' to nature, in the Wordsworthian sense of the pre-human kingdoms. Now that Wordsworth's Lake District has shrunk to a small area of threatened 'environment', Hopkins's 'Binsey Poplars', with its recognition of the scope of human destructiveness, seems prophetic. For better or worse, it is the human kingdom that now reigns on earth, threatening to cut the very roots of the Tree of Life:

> Ten or twelve, only ten or twelve
>   Strokes of havoc únselve
>   The sweet especial scene,
>   Rural scene, a rural scene,
>   Sweet especial rural scene.

But in a far more fundamental sense Hopkins's view of nature begins where Wordsworth's ends. The poem in which he broke that silence self-imposed when he entered the Society of Jesus, 'The Wreck of the Deutschland', celebrates—if that is the word—the encounter of the human soul with nature in her terrible aspect. What hell had been to the older religion, deluge and earthquake and volcano and, above all, shipwreck were to the new 'natural religion', the dark side of the mystery. Hopkins, more realistic than Wordsworth, understood that there could be no piety, natural or supernatural, which leaves out of account 'the raging of the stormy sea and the destructive sword' that Blake called 'portions of eternity too great for the eye of man'. The universe of science seemed to make nothing of the Christian view of man as the object of God's special concern. What to Wordsworth or Turner or Thomas Hardy might seem natural accident within an indifferent universe, the priest must proclaim as the act of God: understood that the God who is, is terrible: 'And here the faithful waver, the faithless fable and miss'.

'The Wreck of the Deutschland' is at once a superb expression of the counter-reformation ideal of sacrifice, and of

nineteenth-century reason wrestling with the nature of an inhuman universe. Hopkins's 'martyr-master' stands with Hardy's
blind President of the Immortals, or Lear's gods, who 'kill us for
their sport':

> I did say yes
> O at lightning and lashed rod;
> Thou heardst me truer than tongue confess
> Thy terror, O Christ, O God.

In such a cry of vanquishment and submission, what an
expression of faith! We must turn to the Psalms or to the Book of
Job for a comparable heroic realism. So understood, this world,
such as it is to human sense and human experience, is the place
of existential encounter with God in his immediate personal
dealings with man. At every time, in every place and situation,
we stand within that confrontation.

> Thou hast bound bones and veins in me, fastened me flesh,
> And after it almost unmade, what with dread,
> Thy doing: and dost thou touch me afresh?
> Over again I feel thy finger and find thee.

No poet was ever more concrete. Perhaps his unmitigated
realism was reinforced by Loyola's Spiritual Exercises, in which
the physical details of the Passion are built up in vivid mental
images. Hopkins re-situated symbol in physical fact. In a ser-
mon he once preached on that potent symbol associated with his
Order, the Sacred Heart, he characteristically insisted on carnal
fact: 'There would', he concedes, 'no doubt be something revolt-
ing in seeing the heart alone, all naked and bleeding, torn from
the breast' but, he goes on, 'Christ's heart is lodged within his

sacred frame and there alone is worshipped.' Not a word about not taking the symbol literally. It is this physicality, this incarnational character, that Yeats understood to be the element in Christianity which scandalised the Greeks. In Yeats's play *The Resurrection* a Greek touches the side of the risen Christ; he recoils with the cry, 'The heart of a phantom is beating'; for, to the Platonic Greeks, the Resurrection of the Body is an outrage. The followers of Yeats's Dionysus sing 'As though God's death were but a play'; but for Hopkins the test of all reality is by flesh and blood.

Yet in Hopkins's realism the symbolic dimension is present. The strength of a symbol is its truth on all levels, including the physical; Coleridge spoke of 'the translucence of the Eternal through and in the Temporal'. 'The Wreck of the Deutschland' is no less symbolic than 'The Ancient Mariner'; nor was Hopkins less familiar than Coleridge with that whole range of neo-Platonic symbolism which likens mortal life to the storm-tossed voyage of Odysseus. The symbol survives in the Anglican rite of baptism in the prayer that the child 'may so pass the waves of this troublesome world, that he may come into the land of everlasting life'. But in Hopkins's poem the symbol is fully incarnated in the physical event. No sea-crossing of dream is so real or so soul-searching; as shipwreck on the high seas.

There was no sympathy between the Jesuit and the young Yeats when their mutual friend Katharine Tynan tried to bring them together in Dublin. Hopkins in a letter to Coventry Patmore objected to a poem by Yeats:

Now this Mosada I cannot think highly of. . . . It was a strained and unworkable allegory about a young man and a sphinx on a rock in the sea; how did they get there? what did they eat? and so on: people think such criticisms very prosaic; but commonsense is never out of place anywhere, neither on Parnassus nor on Tabor nor on the Mount where our Lord preached. . . .

Hopkins, Pater's most brilliant pupil, could have been among the Decadents had he so chosen; he was unimpressed by that decadent chimera the Sphinx.

Of course he was too narrow; and in this respect a man of his time. The twentieth century accords to dreams a reality to which the Victorians were blind. Yeats's 'rough beast' has proved none the less real because it came 'out of *Spiritus Mundi*'. But to each poet his excellence. For Hopkins no dragon of the psyche could strike the terror of 'endragonèd seas'; and he found his nightmare where

> Only the beakleaved boughs dragonish damask the tool-
>   smooth bleak light; black.

Even when in an introspective poem he wrote

> O the mind, mind has mountains; cliffs of fall
> Frightful, sheer, no-man-fathomed

it is likely that he had real cliffs in his mind's eye. In July 1884 he wrote to Bridges, 'Yesterday I went to see the cliffs of Moher on the coast of Clare, which to describe would be long and difficult. In returning across the Bay we were in some considerable danger of our lives'.

Perhaps it is his insistence on physical fact, his bringing of all experience to the test of the incarnational here and now of this world made Hopkins seem so much one of themselves to the positivists of Cambridge in the 1920s. Yet in nothing is he more Catholic than in the sacramentalism of his physicality, which brings the encounter with 'the living God' to the proof of the senses. But when we think of 'nature' in Hopkins's poetry we think not of 'the beat of 'endragonèd seas', nor 'cliffs of fall', but of 'rose-moles all in stipple upon trout that swim', of the sensuous sensual delight of 'spring's universal bliss'. May, 'When weeds, in wheels, shoot long and lovely and lush', was Hopkins's month, as it was Shakespeare's in that same Thames valley both poets loved.

Bluebells were his especial flower, described in his journal as they returned each spring in a wood near Stonyhurst. Here is his entry of May 1871:

> In the little wood/opposite the light/they stood in blackish spreads or sheddings like the spots of a snake. The heads are then like thongs and solemn in grain and grape-colour. But in the clough/through the light/they came in falls of sky-colour washing the brows and slacks of the ground with vein-blue, thickening at the double, vertical themselves and the young grass and brake fern combed vertical, but the brake struck the upright of all this with light winged transomes.

Then he gives the bluebells as they speak to other senses:

> The bluebells in your hand baffle you with their inscape, made to every sense: if you draw your fingers through them they are lodged and struggle/with a shock of wet heads; the long stalks rub and click and flatten to a fan on

one another like your fingers themselves would when you passed the palms hard across one another, making a brittle rub and jostle like the noise of a hurdle strained by leaning against; then there is the faint honey smell and in the mouth the sweet gum when you bite them. But this is easy, it is the eye they baffle. They give one a fancy of panpipes and of some wind instrument with stops—a trombone perhaps. The overhung necks—for growing they are little more than a staff with a simple crook but in water, where they stiffen, they take stronger turns, in the head like sheephooks or, when more waved throughout, like the waves riding through a whip that is being smacked—what with these overhung necks and what with the crisped ruffled bells dropping mostly on one side and the gloss these have at their footstalks they have an air of the knights at chess.

There is much more, as if he could find no end to the simple yet limitless reality before his eyes. At Oxford Hopkins had made a special study of the pre-Socratic philosophers, and especially of Parmenides the Eleatic; who, according to Aristotle, believed in none but a sensible reality: '*It is* and that it is impossible for it not to be, is the way of belief, for truth is its companion.' In his student notes Hopkins said of Parmenides 'His feeling for instress, for the flush and foredrawn, and for inscape/is most striking and from this one can understand Plato's reverence for him as the great father of Realism.' In his description of bluebells Hopkins is affirming, with inexhaustible minuteness, with inexhaustible delight, 'It is'. In his notes on Parmenides he comments, 'indeed I have often felt when I have been in this mood and felt the depth of an instress or how fast the inscape holds a thing that nothing is so pregnant and straightforward to the truth as simple *yes* and *is*.' 'I do not think I have ever seen anything more beautiful than the bluebell I have been looking at. I know the beauty of our Lord by it': for only of the bluebell here and now can we say 'it is'. It could as well have been an ash-twig or an ear of green corn, or a bird's feather: whatever is here and now before his eyes is the most beautiful because it alone is fully real. Being is the attribute not of what was—Proust's *temps perdu*—or of what will be, the heaven of the otherworldly; but only of what is present to human sense. This is nature poetry in its essential purity—the poetry of the outer world, the macrocosm, seen in the mirror of the sense, but (so far as is humanly possible) unclouded by subjectivity.

Coleridge had felt the same overwhelming imaginative impact of the Parmenidean existentialism: 'Hast thou', Coleridge wrote in *The Friend*, 'ever raised thy mind to the consideration of existence, in and by itself, as the mere act of existing? Hast thou ever said to thyself thoughtfully "It is" . . . If thou hast indeed attained to this, thou wilt have felt the presence of a mystery, which must have fixed thy spirit in awe and wonder'. It was, I think, Herbert Read who first called Hopkins an existentialist; and here again positivist and sacramentalist meet on common ground. Hopkins looked not for the immortality of the soul but for the resurrection of the body. In 'The Leaden Echo and the Golden Echo', he wrote,

> See; not a hair is, not an eyelash, not rhe least lash lost;
>   every hair
> Is, hair of the head, numbered.

All these are kept, the poem says, 'yonder'; but Hopkins is not really a poet of the other world, Plotinus's 'yonder' of which this world is the lovely image or shadow. 'The comfort of the resurrection' lies in the promise that the 'it is', here so fleeting, will there be made eternal; not another world, but this world experienced after another manner.

How many of the poems affirm the here and now present to the poet's senses, as in 'Hurrahing in Harvest' (the italics are mine): 'Summer ends *now*; *now*, barbarous in beauty, the stooks arise/Around. . . .' or in 'The Windhover':

> I caught *this morning* morning's minion, king-
>   dom of daylight's dauphin, dapple-dawn-drawn Falcon

and in 'The Starlit Night':

> Look at the stars! look, look up at the skies!
>   O look at all the fire-folk sitting in the air!
>   The bright boroughs, the circle-citadels there!
> Down in dim woods the diamond delves! the elves'-eyes!
> The grey lawns cold where gold, where quickgold lies!

It is with no inward eye that Hopkins beholds bird and stars and harvest fields, but in the ever-new immediacy of sensation. Memory, though it may transmute and distil, though it may immerse in the magical atmosphere of dream, can never recapture the inexhaustible 'isness' of sensible reality. It is in the absolute, the ever-new existence of things from which Hopkins took, and to which he gives, that peculiar, intense and vivid delight that we find in no other poet.

Hopkins's most characteristic images are really long complex nominatives—not so much phrases as words, naming the 'It is':

'drop-of-blood-and-foam-dapple/Bloom'; 'Wiry and white-fiery and whirlwind-swivellèd snow'; 'wimpled-water-dimpled, not-by-morning-matchèd face'. Adam in Paradise did not describe but 'named' the creatures; for the nominative is the nearest that man can come to nature. Of these lost names Hopkins recaptures for us a few fragments—for they are limitless as being itself—in his poetry; 'The Windhover' is a complex Parmenidean affirmation:

> dapple-dawn-drawn Falcon, in his riding
> Of the rolling level underneath him steady air, and
> striding
> High there, how he rung upon the rein of a wimpling wing
> In his ecstasy!

What is, according to Parmenides, is 'a finite, spherical, corporeal plenum and there is nothing beyond it'. All exists for ever within the whole, each thing in its place, instressed by 'the bonds of strong Necessity', the laws of nature. The Parmenidean plenum comes very near the modern picture of the universe in which space and time are relative, are dimensions. Nothing therefore can be considered in itself, as if in isolation. There is only one whole—the all; and truly modern is Hopkins's sense of what we now call ecology—the structure of the whole of a landscape, or cloudscape, or river valley. Like Ruskin, like Turner himself, he studied closely not only the 'inscape' of some single leaf or single tree, but whole natural formations of wind and cloud, rock and water. Cloudscape is instressed by wind, as in 'That Nature is a Heraclitean Fire':

> Cloud-puffball, torn tufts, tossed pillows | flaunt forth, then
> chevy on an air-

built thoroughfare: heaven-roysters, in gay-gangs | they
    throng; they glitter in marches.

Or the Binsey Poplars with the play of wind and sun and shadow:

My aspens dear, whose airy cages quelled,
Quelled or quenched in leaves the leaping sun,
All felled, felled, are all felled;
    Of a fresh and following folded rank
        Not spared, not one
        That dandled a sandalled
        Shadow that swam or sank
On meadow and river and wind-wandering weed-winding
    bank.

The 'inscape' is not of the trees alone but of the whole 'sweet,
especial, rural scene'. The characteristic continuous motion of
the long-stalked aspen-leaves, first seen in play against the morning sky as they 'quelled or quenched the leaping sun', then in the
no less lovely play of the shadows, 'sandalled' because they seem
to tread the ground, while others 'swam or sank' in the water,
imparts to a rivery landscape the trees' delicate motion. The
image is not the sum of its parts but a living indivisible whole.

    In his latest poems Hopkins's great unified images have the
coherence of musical phrases. The opening lines of the sonnet
'Spelt from Sibyl's Leaves' is like a single word that utters the
approach of darkness:

Earnest, earthless, equal, attuneable, | vaulty, voluminous
. . . stupendous

Evening strains to be time's vást, | womb-of-all, home-of-all, hearse-of-all night.

Hopkins at Oxford had noted that 'the two [Parmenidean] principles are fire and earth or, as he puts it, "ethery flame of fire, comforting the heart (he is thinking of it perhaps as a vital principle), marvellously subtle, throughout one with itself, *not* one with the other" and "unmeaning (?'???) night, thick and wedgèd body".' Nature's 'million-fuellèd bonfire' is Heraclitean; but those characteristic images of fire breaking from reluctant earth are surely Parmenidean: 'It will flame out, like shining from shook foil'; 'As kingfishers catch fire, dragonflies draw flame'. In 'The Windhover' fire breaks from the clods of earth as

> shéer plód makes plough down sillion
> Shine, and blue-bleak embers, ah my dear,
> Fall, gall themselves, and gash gold-vermilion.

The 'fresh-firecoal chestnut-falls' of nature have their human echo in the splendid image of Felix Randal at 'the random grim forge' striking fire from the 'thick and wedgèd body' of the iron; the man is matched in the 'great grey drayhorse' with his 'bright and battering sandal' whose iron also strikes fire from stone.

As there is no separation of parts in an ecological whole, so the oneness of being is received through every sense at once— sight, touch, taste; and above all through the poet's fine musician's ear. In 'The Sea and the Skylark' the song of the bird is evoked in a single seamless phrase:

> Left hand, off land, I hear the lark ascend,
> His rash-fresh re-winded new-skeinèd score

> In crisps of curl off wild winch whirl, and pour
> And pelt music, till none's to spill nor spend.

In a wonderful letter to Bridges he explains what his friend had found obscure:

> 'Rash-fresh more' (it is dreadful to explain these things in cold blood) means a headlong and exciting new snatch of singing, resumption by the lark of his song, which by turns he gives over and takes up again all day long, and this goes on, the sonnet says, through all time, without ever losing its first freshness, being a thing both new and old . . . the skein and coil are the lark's song, which from his height gives the impression (not to me only) of something falling to the earth and not vertically quite but tricklingly or wavingly, something as a skein of silk ribbed by having been tightly wound on a narrow card or a notched holder or as fishing-tackle or twine unwinding from a reel or winch.

The letter goes on to describe how

> the lark in wild glee races the reel round, paying or dealing out and down the turns of the skein or coil right to the earth floor, the ground, where it lies in a heap, as it were, or rather is all wound off on to another winch, reel, bobbin, or spool in Fancy's eye by the moment the bird touches earth and so is ready for a fresh unwinding at the next flight.

Again, the whole passage is one long nominative phrase. For Hopkins the lark is its song as the windhover is its flight; form—inscape—is the signature of the 'instress' of energy, 'live and lancing like the blowpipe flame', to use the poet's own image of the creative act of God. No bird of Hopkins's could be put in those natural history museums dear to Victorians; for the bone and feather is only the signature of the soaring singing life whose impress it bears:

> Each mortal thing does one thing and the same:
> Deals out that being indoors each one dwells;
> Selves—goes itself; *myself* it speaks and spells,
> Crying *Whát I dó is me: for that I came.*

There is a curious convergence between Hopkins and Blake, both of whom opposed to the materialist view of nature the more ancient—and also more modern—view of each creature as an unique and distinct impulse of life; 'their habitations/And their pursuits as different as their forms and as their joys'—as Blake says.

It was the Rev. M. C. D'Arcy S. J. who once said to me—and I have since wondered if he had Hopkins in mind at the time—that 'all poets are pantheists'; for if Hopkins could not permit himself to think as a pantheist he could not prevent himself from feeling as one.

> The world is charged with the grandeur of God.
>   It will flame out, like shining from shook foil;
>   It gathers to a greatness, like the ooze of oil
> Crushed.

That other nature mystic of the Society of Jesus, Teilhard de Chardin, perceived that transubstantiation, the central mystery of the Catholic faith, must in its nature transform the whole world. He describes in *Hymn of the Universe* a vision which came to him in meditation before a monstrance: 'I had then the impression as I gazed at the host that its surface was gradually spreading out like a spot of oil but of course much more swiftly and luminously'. This flow of whiteness extended until it seemed to be 'illuminating the universe from within, and everything were fashioned of the same kind of translucent flesh. . . . So, through the mysterious expansion of the host the whole world had become incandescent, had itself become like a single giant host.' Had become, in other words, the mystical body; the Parmenidean 'It is' becomes, in the vision of the cosmic Christ, the Biblical 'I am'.

Again there is a strange convergence of Hopkins, Teilhard, and Blake. Blake's masters—Paracelsus, Jakob Boehme, Swedenborg—were all within, or strongly influenced by, the tradition of alchemy, with its consistent refusal—down to Goethe and his most recent follower, Rudolf Steiner—of a mechanistic view of nature. There is a *deus absconditus* scattered, distributed, like the dismembered body of Osiris, throughout the physical world. Like Osiris this hidden god must at last be reassembled and resurrected. In a long magnificent passage inspired by these esoteric teachings Blake wrote that

> Man looks out in tree & herb & fish & bird & beast
> Collecting up the scatterd portions of his immortal body
> Into the Elemental forms of everything that grows

and concludes:

> wherever a grass grows
> Or a leaf buds, The Eternal Man is seen, is heard, is felt,
> And all his sorrows, till he reassumes his ancient bliss.

Blake's Eternal Man is, like Teilhard's Christ, the Emergent Person of the universe; and Hopkins in 'Hurrahing in Harvest' had divined the same cosmic being:

> I walk, I lift up, I lift up heart, eyes,
> Down all that glory in the heavens to glean our Saviour.

As plainly as Blake or as Teilhard, Hopkins saw the world as His body:

> And the azurous hung hills are his world-wielding shoulder
>   Majestic—as a stallion stalwart, very-violet-sweet!—
> These things, these things were here and but the beholder
>   Wanting.

Hopkins even in his earliest writings often observes a tendency in natural forms towards the human countenance. In a journal he writes of clouds: 'fine shapeless skins of fretted make, full of eyebrows or like linings of curled leaves'; 'rotten-woven cloud which shapes in leaf over leaf of wavy or eyebrow texture'; 'Rarer and wilder pack have sometimes film [of vapour] in the sheet, which may be caught as it turns on the edge of the cloud like an outlying eyebrow'. Hopkins as he gazes at these shape-shifting clouds, or at the stars 'fire-featuring heaven', seems to be awaiting some ultimate metamorphosis he felt to be imminent. Blake had written: 'Think of a white cloud as being holy, you cannot love it; but think of a holy man within the cloud, love springs up in your thoughts, for to think of holiness distinct from man is impossible to the affections.' So it certainly was for Hopkins, as here in 'The Wreck of the Deutschland':

> I kiss my hand
>   To the stars, lovely-asunder
> Starlight, wafting him out of it; and
>   Glow, glory in thunder;
> Kiss my hand to the dappled-with-damson west:
> Since, tho' he is under the world's splendour and wonder,
>   His mystery must be instressed, stressed;
> For I greet him the days I meet him, and bless when
>   I understand.

The 'instressing' of the divine mystery again reminds us of Blake, and the Hermetic travail of nature as it struggles to give birth to the Eternal Man. It is in human consciousness—in Blake's 'divine humanity'—that nature's mere being becomes a person; man is the 'beholder wanting'. Blake had said that 'Nature without Man is barren', he was criticising Wordsworth's 'natural religion'. Hopkins too, at once more modern and more faithful to tradition, restores to man the centrality of which nineteenth-century science seemed for a time to have deprived us:

> And what is Earth's eye, tongue, or heart else, where
> Else, but in dear and dogged man?

Dear and dogged man: for the priest, as for the communist, there is only man; one Adam, one Christ. Far from Hopkins was 'the cult of the individual'. He loved the natural man with a priestly and compassionate love. If Wordsworth too often approached common humanity in the spirit of the man with a questionnaire, Hopkins never did so. Felix Randal the farrier is his son in religion; so is the young bugler to whom he gave his first communion:

I in a sort deserye to
And do serve God to serve to
Just such slips of soldiery Christ's royal ration.

In the young boy server of the handsome heart, the brothers at
the Stonyhurst school play, he saw in human nature a beauty
that moved him to exclaim, in 'Brothers':

Ah Nature, framed in fault,
There's comfort then, there's salt;
Nature, bad, base, and blind,
Dearly thou canst be kind;
There dearly thén, deárly,
I'll cry thou canst be kind.

Faithful to his realism, his Christian incarnationalism, he
cared for the body no less than the soul: 'What I most dislike in
towns and in London in particular', he wrote in a letter, is 'the
illshapen degraded physical (putting aside moral) type of so many
of the people.' For him a man is never more human, more fully
expressive of our 'nature', than in physical action. As the bird is
its flight and its song, so a man is what he does: 'Acts in God's
eye what in God's eye he is'. Felix Randal's deathbed thoughts
are dismissed in a manner prosaic and perfunctory: 'Impatient,
he cursed at first, but mended/Being anointed and all;' But the
farrier is made immortal in the physical glory of his act:

When thou at the random grim forge, powerful amidst
    peers,
Didst fettle for the great grey drayhorse his bright and bat-
    tering sandal!

With the eye of a sculptor he sees the beauty of Harry Ploughman's 'sinew service':

> Hard as hurdle arms, with a broth of goldish flue
> Breathed round; the rack of ribs; the scooped flank; lank
> Rope-over thigh; knee-nave; and barrelled shank—
>   Head and foot, shoulder and shank—
> By a grey eye's heed steered well, one crew, fall to;
> Stand at stress. Each limb's barrowy brawn, his thew
> That onewhere curded, onewhere sucked or sank—
>   Soared ór sánk—,
>
> Though as a beechbole firm, finds his, as at a roll-call, rank
> And features, in flesh, what deed he each must do—
>   His sinew-service where do.

The worst outrage against the common man—Tom the Navvy— is unemployment; for so he is unable to enact what he is, is no more himself than 'a dare-gale skylark scanted in a dull cage':

>   by Despair, bred Hangdog dull; by Rage,
> Manwolf, worse; and their packs infest the age.

By the same token there is no heroism of the mind to equal the simple heroism of the soldier who pledges his body to his country's service. We would be wrong to dismiss Hopkins's praise of soldiers and sailors as Victorian militarism: to do so would be to miss the gospel simplicity of the test—a man cannot give more than his life:

>   'So God-made flesh does too:
> Were I come o'er again' cries Christ 'it should be this'.

The young soldier is the type of Christ's sacrifice:

Yes. Why do we áll, seeing of a soldier, bless him? bless
Our redcoats, our tars? Both these being, the greater part,
But frail clay, nay but foul clay. Here it is: the heart,
Since, proud, it calls the calling manly, gives a guess
That, hopes that, makesbelieve, the men must be no less;
It fancies, feigns, deems, dears the artist after his art;
And fain will find as sterling all as all is smart,
And scarlet wear the spirit of wár thére express.

We think of Hardy, of the Trumpet Major and his sailor brother,
or Sergeant Troy who dazzled Bathsheba Everdene with sword-
play, in which Hopkins would have seen something more than
trivial, for 'the spirit of wár thére express'.

He did in fact greatly admire Hardy, unrivalled novelist of
natural humanity, of simple people whose expression is all in
their action: Giles Winterbourne, planter of trees; Gabriel Oak,
shearing sheep. He loved William Barnes, too: 'It is his natural-
ness that strikes me most,' he wrote to Coventry Patmore,

> he is like an embodiment or incarnation or manmuse of the
> country, of Dorset, or rustic life and humanity. He comes,
> like Homer and all poets of native epic, provided with epi-
> thets, images, and so on which seem to have been tested and
> digested for a long age in their native air and circumstances
> and to have a keeping which nothing else could give.

Perhaps because of his almost nostalgic affection for human
simplicity from which he was himself, by birth, education and
vocation so far removed, Hopkins sometimes adopted dialect
words whose richness and aptness in their own context appealed
to him: sometimes splendidly, as 'didst *fettle* for the great grey

drayhorse his bright and battering sandal!' But what in Barnes (or in the speech of lay-brothers and simple parishioners) he admired as 'in keeping' is, in his own educated English diction, sometimes embarrassingly out of keeping; Felix Randal, 'anointed *and all*'; the cockney 'seeing *of* a soldier'; 'his treat' for the bugler-boy's first communion, and the use of native Scotch words in poems written in Scotland by this very English Englishman.

'Duns Scotus's Oxford' praises the philosopher not for his originality but as 'of realty the rarest-veinèd unraveller'— Parmenides' reality, the same for all. In his sonnet on Henry Purcell *'the poet wishes well to the divine genius of Purcell and praises him that, whereas other musicians have given utterance to the moods of man's mind, he has, beyond that, uttered in notes the very make and species of man as created both in him and in all men generally'*. One might say that nineteenth-century Romantic poetry also gives utterance to 'the moods of man's mind'; and in his generation Hopkins stands almost alone as representing the classical view of man. If Romanticism is a flowering of the highly civilised ideal of the fullest possible realisation of the uniqueness of every individual human being—Browning's *Men and Women*—Catholicism (and within its narrower limits Marxism) never loses sight of the classical bedrock of common humanity: man and woman. By a seeming paradox—so Hopkins understood—the greatest genius comes nearest to the universal human nature; having fewer blemishes, perhaps, to obscure the 'image of God' in which Everyman is created.

In the same way he considered the judgement of an educated man to be marked not by that 'originality' so overvalued in the academic world, but by a nearer and truer approximation to the human norm. He reproved his friend Robert Bridges, in a letter, for his singularity: 'So far as I see, where we differ in judgment, my judgments are less singular than yours; I agree more than you do with the mob and with the *communis criticorum*. Presumably I shd. agree with these still more if I read more and so differ still more from you than now'—so he teases his distinguished friend, who for so long withheld Hopkins's poems from publication on account of what seemed to him their singularity and incomprehensibility.

Coventry Patmore too comes in for a rebuke for being too far removed from the old Adam: 'there is an old Adam of barbarism, boyishness, wildness, rawness, rankness, the disreputable, the unrefined in the refined and educated. It is that that I meant by tykishness (a tyke is a stray sly unowned dog) and said you have none of; and I did also think that you were without all sympathy for it and must survey it when you met with it wholly from without. . . . I thought it was well to have ever so little of it,' he concludes, 'and therefore it was perhaps a happy thing that you were entrapped into the vice of immoderate smoking, for to know one yields to a vice must help to humanise and make tolerant.' Hopkins admired Stevenson's *Dr Jekyll and Mr Hyde* and felt, most refined, most sensitive, most cultured of gentlemen and most scrupulous of priests, that he understood it from within.

Why then was Hopkins so merciless on his own 'poor Jackself'? 'My vocation puts before me a standard so high that a higher can be found nowhere else,' he had written to his Anglican friend, Canon Dixon. To blame the Society of Jesus for his self-imposed vow to write no poetry unless expressly ordered to do so in the service of his vocation would be absurd; the Society has fostered (for the greater glory of God) every kind of talent. At most the Society provided a context which permitted, which perhaps approved of, Hopkins's surely mistaken belief that the immolation of his talent was a gift more pleasing to God than its exercise. There is in the history of the Church (we may see it by walking round any gallery of Christian art) a strain of perverse morbidity, an excessive dwelling upon the tortures of martyrdom, as if these tragic consequences of evil were good in themselves. How well Hopkins knew that, in Blake's words, 'energy is eternal delight', not only in flower and bird, but in Felix Randal, in Harry Ploughman; yet forbade it to himself:

> only what word
> Wisest my heart breeds dark heaven's baffling ban
> Bars or hell's spell thwarts.

In Hopkins's invocation of 'lightning and lashed rod' there is both heroism and—I cannot but feel—some unresolved and finally self-destructive morbidity; which in no way lessens the greatness of the poetry in which he has recorded his encounter with the 'martyr-master' of his dark faith, as in 'Carrion Comfort':

> But ah, but O thou terrible, why wouldst thou rude on me
> Thy wring-world right foot rock? lay a lionlimb against me?
>   scan
> With darksome devouring eyes my bruisèd bones? and fan,
> O in turns of tempest, me heaped there; me frantic to avoid
>   thee and flee?

The image suggests Blake's illustration to the Book of Job in which Satan the Selfhood, master of disguises, masquerades, with cloven hoof, as the Most High. The conceit in 'The Wreck of the Deutschland' which compares God's infliction of suffering to the crunching of a ripe and luscious but bitter fruit suggests Moloch rather than Christ:

> How a lush-kept plush-capped sloe
>   Will, mouthed to flesh-burst,
> Gush!—flush the man, the being with it, sour or sweet,
> Brim, in a flash, full!

The 'gush'—'flush' bursting image is repellent as the exquisitely painted bleeding wound of some martyrdom or crucifixion.

Yet in our own extremity, with what fullness, with what dignity of endurance he companions us. As many of the Psalms, or the Book of Job, those ancient poems to which countless generations have turned in their darkest sorrow, Hopkins has in his 'terrible' sonnets found words of utterance for whoever, 'pitched past pitch of grief', finds himself in the utmost solitudes of desolation. The quality, the degree of sensitivity, recalls a passage in Proust whose insomnia made the night seem endless:

> I wake and feel the fell of dark, not day.
> What hours, O what black hoürs we have spent
> This night! what sights you, heart, saw; ways you went!
> And more must, in yet longer light's delay.
>   With witness I speak this. But where I say
> Hours I mean years, mean life.

Nothing is simple: and we may see in Hopkins's seemingly needless self-immolation the heroism of the life-venturing mountaineer or air-pilot who for its own sake succumbs to 'the fascination of what's difficult'. Are not those spirits who explore the utmost limits, the extremes of joy and grief, all the states of the human soul, the growing-point of our humanity? 'The whole

creation groaneth and travaileth in pain until now,' St Paul
wrote; 'His mystery must be instressed, stressed'; and the instress
of creation falls on 'dear and dogged man'. In man nature struggles to give birth to the hidden god, the Person of the universe.
This for Hopkins is the epiphany (as for Blake before him and
Teilhard de Chardin since) towards which, in ecstasy as in grief,
we strive. 'The just man'—and for Hopkins the just man is red-
coat and tar, the seaman of the Deutschland, 'handy and brave'
'pitched to his death at a blow', is the farrier and the ploughman,
the simple people of 'a house where all were good/To me, God
knows, deserving no such thing', the lay-brother who 'watched
the door'—the just man

> Acts in God's eye what in God's eye he is—
> Christ for Christ plays in ten thousand places,
> Lovely in limbs, and lovely in eyes not his
> To the Father through the features of men's faces.

(1972)

Yeats's Holy City of Byzantium

WHAT IS THE city? The city is not to be found in nature—it is an uniquely human creation—indeed it is *the* uniquely human creation. The city is the dwelling-place humanity has created for itself; but that habitation is not the buildings alone. Architecture is more than building, it is an idea which informs the structure of bricks or stone. I. A. Richards, who loved Plato, called poetry 'the house of the soul', and a city is built not for the body alone but for the soul. The city is the embodiment of the human kingdom of the Imagination, in all its regions, and only when the body, soul and spirit of humanity are given expression can we feel ourselves to be its citizens in the full sense.

A. K. Coomaraswamy, in an essay entitled 'What is Civilisation?', describes Plato's idea of a cosmic city of the world, whose structure is the same as that of every individual soul. The same four functions, or energies, or castes (Plato writes) are to be found in the city and in each of its inhabitants; the law which governs the city is the same law which governs human nature. The principle of justice, therefore, is the same throughout, and that is, that each member of the community should perform the task for which he is best fitted by nature. This of course is the original intent of India's long-enduring caste system.

This archetypal city is a 'holy' city for as the 'heart' is the living centre of the body, so the 'heart' of the city is a sacred *temenos*—church or temple or mosque—around which expands as from a centre all the rich differentiation of the city's life in duodecimal zodiac of the 'tribes' of men. And as the one sun lights the whole world, so the one divine Self illuminates the invisible city.

The type of all Cities of God is, within Christendom, St John's New Jerusalem 'coming down from God out of heaven'. The city, that is, is given by revelation, by inspiration to the soul, for the Kingdom of Heaven is within. St John's city is a perfect cube, with three gates on each of its four walls; comparable mandala structures can be found all over the world, and it seems that this plan of the city is innate in the human imagination everywhere. The city of Jerusalem itself, and its Temple, conformed to this pattern in many essential respects; and the city of Byzantium was deliberately built as a holy city in conformity with the Christian archetype. It is arguable that our modern secular cities are not true cities since they do not conform to the innate pattern at whose heart is the *temenos* or sacred enclosure from which the life of the city naturally grows, Iawmaking and administration, all the skills and crafts, the learning and the arts producing whatever of use and beauty humankind needs and enjoys. In the absence of this pattern we feel ourselves in exile. Anywhere in the world this natural structure will begin to form and differentiate itself in a division of labour according to knowledge and skills whose endless refinements have perhaps never so marvellously flourished as in Byzantium—so at least Yeats believed.

The city of Byzantium was established on the older Greek site by the emperor Constantine in the year 352 and continued for more than a thousand years, until its conquest, under Constantine II, by Mohammed II in 1453. Constantine was the first emperor to declare Christianity the official religion of the Roman empire; and he built Byzantium as the first Christian city.

Yeats's master, William Blake, had already made the Holy City his theme in works that Yeats knew well, for he was the first editor of Blake's Prophetic Books. Blake's great mythological poem *Jerusalem* bears the name of the archetypal city itself. This eternal city was to be embodied in Blake's own city of London, 'here on the banks of Thames builded Jerusalem'. Blake describes in great elaboration the fourfold structure of the City of Golgonooza, the 'Spiritual Fourfold/London continually building & continually decaying desolate'. Its builders are all those who practise the virtues of pity and compassion, love and kindness and mercy, devotion and thanksgiving. In many pages he indicts the 'cruelty' of the 'natural religion' which denies the invisible kingdom and its Master. Blake describes in great elaboration the fourfold structure of the City of Golgonooza, the 'Spiritual Fourfold London'. Blake also describes the part played by the arts in building beautiful forms that the generating souls can 'inhabit', the 'houses and gardens and fields' of the imagination. Yeats would not have differed from Blake in these things but was himself a poet for whom wisdom and beauty, rather than Plato's justice and law, or Blake's 'mercy, pity, peace and love' were paramount. In the two poems in which he writes of his 'holy city of Byzantium' we are in a world very different from Blake's Jerusalem; and yet Yeats too pays homage to the same Invisible Master, for he chose Byzantium, a Christian city, as his symbol, although for the 'god within' Yeats does not use the name of Jesus, but rather the Platonic term, 'intellect'.

YEATS'S 'HOLY CITY of Byzantium' is rather that of Justinian than that of Constantine. He had seen (in Italy) the Ravenna mosaics of the reign of Justinian. His two poems 'Sailing to Byzantium' and 'Byzantium' take Byzantium as a symbol which enables the poet to make his own statement, and his own contribution to that universal city of which Plato spoke.

'Sailing to Byzantium' begins by saying what the city is not: it is not a part of nature but that city of the Imagination discerned by the soul. No poet has been more responsive to mortal beauty than was Yeats; and I remember the cold shock with which, in my twenties, I found the poet of 'The Lake Isle of Innisfree' renouncing the beautiful natural world for 'monuments of unageing intellect' which at that time seemed to me abstract and life-denying:

> That is no country for old men. The young
> In one another's arms, birds in the trees,
> —Those dying generations—at their song,
> The salmon-falls, the mackerel-crowded seas,
> Fish, flesh, or fowl, commend all summer long
> Whatever is begotten, born, and dies.
> Caught in that sensual music all neglect
> Monuments of unageing intellect.

But Yeats still hears in renouncing 'those dying generations at their song', that music: for what then is that renunciation made that the poet should see it as an order higher than nature? According to a Platonic fable (*The Politicus*), echoed by Plotinus,

in youth the soul is feeble and the body full of life, while as the
body ages the soul grows younger towards its perfection; and
this is the theme of the second stanza:

> An aged man is but a paltry thing,
> A tattered coat upon a stick, unless
> Soul clap its hands and sing, and louder sing
> For every tatter in its mortal dress,
> Nor is there singing school but studying
> Monuments of its own magnificence;
> And therefore I have sailed the seas and come
> To the holy city of Byzantium.

To the secular West for whom the bodily life is all and its death
the end, where women cling to their fading beauty and men to
their declining powers, an aged man is indeed a 'paltry thing', no
better than a scarecrow, 'a tattered coat upon a stick'.

Therefore Yeats crosses those 'mackerel-crowded seas' to
reach the 'holy city of Byzantium', city of the arts, there to study
the soul's creations, 'Monuments of its own magnificence.' With
that powerful word he declares his own allegiance to another
order than that of nature—the universe of the soul of which all
art is an embodiment. In the absence of any real conviction that
such an order exists at all, the centuries of Western materialism
have clung to descriptions of nature as the theme of art—unlike
spiritual civilisations of the past for whom the invisible order of
the soul's life has been the theme of poets and painters. Yeats
takes as his 'singing school' that order of art which tells not of
nature but of soul's world. Blake too had declared that 'There is
No Natural Religion', and reproached Wordsworth, great poet
as he was, saying 'Wordsworth must know that what he Writes

Valuable is Not to be found in Nature. Read Michael Angelo's
Sonnet, vol. 2, p. 179:

> Heaven-born, the Soul a heaven-ward course must hold
> Beyond the visible world. . . .'

Her own magnificence lies within, and that magnificence is
the image of the heavenly city. In *A Vision* Yeats sets forth his
great unifying symbol of 'the phases of the moon'. In the section
on the movement of the Great Year of history through those
phases he gave his reasons for choosing Byzantium as symbol of
the supreme moment of fulfilment, in 'phase fifteen', when the
moon is at the full and the world of the soul comes to perfection.
'This is a phase of complete beauty', he wrote, 'Now contemplation and desire, united into one, inhabit a world where every
beloved image has bodily form, and every bodily form is loved'.

For more than a thousand years Byzantium was the wonder
of the world. Geographically and culturally situated between the
Mediterranean world of Europe and Egypt, it was open to the
culture of Greece and Persia and in due course to the empire of
the Caliphs, trading with Russia, India and China. As Byzantium
waxed, Imperial Rome waned; unrivalled in power and wealth,
Byzantium contained, in her days of glory, some million citizens. Standing between the Eastern and the Western worlds, she
imported rich silks from China, spices from India, her learning
from Greece, culture from Persia. Works of art from the four
quarters of the known world poured into her treasuries, while
her churches, palaces, theatres, libraries, baths and stadium were
the creation of her builders and craftsmen. The earlier church
of Hagia Sophia was destroyed by fire in the reign of Justinian
and Theodora (sixth century) who thereafter rebuilt, in less than

six years, the great church of the Holy Wisdom which Justinian proudly claimed surpassed the legendary Temple of Solomon in Jerusalem. Now a mosque, the rich mosaics of holy personages have gone, but the lustre of marbles of various colours, jasper and porphyry and precious gems and metals which dazzled the eyes of barbarians from the distant lands of the Roman empire remain. Above all the great dome, an architectural marvel, would then have been inlaid with those mosaic figures who seem to stand in an optical space outside, not behind, the surface on which they gleam. Yeats had himself seen the mosaics of Ravenna, likewise the work of Justinian and Theodora. The Goddess of Wisdom, in her Greek form, had long been worshipped as Pallas Athene when Athens was the great city; and it was not to any of the Christian saints but to the Holy Wisdom that Byzantium's great church was dedicated, and it is the 'sages', not the saints, of Byzantium whom Yeats summons to be the 'singing-masters' of a poet who sought above all for the divine wisdom beyond any sect. Christians do not speak of 'sages', a word that refers rather to the Greek philosophers, and, for Yeats himself, also those of other traditions, those of India especially:

O sages standing in God's holy fire
As in the gold mosaic of a wall,
Come from the holy fire, pern in a gyre,
And be the singing-masters of my soul.
Consume my heart away; sick with desire
And fastened to a dying animal
It knows not what it is; and gather me
Into the artifice of eternity.

Yeats saw the works of the human imagination—the 'artifice' of civilisation—as a copy not of nature but of 'eternity', the timeless world of the soul made according to the archetype 'on earth as it is in heaven'—the task enjoined to humankind by the Lord Jesus himself. From that sacred wisdom—that unifying vision—flow all peripheral forms, as in the Irish holy books, themselves a flowering on the far margins of the civilised world of the art of Byzantium, in the richness of golden lettering and the flowing designs where 'fish, flesh or fowl' disport themselves in the joy of life.

In his essay on the phases of history in *A Vision*, entitled 'Dove or Swan'—the Dove of Christianity or the Swan of Leda from whose eggs came the Greek epic of Troy—Yeats gives his reasons for choosing Byzantium, at

> the moment when Byzantium became Byzantine and substituted for formal Roman magnificence, with its glorification of physical power, an architecture that suggests the Sacred City in the Apocalypse of St John. I think if I could be given a month of Antiquity and leave to spend it where I chose, I would spend it in Byzantium a little before Justinian opened St. Sophia and closed the Academy of Plato. I think I could find in some little wine-shop some philosophical worker in mosaic who could answer all my questions, the supernatural descending nearer to him than to Plotinus even. . . .
>
> I think that in early Byzantium, maybe never before or since in recorded history, religious, aesthetic and practical life were one, that architect and artificers—though not, it may be, poets, for language had been the instrument of controversy and must have grown abstract—spoke to

the multitude and the few alike. The painter, the mosaic worker, the worker in gold and silver, the illuminator of sacred books, were almost impersonal, almost perhaps without the consciousness of individual design, absorbed in their subject-matter and that the vision of a whole people. They could copy out of old Gospel books those pictures that seemed as sacred as the text, and yet weave all into a vast design, the work of many that seemed the work of one, that made building, picture, pattern, metal-work of rail and lamp, seem but a single image; and this vision, this proclamation of their invisible master, had the Greek nobility. . . .

And that, for Yeats, *is* civilisation, whose unity is not a political but an imaginative unity, from that shared vision of the universal archetype.

From the sages of the Holy wisdom we pass to the golden birds and the golden foliage of artifice in the Emperor's palace, type surely of those palaces whose splendour is described in the fairy-tales of all the world, from the poorest crofts and cabins of Western Ireland to the dark winters of Norway and Russia.

Once out of nature I shall never take
My bodily form from any natural thing,
But such a form as Grecian goldsmiths make
Of hammered gold and gold enamelling
To keep a drowsy Emperor awake;
Or set upon a golden bough to sing
To lords and ladies of Byzantium
Of what is past, or passing, or to come.

Here is Gibbon's description of the Emperor's palace, which
reads more like a passage from one of the world's fairy-tales
than from a work of history:

> the square before the sigma was decorated by a fountain,
> and the margin of the bason was lined and encompassed
> with plates of silver. In the beginning of each season, the
> bason, instead of water, was replenished with the most
> exquisite fruits, which were abandoned to the populace for
> the entertainment of the prince. He enjoyed this tumultu-
> ous spectacle from a throne resplendent with gold and gems
> which was raised by a marble staircase to the height of a
> lofty terrace. Below the throne were seated the officers of
> his guards, the magistrates, the chiefs of the factions of the
> circus; the inferior steps were occupied by the people, and
> the place below was covered with troops of dancers, singers
> and pantomimes. The square was surrounded by the hall
> of justice, the arsenal, and the various offices of business
> and pleasure; and the purple chamber was named from the
> annual distribution of robes of scarlet and purple by the
> hand of the empress herself. The long series of apartments
> was adapted to the seasons, and decorated with marble and
> porphyry, with painting, sculpture, and mosaics, with a
> profusion of gold, silver, and precious stones. His fanciful
> magnificence employed the skill and patience of such artists
> as the times could afford.

—and here Gibbon who had little taste for works of the imagination and ranked generals and armies above philosophers and
artists, cannot refrain from scorn—

but the taste of Athens would have despised their frivo-
lous but costly labours: a golden tree, with its leaves and
branches that sheltered a multitude of birds, that warbled
their artificial notes, and two lions of massy gold, and of the
natural size, who looked, and roared, like their brothers in
the forest.

The Caliph of Baghdad possessed the like:

a tree of gold and silver spreading into eighteen large
branches, on which, and on the lesser boughs, sat a variety
of birds made of the same precious metals, as well as the
leaves of the tree, while the machinery affected spontaneous
motions, the several birds warbled their natural harmony.

Yeats saw Eastern (Persian) influence in those golden vines
'whose tendrils climb everywhere and display among their leaves
all those strange images of bird and beast, those forms that represent no creature eye has ever seen, yet are begotten one upon
the other as if they were themselves living creatures'. Yeats might
have been describing a page from one of Ireland's holy books,
themselves reflecting the Byzantine style.

Gibbon may have despised such things but nor so the world-
wide anonymous imagination that builds invisible palaces!
Perhaps it would be better if the poor of the world all received
washing-machines and television sets, but we should remember that the price would be the inestimable treasuries of the
Imagination. The rarest diamonds are after all only pebbles, and
pearls the secretions of an injured mollusc—it is the magic, the
enchantment, of Imagination alone that creates all human splendour. As Yeats understood when he wrote in his Introduction to

Lady Gregory's collection of *Gods and Fighting Men*, a book of Irish myths and legends:

> Children play at being great and wonderful people, at the ambitions they will put away for one reason and another before they grow into ordinary men and women. Mankind as a whole had a like dream once; everybody and nobody built up the dream bit by bit and the story-tellers are there to make us remember.

Yeats knew in the West of Ireland such people, poor in goods but rich in stories; and writes,

> The poor fisher has no possessions of the world and so no responsibility for it, and if he dreams of a love-gift better than the brown shawl that seems too common for poetry why should he not dream of a glove made of the skin of a bird, or shoes made from the skin of a fish, or a coat made from the glittering garment of the salmon? Was it not Aeschylus who said he but served up dishes from the banquet of Homer?—but Homer himself found the great banquet on an earthen floor and under a broken roof.

In the same foreword to Lady Gregory's book he continues,

> I have read in a fabulous book that Adam had but to imagine a bird and it was born into life, and that he created all things out of himself by nothing more important than an unflagging fancy . . . and whatever they do (the legendary people) whether they listen to the harp or follow an enchanter over sea, they do it for the sake of joy. . . .

❁

'BYZANTIUM' WAS WRITTEN in 1930, three years later than 'Sailing to Byzantium'. It is a poem of magical power and beauty but its meaning eludes explanation. In our attempt to pursue a little further the meaning Yeats attached to the 'holy city of Byzantium'—the Byzantium of his imagination—one can but follow clues and comparisons elsewhere in his work.

It must be understood however that any attempt to interpret Yeats in the light of current Western materialist ideologies is doomed to failure. Throughout his life Yeats entirely repudiated such ideologies then and now prevailing, and searched the available sources of an alternative cosmology, both in literature and in his experimental work of magic and psychical research.

Yeats's elaborate symbol of the gyres, received by him through the mediumship of his wife George, is grounded entirely in the Western tradition of the Pre-Socratic philosophers and Plato himself. In a letter written shortly before his death he summarises that symbol:

> To me all things are made of the conflict of two states of consciousness, beings, or persons which die each other's life, live each other's death. That is true of life and death themselves. Two cones (or Whirls) the apex of each in the other's base.

This symbol he attributes to Empedocles, who describes a perpetual alternation of concord and discord, and writes, 'Never will boundless time be emptied of that pair; and they prevail in turn as the circle comes round, and pass away before one another and increase in their appointed turn'. And Yeats comments, 'I recall that Love and War come from the eggs of Leda'. And he quotes Heraclitus, whose 'thought dominates all', who writes that 'mortals are immortals and immortals mortals, "Dying each other's life, living each other's death".' Although Yeats does not mention Plato as a source of the symbol it is unlikely that he did not also know Plato's parable in *Politicus* of the alternations of the Golden Age and the Iron Age, and the spiral revolutions of time. Plato writes:

> Divinity himself sometimes conducts this universe in its progression and convolves it; but at another time he remits the reins of government, when the periods of the universe have received a convenient measure of time. But the world is spontaneously led round to things contrary.

The gyres move in contrary directions, the one increasing as the other diminishes; Yeats plots in his chart twenty-eight phases of the moon, and at phase one all is dark—the ascendancy of the earth-born race—while at phase fifteen the soul reaches its full beauty with the full moon; and both these phases are 'out of nature', the one in darkness, the other in light.

In 'Byzantium' the poet takes up the theme of 'Sailing to Byzantium' but this time less from the standpoint of the glory of the city of the fifteenth phase, the city of the living—the Emperor and the 'lords and ladies of Byzantium'—than as seen from the Otherworld, the perspective nor of the living but of the immortals whose death we live, as they die our life. The great dome of Hagia Sophia we see nor from within, where the 'sages' stand in their 'holy fire' on mosaic walls, but in the light—or darkness—of that greater dome, the night sky. In the earlier poem the poet had prayed to be freed from his mortal self, 'sick with desire / And fastened to a dying animal' and now as it seems comes the moment of reversal of life and death, as the images of day 'recede' and the night sky opens:

The unpurged images of day recede;
The Emperor's drunken soldiery are abed;
Night resonance recedes, night-walkers' song
After great cathedral gong;
A starlit or a moonlit dome disdains
All that man is,
All mere complexities,
The fury and the mire of human veins.

The gyres of time (whether of the individual lifetime or of history) are Yeats's central symbol. The image Yeats uses is the spindle, or 'pern', which happens also to be a name for the honey-buzzard, a raptor akin to the falcon of 'The Second Coming', where the rotating spindle is also implicit in the 'turning and turning' of the bird:

Turning and turning in the widening gyre
The falcon cannot hear the falconer;
Things fall apart; the centre cannot hold

the 'sages standing in God's holy fire' of 'Sailing to Byzantium' also 'pern in a gyre', the word here used as a verb. They are invited to descend from the 'holy fire' of God into the time-world of transience. In an earlier poem, 'Shepherd and Goatherd', a poem on the death of Major Robert Gregory, Yeats writes of the reversal of the course of life in the 'dreaming back' of the newly dead:

He grows younger every second
. . .
Jaunting, journeying, To his own dayspring,

He unpacks the loaded pern
Of all 'twas joy and pain to learn.

To this poem Yeats appends a note: 'When I was a child at
Sligo I could see above my grandfather's trees a little column
of smoke from "the pern mill", and was told that "pern" was
another name for the spool, as I was accustomed to call it, on
which the thread was wound.' The 'loaded pern' is equivalent to
'Plato's spindle' in 'His Bargain':

Who talks of Plato's spindle,
What set it whirling round?
Eternity may dwindle
Time is unwound.

Again time is 'unwound' as the souls travel back their thread
of life, wound by the Fate Lachesis on her spindle from the dis-
taff of Clotho, to be cut by the shear of Atropos, as the journey of life is reversed in death. (Plato describes 'the spindle of
Necessity' turned by the three Fates, in Book Ten of his *Republic*.)
The image in 'Shepherd and Goatherd' of the soul who grows
'younger every second' echoes again Plato's *Politicus* in which
Plato describes how in the Iron Age men pass, as now, from birth
to death, youth to age, in the Golden Age from age to youth; or
it may be understood in the sense that as the body ages the soul
grows younger. In *A Vision* (The Soul in Judgment) Yeats devel-
ops this theme in his elaborate symbol of the 'dreaming back'
of the dead, in which the discarnate relive their lives in reverse
order; as Major Robert Gregory moves towards his 'dayspring'.

In the second stanza of 'Byzantium' the image recurs in the
unmistakable context of the 'dreaming back' of the dead.

Before me floats an image, man or shade,
Shade more than man, more image than a shade;
For Hades' bobbin bound in mummy-cloth
May unwind the winding path;
A mouth that has no moisture and no breath
Breathless mouths may summon;
I hail the superhuman;
I call it death-in-life and life-in-death.

'We live their death, die their life'; 'for who knows whether to live be not to die, and to die to live'. Plato, Euripides, the Platonic tradition as a whole re-echoes these words. To Yeats this teaching was fundamental to his understanding of the incarnate and discarnate states of the soul. Yeats is indeed saturated with this tradition, known to him from Plato, Plotinus, and the Pre-Socratics. Plato in the *Phaedo* makes Socrates say that 'true philosophers make dying their profession because the philosopher will never attain to wisdom worthy of the name elsewhere than in the next world'. One remembers Shelley's line in 'Adonais', 'Die/If thou wouldst be with that which thou dost seek'. Only death frees the soul from contact with the body and its desires, which obscures the soul's innate wisdom. And in 'Blood and the Moon' Yeats summarises Plato when he writes

For wisdom is the property of the dead,
A something incompatible with life; and power,
Like everything that has the stain of blood,
A property of the living; but no stain
Can come upon the visage of the moon
When it has looked in glory from a cloud.

Yeats is here again speaking of the fifteenth phase, the full moon of superhuman perfection.

Who then is the awesome image that 'floats' before the poet? From a passage in Yeats's last work, *The Death of Cuchulain*, it might seem that the image is himself:

> there floats out there
> The shape that I shall take when I am dead,
> My soul's first shape, a soft feathery shape,
> And is it not a strange shape for the soul
> Of a great fighting man?

For a lifetime Yeats had speculated on the discarnate life of the soul, and in *A Vision* writes that 'religion cannot answer the atheist, and philosophy talks about a first cause or a final purpose, when we would know what we were a little before conception, what we shall be a little after burial'.

Again we have the unwinding of the thread of life in the 'dreaming-back', and this time the 'loaded pern' becomes 'Hades bobbin bound in mummy-cloth', for the symbol of the reversal of the gyres here is applied not to history but to the alternation of life and death—Hades and the 'mummy-cloth' tell us no less.

Another possibility I venture to suggest, but very tentatively. Since the poem is entitled 'Byzantium' it seems likely that the symbols would allude to the iconography of that city, and what symbol more central to the civilisation of Christendom than Christ on the cross? Since the central teaching of Christianity is that Christ 'conquered death'—that he 'descended into hell' and returned—what symbol more apt to float before the poet as an emblem of the ruler of the two kingdoms, of the living and the dead? The icon of Christ on the Cross is both 'man' and 'shade'—at once in life and in death—and also 'more image than a shade' because less a historical than an imaginative reality. The icon of the Christos has power not because it commemorates an historical event, but because it is a vision of eternal reality. So at least it would have seemed to Yeats:

> the church decorations where these are visible representations of holy persons were especially dear to those who believed in Christ's double nature, and that wherever Christ is represented by a bare Cross and all the rest is bird and beast and tree, we may discover an Asiatic art dear to those who thought Christ contained nothing human.

A poem on the theme of Byzantium can scarcely disregard the inner universe—the sacred dimension of the city. What indeed can be said of a city, or a civilisation, that excludes that Otherworld? A secular city confined to the needs and activities of the 'dying animal' would not have been called by Yeats a 'holy city'.

Yeats, for all his esoteric studies and his commitment to Indian spiritual teaching in his later years continued to call himself a Christian—as did his first Master, William Blake. Like Blake, Yeats held that 'All religions are one' and, like Blake again held that 'the Religion of Jesus'—if not that of the Church or churches—is that one universal truth. As a member of the Hermetic Order of the Golden Dawn Yeats made, and wore at all ceremonies, the Rose Cross with the dedication inscribed on it 'magister Jhesus Christus Deus et homo'. In 'A General Introduction to my Work', an essay written in 1937, Yeats declared his commitment to the Christian tradition.

A central symbol in the great church of the Holy Wisdom would have been Christ on the Cross, and was not Yeats in choosing Byzantium as his Holy City implicitly making that symbol central also to his poem? I put this at least as a strong possibility.

The third stanza of 'Byzantium' returns to the theme of art that first appeared in 'Sailing to Byzantium'. Again we have those golden birds, but with two new themes introduced—the themes of 'miracle' and of 'Hades', the Otherworld. The allusion to the 'Golden Bough' is to Aeneas' descent into the underworld in Virgil's poem, and again defines the theme:

> Miracle, bird or golden handiwork,
> More miracle than bird or handiwork,
> Planted on the star-lit golden bough,
> Can like the cocks of Hades crow,
> Or, by the moon embittered, scorn aloud . . .
> Common bird or petal
> And all complexities of mire or blood.

The poet is here speaking of something beyond either living bird or metal bird—that is, miracle. The work of art is 'more miracle than bird or handiwork'. Gibbon observed that Byzantine civilisation replaced reason, which had ruled the classical world, with a faith in the miraculous—that is, in the continual possibility—or reality—of divine intervention in earthly events. Gibbon scorns whatever does not conform to rational thought; but not so Yeats.

Blake would have called that divine inspirer 'Jesus the Imagination'; Yeats understood it in the symbol of the miraculous fifteenth phase of the moon which unites the two worlds. In

A Vision he states the 'blessed dead' inhabit the fifteenth phase. They are the *Sidhe* of the Irish Otherworld; and

> When the moon's full those creatures of the full
> Are met on the waste hills by countrymen
> Who shudder and hurry. . . .

In *A Vision* Yeats writes of change from the Roman to the Byzantine civilisation in terms of sculpture. He noted that 'The Greeks painted the eyes of marble statues . . . but the Roman was the first to drill a round hole to represent the pupil, and because, as I think, of a preoccupation with the glance characteristic of a civilisation in its final phase.' But the Byzantine vision was

> no representation of a living world but the dream of a som-
> nambulist. Even the drilled pupil of the eye, when the drill
> is in the hand of some Byzantine worker in ivory undergoes
> a somnabulistic change for its deep shadow among the
> faint lines of the tablet, its mechanical circle, where all else
> is rhythmical and flowing, give to Saint or Angel a look of
> some great bird staring at miracle.

It is in Byzantium that for the first time in the West a civilisation of the inner worlds—of the *mundus imaginalis*—has come into being. The passage continues:

> Could any visionary of those days, passing through the
> church named with so un-theological a grace 'The Holy
> Wisdom', can even a visionary of today wandering among
> the mosaics at Ravenna or in Sicily, fail to recognise some
> one image seen under his closed eyelids? To me it seems that
> He, who among the first Christian communities was little

but a ghostly exorcist, had in His assent to a full Divinity made possible this sinking-in upon a supernatural splendour, these walls with their little glimmering cubes of blue and green and gold.

Artifice is not mere skill—it is 'miracle', and that miracle is the revelation of a vision of the 'supernatural splendour' of the inner worlds of the human imagination that every 'holy city' seeks to embody. The soul of the earthly splendour of Byzantium was the vision of the Christos.

The 'song' of the golden birds has become the 'crow' of the cocks of Hades, a voice of the Otherworld. It proclaims that awesome wisdom which is 'the property of the dead' and 'scorns all complexities of mire and blood', of that mortal 'heart' Yeats had dedicated to be consumed away in 'God's holy fire', as Dante had stepped into the flames of purgatory.

In the stanzas that follow the poet evokes in the exalted language of an initiate the power of the Imagination to summon from the *imaginal* world the miraculous fire, at that magical moment (midnight) which 'unites the sleeping and the waking mind', the world of the human and the superhuman, of the 'blood-begotten' spirits of the living and the spirits of 'flames begotten of flame', the 'breathless mouths' of the spirits of the Otherworld:

> At midnight on the Emperor's pavement flit
> Flames that no faggot feeds, nor steel has lit,
> Nor storm disturbs, flames begotten of flame,
> Where blood-begotten spirits come
> And all complexities of fury leave,

Dying into a dance,
An agony of trance,
An agony of flame that cannot singe a sleeve.

Here the poet transports us into the *mundus imaginalis* itself, that inner universe of poetry and dreams that all forms of magic and enchantment seek to bring to consciousness—rites and ceremonies Yeats himself as a member of a magical Order had performed and experienced. Here we irresistibly think of the Emperor of Byzantium not as Constantine or Justinian, but of the Emperor, the Tarot 'key' which Years must have used in magical ceremonies of evocation of that inner world. It is on the 'pavement' of this world that the 'blood-begotten spirits' of incarnate humanity meet the immortal 'moods' in the fires of inspiration; which is at once a 'death' of the 'trivial daily mind' of the mortal self, and an 'agony of flame' as mortality is consumed away. Yeats had written in an early essay appended to the second volume of Lady Gregory's *Visions and Beliefs* of that 'interworld', which is the region of the fairy-people to the country people of Western Ireland: it is the theme of the Japanese Noh theatre, and Yeats describes the ghost-character of *Motome-zuka*, who has but to lay her hand upon a pillar to make it burst into flame; she was perpetually burning. Japanese drama takes place in that interworld, whose flames 'cannot singe a sleeve' and are yet realities of the *imaginal* world.

To this play he again alludes in *A Vision*. In this later description he uses the phrase 'the dance of her agony', a word repeated in the passage quoted above, where it may be also that the 'sleeve' is an allusion to Japanese theatre costume. This 'interworld' of the Imagination is the meeting-place of the incarnate and the discarnate, the conscious and the unconscious self, described also in *Autobiographies*, where Yeats writes of

> that age-long memoried self, that shapes the elaborate shell of the mollusc and the child in the womb, that teaches the birds to make their nest, and that genius is a crisis that joins that buried self at certain moments to our trivial daily mind. There are, indeed, personifying spirits that we had best call but Gates, and Gate-keepers, because through their dramatic power they bring our souls to crisis, to Mask and Image, caring not a straw whether we be Juliet going to her wedding, or Cleopatra to her death; for in their eyes nothing has weight but passion.

Another clue to this dance between mortals and immortals is to be found in an early story 'Rosa Alchemica', based no doubt upon Yeats's experience of magical work. In this story Yeats points out 'the independent reality of our thoughts', which are nevertheless the divine powers he calls the 'moods',

> shapes trembling out of existence, folding up into a time-less ecstasy, drifting with half-shut eyes, into a sleepy still-ness. The bodiless souls who descend into these forms were what men call the moods; and worked all great changes in the world. . . . In this way all the great events were accom-plished; a mood, a divinity or a demon, first descending like a faint sigh into men's minds and then changing their thoughts and their actions . . . and empires moved their bor-ders as though they were but drifts of leaves.

Here there is a clear echo of Blake's description of the time-less moment of inspiration in his poem Milton:

For in this Period the Poet's Work is Done: and all the Great Events of Time start forth & are conceived in such a Period. Within a Moment, a Pulsation of the Artery.

There follows a magical dance between mortals and immortals. For a moment the narrator 'seemed to be a mask' which 'many persons with eyes so bright and still that I knew them for more than human came and tried me on their faces'—for the poet is only the mask which the immortal moods put on or off for their drama. Then 'I opened the door, and found myself in a marvellous passage, along whose sides were many divinities wrought in a mosaic, not less beautiful than the baptistry at Ravenna but of a less severe beauty'.

Here Yeats is describing the character of his own imaginative world to which the mosaics of Byzantium are the nearest approximation. 'Then a voice cried out "Is the work of the Incorruptible Fire at an End?" and immediately Michael Robartes replied, "The perfect gold has come from the athanor".' Thus we may conclude that the 'flames that no faggot feeds' of 'Byzantium' are by implication the furnaces of the alchemical transmutation in whose 'agony' the base metal of mortality is transmuted into alchemical gold. In the dance that followed, and in which the narrator is now qualified to take part,

> every mortal foot danced by the white foot of an immortal . . . I was dancing with an immortal august woman, who had black lilies in her hair, and her dreamy gesture seemed laden with a wisdom more profound than is the darkness that is between star and star.

In 'Byzantium' the poet has condensed his early romantic fantasy into eight lines of magical power.

The last stanza introduces two new symbols, the dolphin, and the 'smithies of the Emperor'. The dolphin—often found on Greco-Roman sarcophagi—is that vehicle which carries the souls of the dead to the Otherworld and generating souls to this world.

> Astraddle on the dolphin's mire and blood,
> Spirit after spirit! The smithies break the flood,
> The golden smithies of the Emperor!
> Marbles of the dancing floor
> Break bitter furies of complexity,
> Those images that yet
> Fresh images beget,
> That dolphin-torn, that gong-tormented sea!

In a later poem, 'News for the Delphic Oracle' the dolphins are the vehicles of the dead:

> Straddling each a dolphin's back
> And steadied by a fin,
> Those Innocents re-live their death,
> Their wounds open again.
> The ecstatic waters laugh because
> Their cries are sweet and strange,
> Through their ancestral patterns dance,
> And the brute dolphins plunge
> Until, in some cliff-sheltered bay
> Where wades the choir of love

Proffering its sacred laurel crowns,
They pitch their burdens off.

The Emperor of Byzantium—or the Tarot Emperor of the
World—must have had his 'smithies' where the 'hammered gold
and gold enamelling' was wrought, so that the invisible archetype be made visible. And we again think of Blake's 'furnaces of
Los', the spirit 'who kept the divine vision', where

> Some Sons of Los surround the Passions with porches of
>   iron & silver,
> Creating form & beauty around the dark regions of sorrow,
> Giving to airy nothing a name and a habitation
> Delightful, with bounds to the Infinite putting off the
>   Indefinite
> Into most holy forms of Thought; such is the power of
>   inspiration
> They labour incessant with many tears & afflictions,
> Creating the beautiful House for the piteous sufferer.
> Others Cabinets richly fabricate of gold & ivory
> For Doubts & fears unform'd & wretched & melancholy

—so in the 'smithies' of imagined Byzantium, as in Blake's
'furnaces of Los', those works of beauty are created without
which there is only 'the many-headed foam': Blake's allusion is
to Shakespeare's poet who 'gives to airy nothing / A local habitation and a name'. It was the sages standing in God's holy
fire in Byzantium that Yeats summoned to travel the gyres of
history and to be his teachers, for Byzantium was a city of the
arts. Yeats's master William Blake had written of the arts of
Imagination, 'Poetry Painting, and Music, the three powers in

Man of conversing with Paradise which the flood did not sweep away', and wrote of the labourers in the furnaces of Los, the time-spirit, 'with bounds to the infinite putting off the indefinite', 'the sea of time and space'. And so Yeats, admonishing his own nation, the Irish, in 'The Statues' sets art against chaos:

> We Irish, born into that ancient sect
> But thrown upon this filthy modern tide
> And by its formless spawning fury wrecked,
> Climb to our proper dark, that we may trace
> The lineaments of a plummet-measured face.

The vision of all great cities comes from that fertile darkness; for 'who can distinguish darkness from the soul?' Beauty is not a decoration of material wealth but the source, the soul of every true civilisation; and without that vision of beauty civilisations perish.

Such was Yeats's reflection on the theme of civilisation—on the theme of that universal city of which Plato dreamed, the city 'coming down out of heaven from God' of St John's Apocalypse. The human city must have a soul, an inspiring vision, or it will be mere building, all will be chaos again, 'the bitter furies of complexity' that are held in check by the smithies of the Emperor, the marbles of the dancing-floor where mortals meet immortal spirits, those 'images that yet / Fresh images beget'. The soul of the earthly splendour of Byzantium was the Christian vision of the 'invisible master' of miracle.

By attempting to place some of Yeats's great resonant symbols in their context I hope I may have suggested something of the great imaginative scope of his poetic thought. To which I would only wish to add that however great the resonance of his symbolic images, these are always firmly rooted in earthly reality. Even that great Homeric line 'that dolphin-torn, that gong-tormented sea'. Just as the 'great cathedral gong' of Hagia Sophia 'tormented' the waters of the sea of Marmora, so, Mrs Yeats told me, the fishermen of the west of Ireland attract fish to their nets by beating a sheet of iron—a 'gong' whose vibrations attract the shoals of their 'mackerel-crowded seas'. However the resonance of a symbolic image may travel into the superhuman and the miraculous regions of Imagination, every great poet respects the law of correspondence which in every true work unites the sensible image and the invisible worlds it evokes and manifests.

(1979)

Ash Wednesday

I T MUST HAVE been in 1928 or 1929 that I, most naïve of undergraduates, was staying during a vacation with a fellow-student whose father edited a small provincial newspaper. In the editorial office I happened to pick up an unregarded journal entitled the *Criterion* (or was it the *New Criterion* at that time?). No one else wanted it because there were poems in it, I took it; for although I was reading the Natural Sciences Tripos I nevertheless regarded poetry as my terrain. The first poem I read began, 'Lady, three white leopards sat under a juniper tree'. I had never heard of the author, T. S. Eliot, but the poem struck home. It was my first experience of a totally new kind of poetry—I had been brought up on the Romantics and the Victorians and the Georgians and Walter de la Mare and early Yeats—but this was another world, a different music, moving me in somewhat the same way as had Debussy's chromatic compositions when I first encountered music that was not diatonic. I memorised the poem, not perfectly, and in line-by-line terms probably not even generally understood; but something in me of which I had been hitherto unaware totally understood and responded, as if to a shared secret an older generation had not known. I had entered the imaginative world of my generation, who felt that Eliot's poetry had given us a voice, given us the words we needed. On my return to Girton after the vacation I exposed myself to the scorn of Q. D. Roth (later Mrs F. R. Leavis) for not having known about T.S. Eliot. But I am glad I did not because if I had been told of him by others I would never have met him in the secret wood, where poetry rightly belongs, and not in the class-room where it usually wilts and withers.

Like most people in those days I knew my Bible fairly though not exceptionally well, and recognised the dry bones from Ezekiel, though not the juniper-tree; had there been three white leopards under Ezekiel's juniper-tree I hardly think I would have forgotten it. Not having the habits of a scholar I did not think of rereading Ezekiel in order to understand the references bet-ter; no reference book could have added power to the image of the Three White Leopards which, like a dream-image, was self-authenticating if not self-explanatory. Explanation, in those days, was not what we looked for in reading a poem; instead I followed a lifelong habit and memorised it. That too was com-mon to my generation, and I know no better way of testing the imaginative quality of a poem in its unity and totality than to interiorise it in that way. The piecemeal following up of notes was a way of reading that seems to me in retrospect to have come into fashion with Eliot, who provided notes to *The Waste Land*; earlier (romantic) poets would perhaps have agreed with Yeats who thought the poem should when finished be self-explanatory, within terms of a culture shared by a poet and his readers.

I have since wondered whether Eliot's elaborate notes were not intended as much to put his readers off, as to put them on, the scent. What a gift the references-hunt has been to the unimaginative teacher of Eng. Lit.! And of all modern poets

Eliot has best fitted the academic syllabus because his allusions are mainly of a literary kind well suited to the classroom
and within the scope of the culture expected (at all events until
recently) of a University student or lecturer. Indeed our shared
inherited European culture is one of Eliot's main themes—if not
his central theme. Few of the works readers of Eliot need to
look up are, so to speak, 'out of bounds' (even though the word
'shantih' was less familiar to students in those days than now)
and following up references to Dante and the French Symbolists
was a broadening education in itself. I remember discussing
with St-John Perse, whose poem *Anabase* Eliot had translated,
and suggesting that a wide range of allusion was something he
had in common with Eliot; yes, he said, but Eliot's allusions are
to books, his to things—to gear and tackle and trim of boats;
rare plants growing in the Imperial Gardens of Peking; the
mould on rosebuds or the phosphorescent creatures in tropical
seas. Or think of Yeats and what the academics make (or do
not make) of the books Yeats read—Lombroso's *After Death,
What?*, Swedenborg's *Spiritual Diaries*, Kalidasa and Kabir,
Harold Bayley and G. R. S. Mead, the *Kabbala Denudata* and
H. P. Blavatsky, Fludd and Dee and Agrippa, the Cambridge
Platonists, and for that matter Plato and Plotinus themselves,
not themselves *personae gratae* in academic circles, then or now.
All these are on the shelves of Yeats's library along with the
journals of the Society for Psychical Research, and much besides
that has remained inexplicably invisible to academics writing on
his work. But Eliot is eminently teachable within the terms of
a shared culture acceptable to University English faculties. This
is not to deny that he too is a great poet—some might say that
the very fact of his so situating himself within the mainstream

of European culture is one of his great merits, as compared with Yeats who revived an excluded knowledge—yet I cannot but feel fortunate in not having been 'taught' Eliot; having taught him myself I know how easy it is, in his work, not to see the wood for the trees.

I would not go so far as to say that all those allusions and quotations from earlier authors in which he wrapped himself have done Eliot a disservice; but rereading *Ash Wednesday* recently it did seem to me that there is a measure of protective camouflage—perhaps bandages would be a truer simile—by which he covered in a seemly manner deep and bleeding wounds. That which impelled the poet to write *Ash Wednesday* and *The Waste Land* was certainly not love of erudition; and I and my ignorant kind responded to the cry of the heart at the heart of those careful coverings.

What then did I find in the poem, reading it as I did in the lucidity of my ignorance? First of all, the desolation is in the music; and Eliot's free verse was a music we were then hearing for the first time. Again the learned talk about technique has evaded this direct communication of an experience. Rhythmic patterns are a characteristic (whether in music, dance or poetry or in nature itself) of life. Life is rhythmic, one might almost say it is rhythm. A broken rhythm expresses a broken life, and that is something learning a poem by heart can reveal and that source-hunting cannot. In that new broken rhythm we recognised the new experience of our time. Here were poems of renunciation whose form betrayed none of that conviction, implicit in a formal pattern as such, that there is some ultimate meaning even in grief and bereavement. Eliot's free verse has the movement of feet following the dead to the grave.

But the mourner falls into music and rhythm in his litany
(based on the Litany of the Blessed Virgin Mary) to the 'Lady
of silences/Calm and distressed'. Here is at least an echo of life,
for the inspiration is the woman, the feminine who represents
the life-principle itself. It never occurred to me—nor, I think, to
others reading Eliot at that time—to wonder what incident in
the poet's personal life had inspired his lamentation. All that has
now been dragged out into the light of the media without in any
way adding to, or detracting from, the essence of the poetry. But
it is strange, now that I come to think of it after all these years,
that we did not ask such a question.

The reason, I believe, is that the poem, its music and its
theme, essence, quality was such that it seemed to speak not of
the poet's situation but of our own; not because we too had had
our hearts or our marriages broken but on the deeper level of a
collective archetype from which the poem springs and to which it
addresses itself. The symbolic power of the figure of the woman
in the garden is (like that of the Virgin Mary) collective, not individual. The phase of departure in which that figure is situated
was likewise collective at that time, and its resonance is from a
level of experience deeper than any personal sorrow, although
the poet's personal sorrow was clearly for him the gateway to
the archetypal. This is the gift of the true imaginative poet; and
one has but to compare *Ash Wednesday* with a host of subsequent poetic utterances, confessional, self-pitying to however
desperate a degree, to recognise what a world of difference there
is between the depths sounded in Eliot's poems and the cries of
a purely personal anguish. Nor does the literary persona behind
which the poet chose to mask his face (Ezekiel under the juniper tree in the desert whither he had fled from Queen Jezebel)

disguise that archetypal, naked core of the poem. It is not the words of Ezekiel, powerful as these are, 'It is enough, O Lord! Take away my life' (unspoken in the poem but implicit throughout) but the theme of the Lady that gives to the *Ash Wednesday* poems their irresistible magic.

The Lady herself is more than any human vehicle who might have mediated her numinous presence; her power is supernatural—that is to say she belongs not to the natural world but to the inner universe of the imagination. And that presence in the imagination—the goddess one might say—is ill-aspected—she is distressed, exhausted, worried, forgetful; and in the version I memorised the rose to which she is likened is 'The single rose/ With worm-eaten petals'. Doubtless the rose has resonance of Dante, and the paradisal rose in which the figure of Beatrice merges with the all-embracing presence of the Blessed Virgin herself, who in this context represents the Church. But in Eliot's poems the Lady is powerless to redeem and lead the poet to heaven; to make the dry bones live. She is the 'End of the endless/ Journey to no end' and 'the Garden/where all loves end', but the garden is not Paradise but the desert, the Waste Land, the *nihil*; again in the earlier version the lines 'End of remembering/End of forgetfulness' sound an ambiguous echo of death rather than redemption. The Lady, like the Blessed Virgin of whose litany hers is a dark contrary (and whose presence is implicit throughout the *Ash Wednesday* poems—the first poem, 'Perch'io non spero . . .' ends with two lines from the *Salve regina*) is the archetype of all that woman signifies of love, consolation, intercession, compassion, protection, but she is situated—and not for Eliot alone but for a generation—in a station of departure, a parting on that threshold Blake calls 'the margin of non-entity'. From that threshold she is not approaching but receding, vanishing, taking with her the compassionate, merciful, healing presence of the feminine principle. Even in her departure she is that divine figure—or rather she is its absence. The liberated woman and the unisex girl in blue-jeans who have taken her place may seem but are not she, for she represents the sacred; in her the poet has encountered the numinous. In the centrality of that symbol lies, I suggest, the power of the poem and what it communicates, written at a moment when the secular was about to obliterate from modern experience the old vision of human love as something holy, sacramental.

An apt example of how the new way of reading poetry (conceptual rather than imaginative) could lead the followers of Richards and Leavis astray is E. E. Phare's conribution to the reading of the line about the single rose with worm-eaten petals (in a contribution to B. Rajan's Festschrift for T. S. Eliot's sixtieth birthday). Miss Phare comes up with an allusion to a worm-infested rose in a poem by George Herbert, 'Church Rents and Schisms'. In a series of decidedly forced comparisons the 'Brave rose' of the Church is attacked by a worm whose 'many feet and hair/Are the more foul, the more thou wert divine' and 'Onely shreds of thee,/And those all bitten, in thy chair I see'. This ill-chosen comparison may display Miss Phare's familiarity with Eng. Lit. and it also enables her to relate Eliot's rose to Dante's by way of Holy Church and its corruption thereby by-passing Beatrice and love. But what about Blake's 'The Sick Rose', or Viola's damask cheek, or all those many other allusions, in Shakespeare's sonnets and elsewhere, to the worm in the bud and the perishing of love? A signal, if typical, failure to see the wood for the trees by those who read piecemeal.

Eliot's desolation was total because he was the vehicle of a collective archetype. He knew from a deep experience the holiness of what the secularisation of the world was about to banish. The hard-edged generation that followed him—the Oxford left-wing political poets and the scientific positivist school of Cambridge—were not even to miss her for they had entered totally the realm of the secular. They had never known the Lady of Silences. Between the violet and the violet, between vernal sweetness and 'the violet hour' of nightfall, between the lilac blossom and the yew tree, between presence and absence, a threshold is crossed. She has gone, 'White light folded, sheathed about her, folded', the veiled bride shrouded for death. The music of *Ash Wednesday* recalls the valedictory music Mark Antony heard in Egypt when the God Hercules left him.

Doubtless the *Four Quartets* are great poems, in many respects more mature in their artistry than *Ash Wednesday* and *The Waste Land*. Many have found consolation in the poet's wise words and Christian sentiments and insights. I confess with regret that much of this seems, in the balance with that archetypal figure of the departing Lady—and she moves through the later poems also—a resolute attempt to endure with patience and dignity—an intellectual and moral act of will—rather than an imaginative transformation or transmutation. The words the poet gave to a sense of loss spoke from the heart:

> Because I do not hope to turn again,
> Because I do not hope,
> Because I do not hope to turn

Whatever reassurance Eliot's later poems may have brought to many of my contemporaries with their religious message of acceptance and patience, my personal debt to him is rather for the words he gave to the abandonment of hope. He saw, at a certain time, what gate it was our world was about to enter. For me it is other voices among my contemporaries—and I do not mean only Yeats but also Edwin Muir, Vernon Watkins, David Gascoyne, even perhaps that other Christian poet David Jones— who have spoken of the abiding transcendence of the sacred; but of these none has borne witness with comparable eloquence to its loss.

(*c.* 1985)

Edwin Muir

WHEN EDWIN MUIR died, in January 1959, at the age of seventy-one, he was still at the height of his poetic powers, and many of his finest poems are among his last. Time, that so remorselessly fades some poems which in their day seemed impressive, makes others, at first little noticed, seem to glow with some inner light. Edwin Muir's poems belong to the second kind: time does not fade them, and it becomes clear that their excellence owes nothing to the accidental circumstances of the moment at which the poet wrote, or we read, his poems; they survive, as it were, a change of background, and we begin to see that whereas the 'new' movements of this or that decade lose their significance when the scene changes and retain only a historical interest, Edwin Muir, a poet who never followed fashion, has in fact given more permanent expression to his world than other poets who deliberately set out to be the mouthpieces of their generation.

He was not a political poet; and yet his record of the state of Europe before and after the Second World War is not only more imaginatively perceptive, but more first-hand than that of the political poets of the thirties. He belonged to no church and subscribed to no formulated doctrine; yet he has written poems that sound depths of certain Christian themes never touched by poets of the Anglican revival. He was not a Scottish nationalist and after some early exercises never wrote in any Scots dialect; and yet he stands out as the greatest, and perhaps also the most typical, Scots poet of his time. All this because of an unswerving inner certainty, an integrity, an indifference to fashion, that made him never seek to impress or please, but only to bear witness to the truth that was in him.

It is easier to explain why we admire some poem than why it moves us; for what is finally moving is just that in it which cannot be explained. The final Yes that we give to a living poem is more than an intellectual response—though it includes intellectual assent as well. It involves both the conscious and the unconscious mind. Muir, at all events, would have accepted some such statement. He once described to me a dream that at the time seemed to convey to him the deepest truth about writing. The dream was a very simple one: it consisted of a semicolon. The meaning of this semicolon, as it revealed itself to the dreamer, was that the poet never knows all that he writes: he writes only, as it were, as far as the semicolon; beyond the statement is something more, that completes his meaning. We can never define it, yet it is part of the poem, and part of what the poet communicates to the reader.

In one of his first published works, *Latitudes*, there is an essay entitled 'Against Being Convinced'. In this essay, Muir criticises the philosopher, as one who can 'give an answer with certainty—certainly at least by definition—to the question "what is thought?" but he can give no certain answer to the question "what is life?"' Though he does not say so, he implies that to answer this question belongs to the poet; the poem

communicates life, essence, which is indefinable; for the opposite of the philosopher, he says, would be 'a thinker of an incredible simplicity, a spontaneity which would appear to be a piece
of nature's carelessness'. 'A philosopher is a man who thinks
in and out of season,' he wrote in the same essay; and he knew
with a sureness given to few poets how to entrust himself to the
wisdom that has nothing to do with dialectic but everything to
do with life. In one of his last poems, 'The Poet', he wrote of the
poet's task.

> What I shall never know
> I must make known.
> Where traveller never went
> Is my domain.
> Dear disembodiment
> Through which is shown
> The shapes that come and go
> And turn again.

In many poems, as in 'Day and Night', he writes of the two wis-
doms, that of the conscious day, and that of the night, ancestral,
impersonal, yet deeply familiar, and wise with the wisdom of
countless generations. Of this wisdom the poet is not the author
but the transcriber; 'the authors', as Blake says, 'are in eternity'.

The last poem that Muir wrote opens with the line 'I have
been taught by dreams and fantasies,' and ends with a declaration of faith

> That Plato's is the truest poetry,
> And that these shadows
> Are cast by the true.

But the dreams and fantasies came long before Muir had studied the Platonic philosophy. The world of ideas for him was not a doctrine but an experience. In his *Collected Poems*, published in April 1960 but chosen, all but some fragments left unpublished when he died, by Muir himself, he had reprinted two early poems, 'The Ballad of the Soul' and 'The Ballad of the Flood'. Technically they are not very successful exercises in the tradition of the supernatural ballad, and the influence of 'The Ancient Mariner' is strong—a poem that might also have been called 'The Ballad of the Soul', and no doubt Muir recognised that Coleridge had seen into the same world as himself; for these poems are an attempt to describe in verse a vision, whose circumstances are described in the poet's *Autobiography*. This vision seems to have been his poetic initiation, an opening of the imaginative eye that he never afterwards forgot. He seemed—not in sleep, but in a state of waking trance—to be the spectator and participator of a great cosmic drama. Years later, he was able to write that he remained certain that 'it was not I who dreamed it but something else which the psychologists call the racial unconscious, and which has other names'. It is the test of the authentic poet at all times that his work should draw its inspiration from this source.

What Muir saw in his vision that was to shed its peculiar light upon all his subsequent poems he called the Fable, and entitled his first autobiography *The Story and the Fable*. In that title we again find the distinction between the wisdom of the day and of the night, the sleeping and the waking mind, that which comes before and after the semicolon. For the Story is the life of the individual—of any individual; but the Fable is that which every life seeks, more or less imperfectly, to realise, to reflect, to embody—something we know by inheritance, a pattern built up, it may be, by, 'the endlessly repeated experience of the race'. He wrote:

> It is clear that no autobiography can begin with a man's birth, that we extend far beyond any boundary line which we can set for ourselves in the past or the future, and that the life of every man is an endlessly repeated performance of the life of man. It is clear for the same reason that no autobiography can confine itself to conscious life, and that sleep, in which we pass a third of our existence, is a mode of experience, and our dreams a part of reality. In themselves our conscious lives may not be particularly interesting; but what we are not and can never be, our fable, seems to me inconceivably interesting. I should like to write that fable, but I cannot even live it. And all I could do if I related the outward course of my life would be to show how much I have deviated from it; tho' even that is impossible, since I do not know the fable, or anybody who knows it.

But the Fable is enacted and reflected, again and again, in the differing situations of time and in history. If this were not so, individual life would be meaningless and poetry unnecessary—a few old myths would have said all. But the Fable is both old and ever new, and must be rediscovered, retold, reclothed in every age, indeed in every life. Edwin and Willa Muir were the translators of Kafka, the most contemporary, in the dress in which he clothes the Fable, of all symbolist writers; Kafka's supernatural labyrinth is superimposed upon a bureaucratic modern European society with such imaginative power that the symbolism gives meaning to the actual while at the same time the actual gives to

the Castle and the Courts of Judgement the aspect of the contemporary. The two early ballads I have mentioned are, as Muir
himself must have realised (for he did not reprint them for many
years) interesting failures. They are so because the archetypes
are not sufficiently incarnated; but, while the visionary insight
remains as strong as ever at every return to his cosmic revelation,
Muir added some new human or historic concreteness, wedding
the archetypal to the real as only those poets can do for whom
the real is the signature of the Mystery.

A very great proportion of his poems are about history and
about politics (as were Yeats's also), but always he sees the
events of history as episodes in the Fable: and this enabled him
often to see the immediate with a steadier gaze than, say, the
political poets of the thirties, whose sense of proportion was less
true for want of that imaginative orientation. Certainly Spender
and Day Lewis felt strongly about world events; and Auden
equals, indeed surpasses, Muir in descriptive vividness; but in
Muir alone do we find 'those hard symbolic bones' that Yeats
found in Dante and Blake—political poets also—that give events
their enduring aspect.

Edwin and Willa Muir passed like pilgrims through some
of the worst horrors of Europe; in Czechoslovakia before the
Anschluss and after—they returned there as the tide of German
occupation had barely receded, and in time to witness the
Communist *coup d'état*—but in such poems as 'The Cloud' we
may see how the perception of the Fable enabled the poet to
see man in a given political situation, if not unmoved, then at
all events unshaken. The anonymous man of the modern collective farm is none the less a child of Adam and his great spiritual
destiny for not knowing himself to be so; the belief that man is

only 'dust of the earth' does not make this true, though millions share the error:

> At a sudden turn we saw
> A young man harrowing, hidden in dust; he seemed
> A prisoner walking in a moving cloud
> Made by himself for his own purposes.

It was in German literature, from his early readings of Heine and Nietzsche, to his later studies of Kleist, Hölderlin, Kafka, and Hofmannsthal, that he probably found his deepest affinities. He expresses, in his own work, much rather the European than the English experience of the war years. The invasion of human feeling and natural kindness by those successive tides of ideology and power which reached England only as hearsay, Muir saw, and felt, at first hand.

If Edwin and Willa Muir passed through the world like pilgrims, that argues a certain kind of detachment, but not, certainly, the detachment of the privileged unparticipating observer. They were always poor, and Edwin Muir came from the poorest of the poor. He was the son of a small farmer on the small island of Wyre, in the Orkneys. There he lived only long enough to learn what was to be, for him, the landscape of Eden, that recurs in so many of his poems, always with that peculiar radiance in which the imagination clothes the childhood of poets,

> That dread country crystalline
> Where the blank field and the still-standing tree
> Were bright and fearful presences to me.

It was no sheltered life he lived there; his father was driven from the first farm by the exactions of a bad landlord, and after a succession of poorer farms, off the land altogether. As boyhood ended, Orkney was exchanged for Glasgow; he was to learn that there is poverty and poverty.

Glasgow gave him a precise imagery of Hell. There is a passage in the *Autobiography* that captures the terror of that landscape:

> The same attraction to squalor drew me to the football matches on Saturday afternoon. Crosshill was a respectable suburb, but there were vacant lots scattered about it, chance scraps of waste ground where the last blade of grass had died, so that in dry weather they were as hard as lava and in wet weather a welter of mud. On these lots teams from the south side played every Saturday afternoon with great skill and savage ferocity. . . . Some of the teams had boxers among their supporters; these men stood bristling on the touchline and shouted intimidations at the opposing players. I first saw one of these games shortly after I came to Glasgow; a brown fog covered the ground, and a small tomato-red sun, like a jellyfish floating in the sky, appeared and disappeared as the air grew thicker or finer. . . . There was a grimy fascination in watching the damned kicking a football in a tenth-rate hell.

Years later some such memory became infused into the poem whose title is 'Milton'; but the poet is in truth Muir himself. He does not, as Auden would have done, describe Glasgow; though from the prose description quoted, we cannot doubt his descriptive powers. For him, that 'tenth-rate hell' is but a symbol, and in two lines he evokes only as much of its essence as he needs:

a mass of blackened stone
Crowned with vermilion fiends like streamers blown
From a great funnel filled with roaring flame.

Shut in his darkness these he could not see,
But heard the steely clamour known too well
On Saturday nights in every street in Hell.

He uses only as much imagery as is needed to give a Here and
Now to the symbolic statement and to remind us that the Fable
goes on, in the world we inhabit, never more realised than in
those regions that have most forgotten it.

Both the Orkneys and Glasgow, the places that give Muir the
landscape of his poetry are, of course, Scotland, not England. He
wrote in English, but when he wrote of England, or of English
writers, he wrote as a Scot, seeing all south of the border as
a country whose ways of thought were alien to him—perhaps
more alien than those of other European countries. The Scottish
Nationalist movement held it against Muir that he did not write
in what is nowadays called 'lallans'—lowland Scots. But the
question of language was one of which he was deeply aware;
and he even wrote that 'No writer can write great English who
is not born an English writer and in England—and born moreover in some class in which the tradition of English is pure, and
it seems to me, therefore, in some other age than this.' (This last
quiet phrase is characteristic of his almost imperceptible manner of making quite devastating critical pronouncements.) 'It is
improbable', he added, 'that Scotland will produce any writer
in English of the first rank—or at least that she will not do so
until her tradition of English is as common, as unforced and

unschooled as if it were her native tongue.' He criticised the
alien facility of Stevenson; yet he had to write in English, for
he regarded 'lallans' as an artificial language. He himself came,
besides, from the Orkneys, where the speech is as remote from
lowland Scots as English is; a speech and a language whose affinities are Norse. History made the use of English for him inevitable; in the same way as he felt that for the political problems
of Scotland—the problem of Glasgow, for example—Socialism,
not Scottish Nationalism, could now provide the only answer.
We have to go forward in time.

In *A Note on the Scottish Ballads* he defined some of the
attributes most characteristic of Scottish poetry as he saw it,
'this terrific sad, and simple vision of life'. English poetry, he
believed, most excels when most subtle, delicate, and complex,
Scottish when most intensely simple: the best English poetry is
the work of an aristocratic culture, whereas the great poetry of
Scotland—and not only her ballads—has been produced by men
in the ordinary sense uncultivated, the sons of the land and of
the sea. Muir himself was thus in the tradition of his race, the
son of a farmer, and deeply wedded to the rocks and isles of
Scotland. He writes, besides, from, and for, a tribe, a race. The
Fable belongs to the race, to the ancestors: but so does Muir's
speech, so do his images, and his loyalties.

There is an archaic splendour, as of the ballads, in his heraldic
images of animals, flowers, roads, mountains, images strength-
ened and clarified by the imaginative simplification of those
experiences most intensely and universally shared. The genius of
the race is not for the subtle deviation but for the simple essence.
'The unquenchability of desire, the inexorability of separation,
the lapse of time, and all these seen against something eternal

and as if, expressed in a few lines, they were what human beings have felt from the beginning of time and must feel till time ends: these things, uttered with entire simplicity, are what at its best Scottish poetry can give us.' At his best, Muir achieved a poetic language at once powerfully mythological, yet concrete; symbolic, yet poignant with a particular joy or anguish.

In Muir's poetry the personal gives immediacy to the universal, which in turn gives meaning and stature to the personal. There are poems equal to 'The Brothers'—one of the last he wrote—but none which better realises that synthesis of the story and the fable, an individual talent and an imagination at one with that of a race. The poet describes a vivid dream of his two brothers, long dead, as they had been as boys; yet the image is at the same time simple in its universality, and written within the tradition that still attaches to blood-kinship a kind of formal dignity almost unknown in modern society. The vividness of the supernatural that exceeds in its intensity anything in nature is perhaps common to all primitive races; but the image of the two radiant children picks up purely Scottish echoes, from such ballads as 'The Cruel Mother'—a story of the unwedded girl who bears twin children, and kills and buries them to cover her shame. As she returns home,

> She lookit out owre her castle wa'
>   Fine flowers in the valley
> And saw twa naked boys at the ba'
>   And the green leaves they grow rarely.
>
> 'O bonny boys, gin ye were mine
> I wad clad you in silk and sabelline.

O I would dress you in the silk
And wash you ay in morning milk.'

And they reply that it was not so when they lived,

'O mother dear, when we were thine,
You didna prove to us sae kind.

O cruel mother, we were thine
And thou made us to wear the twine.

But now we're in the heavens hie,
   Fine flowers in the valley
And ye have the pains o' hell to drie
    And the green leaves they grow rarely,
Ten thousand times good night and be wi' thee!'

Muir's poem is different in tone, but it plays upon an imagination whose contours have been formed by such burning images:

Last night I watched my Brothers play,
The gentle and the reckless one,
In a field two yards away.
For half a century they were gone
Beyond the other side of care,
To be among the peaceful dead.
Even in a dream how could I dare
Interrogate that happiness
So wildly spent yet never less?
For still they raced about the green
And were like two revolving suns;
A brightness poured from head to head,

So strong I could not see their eyes
Or look into their paradise.
What were they doing, the happy ones?
Yet where I was they once had been.

The poet then takes us beyond that age-old magic of the
supernatural, into the metaphysical, in a statement moving in its
simplicity, of the incorruptibility of the soul:

I thought How could I be so dull
Twenty thousand days ago
Not to see they were beautiful?
I asked them Were you really so
As you are now, that other day?
And the dream was soon away.

Still keeping close to the pattern of the old ballad and its intensity of guilt as the individual confronts the eternal, he brings the
archetypal image to bear upon the actual world:

For then we played for victory
And not to make each other glad.
A darkness covered every hand,
Frowns twisted the original face,
And through that mask we could not see
The beauty and the buried grace.

Muir possessed a birthright rare in the modern world, and
perhaps irrecoverable, in being able to write for his tribe, to
speak with the voice of the ancestors. Modern man lives as
though without a past; but Muir wrote, 'I think that if any of
us examines his life, he will find that most good has come to

him from a few loyalties, and a few discoveries made many generations before he was born.' Fast vanishing in Ireland and Scotland, all but gone in England and America, this vital sense of the life of a race that bears, as if a single life, a destiny to unfold and fulfil, is still to be found among those Jews who are loyal to their inheritance; and many of Muir's finest poems take the Hebrew patriarchs for themes—Moses on Pisgah Hill watching his people below entering the Promised Land; the nomadic wanderings of Abraham, Isaac, and the still-journeying, still-suffering race.

Time, and the continuity of man through time, the poignancy of the individual life that for a while bears the burden, the calm patient continuance of the race from Adam—and before Adam—to the return to Eden at the end of the journey, these things were the essence of his vision. Often the poet writes in the first person plural—'we'; but his 'we' is not, as with Auden (another poet much given to this plural) a group of friends or like-thinkers, or a political team, but the greater 'I' of the tribal life of Man. Conversely his 'I' embraces 'we', as the journeying spirit that travels from the beginning of the cosmos to its end.

In writing his Fable of Man, Muir turned naturally to those great symbolic figures who are not men, but Man—Adam, and Prometheus; the Israelites, with their strange god-bearing destiny and, inevitably, the figure of Christ, though that figure emerges late in Muir's verse. History itself becomes a symbolic story as a pattern emerges, or is imposed, by the human experience repeated time and again. The eternal battlefield of Troy, the flight of Hector, the sack of the city, the constancy of the wife who waits. It is Penelope, wife to the wanderer, not the static

Platonic image of Helen, who is Muir's figure of woman. In 'Telemachus Remembers', he writes of the weaving and unweaving of the unfinished figures of the loom, as an emblem of that daily life which is always an imperfect realisation of the Fable. The loom cannot, indeed must not, be finished, yet life must never be relinquished. Penelope's greatness lies in her acceptance of the imperfection, and her loyalty to the task of producing the partial, the imperfect, the never completed.

> A horse's head, a trunkless man,
> Mere odds and ends about to be,
> And the thin line of augury
> Where through the web the shuttle ran.

Woman as the weaver of lives is an old theme; but again, it is a Scottish theme; Gray's 'Fatal Sisters' is based upon the story of 'a man from Caithness' who saw women in a hollow hill weaving men's entrails into the web of fate; but Muir could take such symbols, and in his hands they seem neither old nor new. The homeliness of 'odds and ends about to be' makes us accept the 'thin line of augury' as something no less simple and inevitable— as indeed it is; though Yeats, one reflects, would have said it differently. Muir never mounted 'that high horse'; it is often only on a second or a third reading that we realise just how much he has said.

But the story of the Journey goes back long before man; and perhaps Muir's greatest poem is the sequence he called *The Journey Back* that opens with the line, 'I take the journey back to seek my kindred', and traces the long travelling through the animals, the earth itself to the stars and the first stuff of the material world.

It may be that modern man's sense of chaos comes in part from his loss of that pattern of which his necessarily fragmentary individual life is a part. Blake write of the 'chaos' of the individual experience, which he contrasts with the beautiful order of 'eternity'. Have we lost our sense of that order because we have let go the myths that best embody it, or have we relinquished the myths because we have lost sight of the order that they exist to make known?

Yeats, it may be, rediscovered the order through the study of myth and symbol; but Muir's poetry springs in the first place from intuitive perception. At first his poetic images arose within his dreams, and owed little to religious or aesthetic tradition. 'I do not know the fable, or anybody who knows it', he wrote, but then he added, 'One or two stages in it I can recognise: the age of innocence and the Fall and all the dramatic consequences of the Fall. But these lie behind experience, not on its surface; they are not historical events; they are stages in the fable.' Here the poet is acknowledging that the Fable has in part been known, in part stated in those mythological forms we inherit: Eden and Adam, and 'those dramatic consequences', the Incarnation and the Redemption.

Rather late in life a friend pointed out to Muir that he was a Christian. It had not occurred to him, yet, when put to him, he acknowledged that this was so. Some writers on his work have made too much of this; for if he was a Christian poet he was so by convergence of symbol, not (as, for example, T. S. Eliot) by subscription to doctrine. His wine could never be measured in any pint-pot of orthodoxy; for in revealing in part the mystery he leaves it still a mystery. The most certain thing he knew of it was that it is unknowable. He did in fact increasingly use a traditional symbolism as he discovered that his vision itself placed him within age-old traditions; that what he had glimpsed in dreams had been man's theme for countless centuries.

His poem of the Annunciation is as profoundly spiritual, in its way, as Fra Angelico (whose painting he had in mind), yet it is not because he was a Christian but because he rediscovered the symbols from within that this is so. For him, the meeting of the Angel and the woman is essentially a poem about the eternal nature of love, not a poem describing an unique historical event. The theme is none the less holy for that; for Muir, like Plato, understood that lovers are winged—that is to say uplifted into a spiritual order, whose mystery is reflected in the earthly event:

> See, they have come together, see,
> While the destroying minutes flow,
> Each reflects the other's face
> Till heaven in hers and earth in his
> Shine steady there. He's come to her
> From far beyond the farthest star,
> Feathered through time. Immediacy
> Of strangest strangeness is the bliss
> That from their limbs all movement takes.

Muir never employed so great a wealth of traditional symbols as did Yeats; yet inevitably he discovered that in exploring the Fable he was travelling in a frequented land; for the symbolism of all religions and mythologies, not least Christianity, exists only to make that country known. He discovered late what was known early to Dante and Milton, and discovered in the course of their poetic thought by Coleridge, Shelley, Blake, and Yeats, the great symbolic language of tradition. The world-tree and its fruits, the birds of the soul, sun, moon, river, loom, dragon, gate, and dark tower, may be likened to words of that language, whose meanings, though not otherwise definable, are exact. Knowledge of these symbols is essentially a kind of learning, but it is the learning of the imagination, not of the merely conceptual mind. It is the learning of the poets.

Muir came to the great source of vision without this learning, with little knowledge of the traditional forms. He was a symbolist poet by natural gift, not one who, like Yeats, had 'Set his soul to study in a learned school'. But the learning of tradition, for him, was less important than for Eliot, less than for Yeats, just because that which tradition preserves and transmits was so much nearer to him. 'We receive it from the past, on which we draw with every breath, but also—this is a point of faith—from the source of the mystery itself.'

But even when his symbols are drawn direct from *Anima Mundi* they are never vague, never obscure. Muir in his own way insisted as strongly as Yeats on the necessity of form. In *A Vision*, Yeats speaks of the symbol as 'uniting the sleeping with the waking mind', and Muir would have agreed with him; the symbol masters the unknown and the chaotic. He criticized D. H. Lawrence, whom in many respects he admired, because he saw in him an expression of the tendency of the time towards chaos, towards allowing the 'human form divine' to be lost in some vague life-force. What Lawrence expresses (and Muir links him in this respect with Shaw) 'is faith in all life that is not the life of personality, of synthesis, of order, of fulfilment . . . they are nihilists and the more dangerous for not knowing it. Their popularity is disquieting; it points to a disintegration of personality which must be general.'

But no symbolist artist can ever be on the side of vagueness, of disintegration. Muir's wisdom of the night, is not a capitulation to chaos. It is, he believed, man's characteristic vital achievements, as man, to give form, to impose pattern and order upon what he experiences and perceives. Plato held that form belongs specifically to intellectual order; that matter, until the mind projects upon it those forms, is mere chaos, *non-ens*. Mathematical relations—the triangle, the square, and the rest—belong to the order of the mind. And Muir, with his love of clarity of form likewise cites mathematics as a pure instance of the peculiarly human gift of imposing harmonious order upon the chaos of the world.

I think he loved the heraldic imagery he so often uses for some such reason, for every heraldic form both defines and celebrates some mastery over the natural and animal flux and chaos that is around and within man.

> Who curbed the lion long ago
> And penned him in this towering field
> And reared him wingless in the sky?
> And quenched the dragon's burning eye,
> Chaining him here to make a show,
> The faithful guardian of the shield?

But these still, heraldic forms are not merely invented in order to master the flux: they are pre-existent, they belong to the order of the Fable that was and 'in the beginning'—whatever the beginning may be:

> The frieze of fabulous creatures winged and crowned,
> And in the midst the woman and the man—

Lost long ago in fields beyond the Fall—
Keep faith in sleep-walled night and there are found
On our long journey back where we began.

In the imagination the creatures are 'winged', as Plato's lovers or angels are, with spiritual life, and 'crowned' with all that kingship conveys of glory, uniqueness, inherent power and entire reality, overwhelming presence and entity. It is the poet who can reveal their, as Blake would say, 'eternal lineaments'. I am one of those who hold the unfashionable belief that talent cannot make a poet, and that the *what* of art is more important than the *how*; and also that 'technique' does not exist in itself but only as a means to an end, an idea that is to be realised. Nor are all poetic ideas of equal value. Donne or Dryden cannot be as great as Milton or Dante because these poets do not attempt themes that bring into play so great a range of imaginative experience. The themes of major poetry are epic, and cosmic; Muir wrote no epic nor could he have attempted a coherent whole on the scale of the *Sagas* or the *Iliad*, yet an epic sense haunts his work; and nearly all he wrote has the luminosity of an inspired vision.

His themes—here again he is in the tradition of the Scottish and border ballads—are epic themes, the tribe, its wanderings in exile, its cities and their fall, its heroes and those anonymous bearers of its destiny who watch and remember. Beyond the epic lies the cosmic, the world of the gods in whose presence the human scenes take their due proportion. 'Religious' poetry is not necessarily of this kind. The devotional poets of the seventeenth century, or Hopkins, are beautiful minor poets whose experiences of the divine are (in no moral or pejorative sense) self-centred; whereas Blake, Milton, Dante, and the author of

'Byzantium' speak from beyond the human personality, from that life of which the individual man is no more than a form or organ. Visionary as he was, Muir is perhaps at his surest when he writes of middle earth; yet he never writes of the human scene without some haunting of the larger presences of the gods; and sometimes he writes of the gods themselves, catching an echo from Hölderlin:

> About the well of life where we are made
> Spirits of earth and heaven together lie.
> They do not turn their bright heads at our coming.
> So deep their dream of pure commingled being.
> So still the art and the level beam that flows
> Along the ground, shed by the flowers and waters:
> All above and beneath them a deep darkness.
> Their bodies lie in shadow or buried in earth,
> Their heads shine in the light of the underworld.
> Loaded with fear and crowned with every hope
> The born stream past them to the longed for place.

(1961)

The Poetry of Vernon Watkins

I MET VERNON WATKINS on only three occasions; on the first I introduced him at a reading of his poems at the Institute of Contemporary Arts (I think it was in 1949). I no longer remember which of his lyrical poems he read, but 'The Ballad of Sodom' remains in my mind from that time. I knew him, then, rather as the author of *The Ballad of the Mari Lwyd*, than, as I later realised, the greatest lyric poet of my generation.

My second sight of Vernon Watkins was in 1966 when at the Leicester Poetry Festival he, William Empson and myself were on the platform together, reading our poems. The occasion was—probably for all of us—one not to be forgotten; for we had all three been fellow-students at Cambridge during the late Twenties. William Empson and Vernon Watkins had both gone up to Magdalene, William Empson to become Dr I. A. Richards's most distinguished student at a historic moment in the annals of the Cambridge English school; and Vernon Watkins to make the more impressive choice of leaving Cambridge, which he foresaw had nothing to give a poet of the Imagination. The then Master of Magdalene, A. C. Benson, said to him at the time that if he followed his intention of becoming a poet he would 'curse the day he was born'; his reply was no less melodramatic: 'I have already done so'.

On the platform of the ancient Hall of Justice in Leicester where Shakespeare's company had played, I listened to my two contemporaries; to my old friend William Empson reading poems I had known by heart in that remote Cambridge world; and to Vernon Watkins whose poetry I had only much later come to know. William Empson's poems vividly recalled a period and an unrecapturable moment of youth; for the first time I saw these intellectually brilliant *jeux d'esprit* as belonging essentially to an undergraduate world. Vernon Watkins's poetry I knew, as I now heard it read by the poet, belonged to the timeless and ageless order of great art. Both poets were fine readers: William in his impassioned volcanic style; Vernon Watkins's voice, like the music of Haydn, speaking 'not to the sensual ear/But to the spirit'. For the first few minutes the ear was not attuned, as if to the speech of some celestial hierarchy not normally perceptible to human attention; but presently one heard, and the voice of the poet became audible at once in the music and in the meaning of the poetry. I do not mean that he was an especially good reader in the professional sense; his friend Dylan Thomas could do what he would with any audience, whether attuned to poetry or no; whereas Vernon Watkins, I imagine, could remain inaudible (spiritually) for those of his auditors who failed to make the transition of attention which on that evening lifted my mind entirely into his poetry.

A year or two ago I published on Vernon Watkins's poetry an essay full of admiring respectbut which somehow missed the essence which upon the occasion of that reading I felt so strongly; 'an unworldly, or inhuman quality', so his wife, Gwen

Watkins, wrote to me in a letter. I replied surely not inhuman but perhaps trans-human; and she, 'I think the impersonal or "trans-human" quality of his work—and in a way in his attitude to personal relationships—was due to the fact that he saw people as immortal souls, not as personalities; and presumably the soul, though beyond personality, has put off things such as sex and age which it needed in time.' At some time after his dramatic interview with A. C. Benson, Vernon Watkins destroyed all his early work because it was, as he said, 'dominated by time'. (It was also derivative, from Shelley and Blake in particular.) This act followed a visionary epiphany which revealed to the poet some reality beyond time; the culmination of a 'breakdown' which seems to have followed the classical Pauline pattern of spiritual stress followed by enlightenment. It was in any case a realisation upon which he never went back. At the present moment, when the temporal personality seems all-important (as it must necessarily become when the immortal soul is denied) such a decision must to many seem incomprehensible. Perhaps in this rejection of the temporal lies the explanation of a fact which has often surprised me, the failure of quite a number of 'literary' people to see what an incomparable poet Watkins was. There is in all his work that quality at once remote and compelling which belongs to that part of us which is outside sex and age and the temporal person.

Vernon Watkins is perhaps 'a poet's poet', yet in this sense there are readers who are poets and writers who are not. The best of his work, with the possible exception of his ballads, is Shelley's 'language of the imagination'. Like white light or distilled water his invisibility to the common kind and degree of attention is an attribute of this poetic purity. The common reader very often prefers verse which, because it has little or none of this quality, comes within the range of ordinary attention.

Indeed I have read his poems at times without the miraculous shift of focus and found their intricate flowing patterns of words and images impossible to follow; nothing in their woven veil for logic to hold on to, no more than in the sound of a waterfall. But then the attention is caught up and, committing ourselves to the swift yet gentle current, we flow with the verse; and perceive that the order of the poetry is not below that of reason but above it; not formlessness but an interplay of forms and ideas so subtle and so finely interwoven that only the poet can hear what the poet speaks. Reading his work I no longer seek to apply the relatively crude instruments of *Practical Criticism* or *Seven Types of Ambiguity*, but await the miracle. Once attuned, the 'minute particulars' come into focus; for in addressing the spirit no poet could be less abstract, less theoretical, less devotional, less 'religious': we are shown the visible, sensible world in all its precision of form, but in a different focus, so that at first we do not recognise in a transfigured landscape familiar headlands and hills.

I belong to a generation for whom iconoclastic avant-gardism was the norm, the accepted convention; it holds no surprises. All my illuminations have come from the astonishment of discovering, in Eliot, in David Jones, in Yeats, Edwin Muir, Vernon Watkins, the roots of tradition unsevered. Vernon Watkins's choice to live his life on the Gower peninsula was in itself an affirmation of traditional loyalty. 'The history of Welsh poetry has been dominated by the sense of tradition,' H. I. Bell wrote in *The Development of Welsh Poetry*, 'a persistent loyalty to the past.' Vernon Watkins, though writing in English, had this loyalty in its most extreme degree, a cosmic loyalty extending to the pre-human rock and water and light of Gower, which lifts his sense of the past out of time altogether and back full-circle into the ever-present; a quality his poetry has in common with the *Lay of Taliesin* which must be, for any Welsh poet, rather than the Greco-Roman or Renaissance poetic tradition, his classical ground.

The bards and *fili* of Wales and Ireland served a long apprenticeship in learned schools where they were taught not only complex rules of versifying, but also the proper themes of poetry. These included the history of families and of places, by which, with the addition of new heroic episodes and eulogies (which it was part of the poet's role to compose), the national sense of identity was created and preserved. The spiritual knowledge of the Druid tradition was also preserved and transmitted in a symbolic language clear to the initiate, obscure to the vulgar. It must even now be impossible—and in this they are greatly to be envied—for any Welsh poet, whether writing in English or Welsh, to be altogether outside this bardic inheritance from that Hyperborean Abaris to whom Pythagoras said he had nothing to teach, for he already possessed full knowledge of the Mysteries.

Robert Graves in his finest work, *The White Goddess*, writes of 'the Theme' of true poetry. It is not generally held, at the present time, that there is any one particular theme more than another proper to poetry. Shelley called poetry the language of the imagination, which, though true in any sense, seems to make the choice a personal one. Here again the Welsh inheritance gives a more objective and a more instructed meaning to the Theme. Graves writes 'the Welsh poet Alun Lewis who wrote, just before his death in Burma, in March 1944, of 'the single poetic theme of Life and Death . . . the question of what survives of the beloved'. Granted that there are many themes for the journalist of verse, yet for the poet, as Alun Lewis understood the word, there is no choice. The elements of the single, infinitely variable theme are to be found in certain ancient poetic myths which though manipulated to conform with each epoch of religious change—I use the word myth in the strict sense of 'verbal iconograph' without the derogatory sense of 'absurd fiction' that it has acquired—yet remain constant in general outline. Perfect faithfulness to the theme affects the reader of the poem with a strange feeling between delight and horror, of which the purely physical effect is that the hair literally stands on end.

Poetry to the uninitiated, Graves concludes, must seem 'a preposterous group of mare's nests'; the metaphor is deliberately chosen, for the Night Mare—Vernon Watkins's *mari*—is 'one of the cruellest aspects of the White Goddess', the Muse.

Robert Graves's own cult of the Muse is perhaps idolatrous; directed, that is to say, towards the externals of the symbol; which nevertheless has upon his imagination, even while he denies its metaphysical context, an irresistible power. Vernon Watkins experienced the *mari* numinously; and his ballad does, more than any poem known to me, make the hair stand on end. *The Ballad of the Mari Lwyd* embodies and transmits an ancient knowledge whose roots are in a forgotten past, which the poet has inherited rather than adopted. Unexplained, inexplicable, the truth of poem and poet to 'the Theme' is something more radical than a belief or poetic enthusiasm. Neither is the Theme historically determined or bounded by any one period more than another within the centuries through which it has been transmitted; with a living tradition archaeological purism is incompatible. The pre-Christian *Lay of Taliesin* has taken into its continuity the Christian revelation; and Vernon Watkins, himself within the continuity of Taliesin, expresses a vision unambiguously Christological. Throughout all the intricacies of its weaving, every moment of time and atom of space (to take an image from Blake, one of Watkins's poetic masters) within his cosmos is oriented within that Revelation. In mood, often even (as in *The Death Bell*) in his 'metaphysical' imagery, Vernon Watkins calls to mind Vaughan or Herbert or Traherne; but the scope of his vision belongs peculiarly to his own time, within the cosmology of Teilhard de Chardin and the poetry of St-John Perse.

Dr Bell, whom I have already quoted, says that 'Welsh poetry as a whole suffers from a lack of the architectonic faculty'. The Theme does not in its nature lend itself to the kind of forms to which Greco-Roman rationalism have accustomed us; it is elusive and pervasive rather than definable. The vision of such writers as David Jones, Dylan Thomas and Vernon Watkins lends itself to other forms, and to look for the architectonic is to miss the peculiar and fluid beauty of their kind. 'It is on the line, the couplet, the stanza, the units of which the poem is composed, that the poets of Wales usually lavish their attention.' Not Yeats himself could spin those gossamer lines, strung with their words like perfect spheres of dew, that characterise Vernon Watkins's finest lyrics; yet that gossamer is held by forces strong and coterminous with the universe. All his best poems seem—as Robert Graves suggests as a characteristic of poets dedicated to the Theme—like parts of a single poem; his elegies flow into an affirmation of rebirth, his poems for a birth or a christening are rooted in the world of the dead within the rocks, and out of the graves flowers grow for some epithalamium, or foals are born to the shadowy *mari*. He sought always, it seems to me, as in his 'Ballad of the Mari Lwyd', a unity of vision which should include life, death and rebirth; but in his work the theme is not doctrine but experienced in a manner wholly poetic. He communicates this Pythagorean life-in-death, death-in-life, terrible in the darkness of the 'Mari Lwyd', joyous in the birth of foal or child, bird, bud and blossom into the light, but always numinous, as it must have been experienced in the archaic rites of the Goddess. His poetry whether of death or rebirth is without nostalgia, like a field of flowers whose roots are always in the graves; an everpresent paradise beyond pathos and beyond tragedy.

Vernon Watkins's respect for tradition was not confined to his bardic inheritance; he was a learned poet, well read in French and German literature. He translated, besides Heine and Hölderlin, from Baudelaire, Paul Fort, Francis Jammes, Tristan Corbière and others. He lacked nothing the finest English culture (that Public School education which in another generation will have virtually ceased to exist) could impart to an heir of the Bards. Doubtless he was influenced, like all his generation, by the critical writings of T. S. Eliot. Yeats, certainly, was nearer to Vernon Watkins in his understanding that tradition is not anything and everything that has historically occurred, but a few heroic and religious themes, passed on from age to age; yet Eliot's more historical view of tradition he would certainly not have rejected; the poet may inherit the Theme, but he is free to choose his themes; history and tradition are not identical, yet each has its own importance. Vernon Watkins was well read throughout the whole range of European literature; Dante, Blake, Heine,

Browning, Yeats are names that stray often into his poems; he admired and read French poetry no less than German; his skill in the use of Sapphics and Alcaics came from his appreciation of Greek lyric poetry, which he read (though he knew some Greek) generally in translation. He spoke of some avant-garde versifier who had reproached him for his excessive interest in writers of the past; 'They won't help you,' this knowing one pointed out; on the contrary, Watkins replied, it was precisely to these that he owed everything. As a young man he visited Yeats, who received him perhaps more kindly because he was not an Englishman, or associated with the Auden–Spender–Day Lewis school, which he found antipathetic. It was like him, too, to have gone to much trouble, in Venice, to get the key to Browning's Palazzo, which he visited in the spirit of pilgrimage. It was of such things he spoke upon my rare meetings with him.

Much could be said of Vernon Watkins's verse, of his skill in the use of many forms both English and Classical. Perfectionism of verse has been the heritage of Welsh-born poets down to Vernon Watkins's generation, perhaps the last inheritors. English poets, whose ears are attuned to blank verse, sonnet and couplet, may envy poets of the Celtic tradition the intricate rhymes and assonances of the *cynghanedd*. Vernon Watkins was not a Welsh speaker, though his parents were; but he remained within earshot, so to say, of the language. We can already see in retrospect that the innovations of modern poetry have not been those much-publicised rejections of traditional forms, the 'free' verse introduced by Pound and Eliot, French prose-poetry, or the succeeding chaos, but (in these islands, for America is another matter) the skilful, careful and gifted prosody of poets within the Celtic tradition of Wales and Ireland, and perhaps of the 'makars' of Scotland. Hopkins, an Englishman, studied Welsh verse. In his use of verse Vernon Watkins comes perhaps nearest to his early friend Dylan Thomas, with whom he shared the years of learning the poet's craft. Yet it is not in these poems in which he most resembles Dylan Thomas that Vernon Watkins is at his best—rather the reverse—and the same is true of the influence upon him of Yeats, whom he already had taken as a model while his Cambridge contemporaries were concerned only with Pound and the Imagist theories of T. E. Hulme. His note is his own; yet at the same time a voice more of the race than that of Dylan Thomas.

Like Dylan Thomas he was a perfectionist, never allowing any poem short of attainable perfection to appear in print; he left unpublished as many poems as he ever passed for publication. Like David Jones it was his habit to keep poems and to work over them at long intervals until he was satisfied that they were right. He was cut off in the prime of a talent slowly and continuously developed.

So much of his best work is so recent that it is hard to realise his death. Yet in another sense death has set a seal of perfection on Watkins's work in a sense beyond the universal finality of death. Because the wholeness of life and death within immortality was the theme of his work, the poet seems now to have been writing from his own experience no less of death than of life; which was not nor could have been so while he was working on the pattern from the side of life. To say his poetry 'foresaw' his own death is too personal a way of expressing the integrity of what was a universal vision of the human condition, comparable with that of Henry Vaughan or Thomas Traherne. Like these, Vernon Watkins had discovered that mysterious light or life of which the visible world is woven; the ultimate alchemical mystery whose realisation brings to those who achieve it a supreme joy, and the all but lost sense of 'the holy' which illuminates the work of Vernon Watkins, as it does the finest work of Dylan Thomas.

(1970)